Rural Studies Series

Series Editors

Charles Watkins, *Department of Geography, University of Nottingham*
Michael Winter, *Countryside & Community Research Unit, Cheltenham*

As a consequence of the explosion of interest in environmental matters, the phenomenon of counter-urbanization and the successive crises of the Common Agricultural Policy, rural studies has expanded rapidly in the past decade. With roots in geography and sociology, as well as in the new subjects of environmental studies and countryside management, this series is based on inter-disciplinary perspectives.

Revealing Rural 'Others'

Representation, Power and Identity in the British Countryside

Edited by
Paul Milbourne

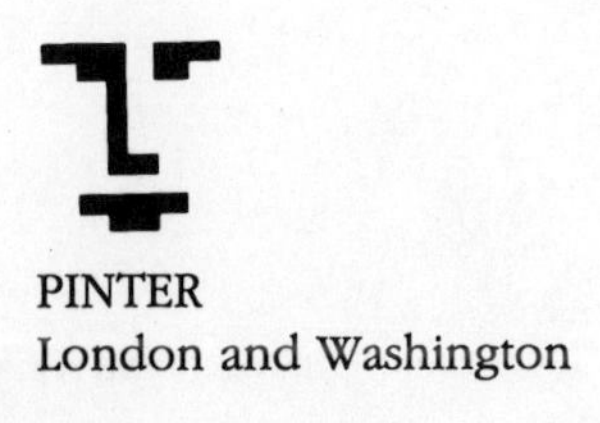

PINTER
London and Washington

First published 1997 by
Pinter
A Cassell Imprint
Wellington House, 125 Strand, London WC2R 0BB
PO Box 605, Herndon, VA 20172

British Library Cataloguing-in-Publication Data

Revealing rural 'others': representation, power and identity in the British countryside. - (Rural studies series)
1. Land use, Rural - Great Britain 2. Sociology, Rural - Great Britain 3. Great Britain - Rural conditions
I. Milbourne, Paul
307.7'2'0941

ISBN 1-85567-424-6

Library of Congress Cataloging-in-Publication Data

Revealing rural 'others': representation, power and identity in the British countryside/edited by Paul Milbourne.
p. cm.—(Rural studies series)
Includes bibliographical references and index.
ISBN 1-85567-424-6
1. Great Britain—Rural conditions. 2. Social change—Great Britain. 3. Social structure—Great Britain. 4. Rural development—Great Britain. I. Milbourne, Paul, 1966- . II. Series
III. Series: Rural studies series (New York, N.Y.)
HN385.5.R48 1997
307.72'0941—dc20
96-9773
CIP

Typeset by BookEns Ltd, Royston, Herts.
Printed and bound in Great Britain by Biddles Limited, Guildford and King's Lynn

Contents

List of Illustrations

List of Contributors

Judy Clark is a Research Fellow in the Department of Geography at University College, London. Her research interests focus on the relationships between science, nature and society.

Graham Cox is a Senior Lecturer in Sociology in the School of Social Sciences at the University of Bath. He has researched extensively on agricultural and environmental change and is presently working on the politics of rural leisure activities and property rights in the countryside.

David Crouch is Professor of Cultural Geography and Head of the Leisure and Rural Development Group at Anglia University. His work has concerned the reinterpretation of the process of geographical knowledge through a series of projects at the interface of cultural geography, leisure/tourism studies and landscape, often focused through rural examples. This series of studies has included allotment holding, Stonehenge, locally sustainable rural tourism, caravanning, the culture and landscape of people living in Weardale, and an investigation of the geographical knowledge in the work of mid-century St Ives artist, Peter Lanyon.

Jim Davis is team leader of a Children's Society project in Somerset which is using community development techniques to develop child-focused services in rural and urban areas. The project incorporates a traveller support programme that works with New Age travellers in the South West.

Nick Fiddes is a Research Fellow in the Department of Social Anthropology at the University of Edinburgh. He is currently working on an ESRC-funded project, entitled *Environmental Activism: an ethnography of ecological 'direct action'*. He has previously published a book *Meat: a Natural Symbol* (Routledge 1991).

Annie Hughes is a Lecturer in the School of Geography at Kingston University. Her doctoral research considered the diversity of contemporary female experience in rural Britain. She is the author of 'Rurality and "cultures of womanhood": domestic identities and moral order in village life' in P. Cloke and J. Little (eds), *Contested Countryside Cultures* (Routledge 1997).

Noragh Jones is a freelance writer who has lived in rural Ceredigion since 1986. She was formerly a librarian and lecturer in the North and South of Ireland, and in Yorkshire, before moving to rural Wales. Her book *Living in Rural Wales* grew out of her personal experiences and encounters as an incomer in a fragmented rural community.

Phil Kinsman is a Research Officer in the Department of Geography at the University of Nottingham. His research interests include issues of race, landscape and national identity - particularly as seen in the images of the photographer Ingrid Pollard and the work of the Black Environment Network pressure group. This research has involved looking at diverse issues such as the history and contemporary use of the idea of race, British national identity and nationalism generally, environmentalism and ecology, photography, post-colonial and crime literature, and cultural studies.

Philip Lowe holds the Duke of Northumberland Chair of Rural Economy and is Director of the Centre for Rural Economy at the University of Newcastle upon Tyne. His research interests cover a broad range of countryside and environmental issues, including rural development and agri-environmental policy on which he has published extensively.

Paul Milbourne is a Research Fellow in the Countryside and Community Research Unit at Cheltenham and Gloucester College of Higher Education. His research interests include rural housing and homelessness, poverty and marginalization, and cultural change in the Welsh countryside. He is co-author of *The Condition of Rural Wales: Marginalisation in the Contemporary Countryside* (1997), published by University of Wales Press, and is currently co-directing an ESRC-funded project entitled *The Homeless Poor in Rural Areas*.

Jacqueline Sarsby is a Research Associate in the Countryside and Community Research Unit at Cheltenham and Gloucester College of Higher Education. She is a social anthropologist with a background of published research in subjects which include romantic love, multi-problem families and the cycle of deprivation, and the work and home lives of women pottery workers. Since 1990, she has been photographing her work: in the Potteries, where she had done oral history fieldwork in 1981, and in Devon, where she has combined oral history and photography, to research and document the lives of women on Devon farms.

Susanne Seymour is a Lecturer in the Department of Geography at the University of Nottingham. Her research interests focus on cultural understandings of the environment and landscape and environmental policy. She has recently published work on 'Church, landscape and community' with Charles Watkins in *Landscape Research* (1995).

Neil Ward is a Lecturer in the Department of Geography at the University of Newcastle upon Tyne and his research interests include technological change, agriculture and environmental regulation, pesticide pollution and the implementation of EU environmental policy. He has recently published work on 'Technological change and the regulation of pollution from agricultural pesticides' in *Geoforum* (1995).

Michael Winter is Professor of Rural Economy and Society in the Countryside and Community Research Unit at Cheltenham and Gloucester College of Higher Education. His sociological interests in the countryside include hunting, shooting, agricultural change and religion. He has also widely researched and published on agri-environmental policy and politics. His most recent book is *Rural Politics: Policies for Agriculture, Forestry and the Environment* (Routledge 1996).

Acknowledgements

Thanks are due to many people who helped make possible the production of this book: the Rural Economy and Society Study Group for providing the forum for a stimulating session on 'rural others' at the 1994 annual conference in Cheltenham; the actual contributors to the book who have endured the learning experiences of a first-time editor, and finally, those individuals whom I met during their campaign in the countryside around Newbury in January 1996 - their actions provided the impetus for completing the introduction of this book.

Paul Milbourne
Cheltenham, October 1996

Introduction: Challenging the Rural: Representation, Power and Identity in the British Countryside

PAUL MILBOURNE

On 16 November 1995 Sir David Steel announced the launch of the Countryside Movement, a new organization for the countryside which aims to improve awareness and understanding of rural issues through intensive programmes of education and campaigning. During its media launch it was claimed the Movement would seek 'for the first time to offer the countryside the opportunity to speak with a single voice'.[1] However, an examination of the nature of this single voice reveals not a new voice – although membership of the Movement is open to all groups – but the voice of traditional hegemonic groups within rural Britain. Its executive includes the president of the National Farmers' Union, a past president of the Country Landowners' Association, the chairman of the Game Conservancy, and the Duke of Westminster, who is one of the largest and wealthiest private landowners in Britain. Furthermore, Keeble (1995) suggests that up to £3 million of initial funding for the Movement has been provided by a range of businesses and private individuals involved in country (blood) sports. Within the Countryside Movement then, we hear the voice of traditional power and privilege, of field sports, farming and landed property – a voice which is attempting to re-position and re-establish its vested interests within a rapidly changing rural Britain.

This collected volume is intended to challenge such hegemonic views of the British countryside by exploring a range of diverse voices writing on and living within rural areas. The chapters originally appeared as papers which were presented at the 'Revealing Rural "Others" ' session of the 1994 Rural Economy and Society Study Group annual conference held in Cheltenham. The session aimed to bring together different styles of research and writing on the rural, and this aim has remained within this book: it draws on work from different areas within the academy - human geography, sociology and social anthropology - and from outside; some combining qualitative and quantitative research, most adopting a variety of qualitative methods; predominantly presented through the medium of the written word, although including photographic representations of research.

This edited text attempts to uncover the experiences of a range of groups and individuals using rural space, whether on a permanent or temporary basis, whose voices remain largely softened, deflected or silent within mainstream writings on the rural. Many of these voices remain unheard because they cut against dominant cultural and political constructions of English[2] rurality which are (re)produced and (re)presented within various academic, policy and lay discourses - constructions associated with specific notions of class configuration, nature - society relations, ethnicity, gender relations, power, affluence, national identity and so on. We see, within such constructions, notions of harmonious rural communities in which each person accepts her or his own class position within a hierarchical society; the 'countrywoman' happily restricted to informal work within the domestic sphere; a contented rural poor looked after by fellow villagers; field 'sports' providing a continuity of traditional country practices into the present; and a sea of white faces living within rural spaces which invoke powerful and mythical symbolism as 'our green and pleasant land'. But there is also considerable political power bound up with these images of the English countryside, and elements of such images can be seen to be embedded within political power relations in Britain. There is both power in the rural, and notions of rurality within the minds of power-holders - certain versions of the rural become elevated to positions of privilege, worthy of protection and actively reproduced.

Over recent years, however, many rural areas have witnessed dramatic transformations of social structure, with many newcomer groups importing different attitudes towards certain aspects of rural life, while tending to reinforce other elements. For example, relatively few rural dwellers now have any direct linkages with the productionist countryside, predominantly involving agriculture, which is leading to a series of high profile challenges to taken-for-granted smells, sounds and sights of agricultural activities. From the court injunction taken out against the owner of Corky the Cockerel in 1993 for crowing too noisily (Stokes, 1993) to the recent contestation of a pig farm extension in Somerset, Midgley (1995) has commented on these changing attitudes to the rural, as the countryside is increasingly transformed into an arena of (cultural and environmental) consumption:

> A battle royal is being fought in the countryside. You might not know it but in parish councils, planning committees and farms up and down the country, the green wellie brigade is putting the boot into the old guard black-wellie fraternity. (p. 10)

More generally, we can point to changing nature-society relations and a series of shifting attitudes towards the environment within Britain - a rejection of intensive farming methods and a growth in vegetarianism; protests against live animal exports, blood sports and road developments across environmentally sensitive areas; and a growth in numerous New Age groups, such as travellers, which aim to strike up new relationships with nature. These attitudinal changes have led, in many ways, to direct challenges to traditional nature-society relations in the countryside - demonstrations outside farms, disruption of foxhunting, open-air festivals and environmental non-violent direct action against major road bypasses.

These different ways of viewing the countryside and alternative ways of using rural space though, have themselves been challenged recently by the introduction, in November 1994, of the Criminal Justice and Public Order Act - exactly twelve months prior to the launch of the Countryside Movement. Within this wide-ranging piece of legislation, we can identify an attempt to re-establish the 'legitimate' claims of certain groups over others in the 1990s countryside - privileging, for example, the claims of the large private landowner over rambler, the hunt practitioner over protester, morris dancer over raver, Caravan Club member over New Age traveller. Michael Howard, the Home Secretary, emphasized the importance of defending one of these 'legitimate claims', blood sports, in the run up to the Criminal Justice Bill receiving Royal Assent in 1994:

> They [the hunt saboteurs] should stop their appalling behaviour and leave people to enjoy their traditional - and entirely legal - country sports. (quoted in Bennetto, 1994, p. 1)

Thus, with the recent formation of the Countryside Movement and the introduction of the Criminal Justice and Public Order Act, we see a concerted effort on the part of Government and traditional rural elites to re-impose ordered notions of rurality; to protect certain notions of the (English) countryside from perceived outside, often urban, threats of alternative ways of seeing and using rural space. As Sibley (1992, 1994) has highlighted, such attempts at (re)establishing order in the countryside can be seen as linked to dominant notions of rurality as 'purified space', and views of the countryside as an arena of conformity in which difference is constructed as deviance. The chapters included within this book attempt to move beyond these traditional, elitist, ordered gazes of rurality; to engage with different ways of viewing, different ways of experiencing the rural. Some of the chapters focus on groups affected (or more accurately targeted) by the Criminal Justice Act (road protesters and New Age travellers), others engage with sets of neglected experiences of rural living concerning gender, poverty, ethnicity and other cultural identities, while others still discuss changing power structures which may be acting to transpose traditional rural elite groups, such as hunters and farmers, to the position of 'other' within the 1990s countryside.

In the process of challenging powerful images of, and voices on, the rural, many of the authors within this volume engage with recent debates within the social sciences generally and rural studies more specifically (and also rather belatedly) concerning issues of representation, power and identity within academic research and writing. Central to such work has been the notion of authorial power; that much of academic writing and research has privileged certain accounts over others - certain methods of enquiry, certain subjects and certain spaces. Within such a critique of the academy though, it is also possible to view the rural arena generally as a neglected space for critical research within the social sciences (see Whatmore, 1993), as writers have tended to privilege 'the urban' as case study. However, it has been through an initial review essay by Philo (1992) and subsequent engagements between Murdoch and Pratt (1993, 1994) and Philo (1993) that a growing number of rural researchers, but particularly rural geographers,[3] have begun to take more seriously issues concerning difference, marginalization, identity and power within the rural arena. Within recent rural (geographical) research and rural (geographical) conferences we see evidence of a more active engagement by certain researchers with a range of qualitative methodologies in an attempt to explore individual experiences and different cultural identities within rural Britain. These researchers are increasingly recognizing their own (privileged) positions within their research projects, and, like other post-modern writers, are attempting to decentre the 'privileged sites from which representations emanate' (Duncan and Ley, 1993, p. 2) and move towards a 'polyphony of voices' (*ibid*, p. 8). However, as Duncan and Ley (1993) have commented, we need to be wary about just how far we (as academic researchers and writers) can claim to have lost representational control, given that it is almost always the academic who has initially defined the research project, who is *allowing* individuals and groups into her or his research, and who maintains overall organizational control over representation. Indeed, the vast majority of academic research and texts - including this present volume - has been carried out by, written for and consumed by other academics, a process which privileges the spoken and written word in both the practice and (re)presentation of research. Clearly, an edited text such as this one is able to be doubly criticized on this count; criticisms which I have been well aware of during the process of producing this book for an academic publisher. Notwithstanding this editorial process though, it is hoped that the collected chapters within this book capture something of the diversity of research on, and the diversity of voice of, groups within the British countryside.

Finally, in an edited text which focuses on neglected facets of rural research, peoples and experiences, it is necessary to stress that this book has inevitably failed to engage with other marginalized voices within and on the rural, and has also omitted some other rural spaces. For example, the book has tended to ignore identities of sexuality within the countryside (but see Bell and Valentine, 1995), and the experiences of being young, elderly, homeless or disabled in rural areas, and while I am aware of on-going projects in each of these areas, it has not been possible, for a variety of reasons, to incorporate such research writings within the covers of this single text. It is also the case that the research referred to within this book has been restricted to areas of rural Britain and, in most cases, areas of the English countryside. Moreover, recent research on 'other' groups and 'other' experiences in rural areas has focused predominantly on particular types of rural space - generally the geographically bounded village situated within a predominantly agricultural landscape. Little research has focused on other types of rural spaces: for example, areas of industrial and post-industrial countryside which tend to be characterized by distinctive sets of nature–society relations, often involving an exploitation of local landscapes by extractive capital; or the inter-connections between 'urban' and 'rural' spaces - the urban within the rural (small towns within rural hinterlands) and the rural within the urban which, it can be argued, represents the dominant direct experience of 'the rural' for the vast majority of the British population (the Country Park, municipal park, green belt footpath, allotment,[4] golf course, school playing field or domestic back garden).

The Structure of the Book

Although the writings within this book do not fall neatly within any simplistic themes or categories, the first four chapters address a series of environmental issues within the British countryside. Each of these chapters explores some key changing nature–society relations, albeit from different perspectives, as new groups move into rural areas holding on to different notions of nature and environment, and others from both within and without the rural begin to question key notions associated with environment in a rural context. In Chapter 1, Phil Kinsman charts the work of the Black Environment Network (BEN), which since 1988 has attempted to place issues of multiculturalism and representation of minority ethnic groups on the agendas of a range of environmental and countryside groups. Here, notions of race, landscape and national identity are discussed in relation to the categories of rural and countryside, as BEN has begun to uncover the hidden and erased historical presence of black people in rural England. However, while BEN has focused predominantly on issues of national identity from an urban perspective, the everyday concerns of many minority ethnic people, its rural work has attracted most attention from the media. Kinsman suggests that such a preoccupation with BEN's work on countryside issues is due to the fact that the rural represents an ideological terrain within England in which ideas of identity are frequently disputed.

Nick Fiddes, in Chapter 2, examines another challenge to existing power structures within rural (and urban) areas, through a discussion of recent environmental protest in Britain. Focusing mainly on road protests in the 1990s, attention is given to a rise in grassroots activism and the growing use of non-violent direct action (NVDA) to delay building work. The chapter explores the characteristics, ways of life and beliefs associated with those involved with such protests, and highlights important contested understandings of property rights and ownership, and a variety of ways in which power is negotiated. Fiddes suggests that a central underpinning of the philosophies associated with such protests is that 'we all belong to the land', that attachment to one's habitat is a fundamental part of society. Such ideas clearly challenge traditional views of land as commodity and the traditional private property rights of powerful landowners within Britain. Inevitably though, the gravity of such challenges initiated a response by central government which came, in part, with the Criminal Justice and Public Order Act 1994, and as Fiddes suggests, this particular piece of legislation will bring those groups who believe in the legitimacy of NVDA into direct conflict with those who are the traditional holders of authority. However, Fiddes concludes by arguing that the ultimate success of the NVDA movement should not be measured in terms of the number of road schemes halted, but instead by the extent to which its beliefs and values inform broader public opinion.

Chapter 3 explores the changing situation of a group which is frequently viewed as a traditional elite within rural areas - farmers - through a discussion of the shifting meanings attached to river pollution in Devon. Susanne Seymour, Philip Lowe, Neil Ward and Judy Clark engage with recent debates in rural studies concerning 'neglected others' in the countryside, suggesting that recent processes of rural social recomposition have acted to question the cultural authority and landowning power of many farmers, particularly in relation to environmental issues and debates. The chapter highlights the ways in which public and environmental pressure groups, which have been traditionally marginalized in many rural areas and detached from decision making, have become more respected and powerful over recent years. Such shifts have restricted many farmers to positions of 'outsiders to an emerging social consensus which regards damage to the environment as morally wrong'. The authors explore these changing power relations between a previously 'othered' environmental interest and traditional production 'elites' concerning water pollution from dairy farming in Devon. Drawing on an actor-network approach, the chapter examines a range of 'stories' constructed by different actors about farm pollution in an attempt to assess the extent to which debates surrounding pollution challenge traditional power relations in the countryside.

Graham Cox and Michael Winter in Chapter 4 reconsider the position of another traditionally perceived powerful elite in rural areas - the hunting community. They suggest that current national opinion on field sports and an influx of ex-urban residents to many rural areas have resulted in a situation whereby many within the hunting community now feel beleaguered rather than privileged. Using the examples of the Devon and Somerset Staghounds and the Quantock Staghounds, the chapter highlights some key social and economic characteristics of these hunts and a range of conflicts between local authorities and hunting. However, attempts to ban hunting have been thwarted by the existing legal system and parliamentary cross-party political alliances, while the recent introduction of the Criminal Justice and Public Order Act in 1994 has shifted further the balance of political and legal forces in favour of the hunting community re-establishing its privileged position, although arguably, a beleaguered privilege within rural Britain.

Issues of poverty in the British countryside are explored by Paul Milbourne in Chapter 5, who suggests that rural poverty can be seen as a doubly neglected part of research within the social sciences. The chapter reviews some key ongoing debates within the general poverty literature, focusing in particular on the shifting and competing meanings and definitions attached to poverty, before exploring something of the hiddenness of poverty in rural Britain and America. Here attention is given to recent research projects which have pointed to such factors as a general urban bias within the social sciences, physical settlement patterns and cultural constructions of rurality as acting to reduce the scales of visibility of poverty in rural areas. Drawing on one particular study of rural lifestyles in England and Wales, the chapter provides a multi-method approach to rural poverty research by exploring the incidence, nature and multifarious experiences of poverty within areas of the British countryside. While Milbourne highlights a widespread occurrence of poverty in rural areas, he suggests that the nature of this poverty would appear to differ markedly from that revealed within urban studies. Moreover, the lifestyles research has pointed to a range of, often contradictory, understandings of rural poverty among residents in the countryside, as well as highlighting some broader notions of rural socio-cultural marginalization.

Jim Davis discusses his recent work with New Age travellers in south-west England in Chapter 6. Using articles taken from local newspapers, he illustrates something of the feelings of hatred and fear associated with the relocation of these more mobile residents to many rural areas. However, such individual feelings of fear have been reinforced recently within political circles; by John Major's infamous party conference speech and the vociferous voices of MPs with constituencies in the English shire counties. The Government's response to this perceived 'invasion' of rural England by travellers was contained within the Criminal Justice and Public Order Act 1994, legislation which has transformed aggravated trespass into a criminal offence and given greater powers to the police and local authorities to evict travellers from illegal sites. Based on interviews with over 100 travellers in the rural South West, this chapter explores the motivations behind and experiences of travelling in the pre- and post-Criminal Justice Act period. This research has highlighted that over half of the travellers within the study had previously been homeless, with most having no alternative accommodation to their vehicle, and that the Criminal Justice Act has brought about an increased scale and frequency of traveller movement across predominantly rural areas. However, the chapter also points to several examples of traveller groups who have integrated into rural communities, highlighting an alternative vision of rural living - one which thrives on the richness of cultural diversity.

In Chapter 7, Noragh Jones writes about her experiences involved in moving from Belfast to the village of Cwmrheidol in west Wales, a piece of writing that can be described as practical or everyday ethnography. In the process of 'getting to know' her new valley and its people she began to record her conversations with a range of local residents, conversations which were subsequently published as a collection in a book, ***Living in Rural Wales*** (1993). Through the extended commentaries of local residents presented within the chapter, we see some different ways of seeing this area of the Welsh countryside; we encounter, among others, Ieuan, a Welsh-speaking hill farmer, Crow, a New Age traveller, and Alison and Phil, a couple of green incomers from an English city. Drawing on Etzioni's (1993) communitarian perspective, she also highlights a series of bridge-building individuals who are attempting to maintain a sense of community - between new and old, straight and alternative groupings - within this rapidly changing rural area. The chapter highlights unusual alliances that are acting to cut across traditional cultural polarities and proposes a set of new attitudes towards 'others' within rural Wales which draw on the old Celtic symbol of the Fifth Province.

Jacqueline Sarsby discusses some different methods and presentation styles within rural research in Chapter 8. Engaging with her academic training in social anthropology and her interest in photography, she highlights how she has attempted to combine taped life histories, still photographs and exhibitions within her work with farming communities in rural Devon. The chapter explores different world views of rural Devon from the perspectives of the farmers within her photographs, visitors and curators involved in her photographic exhibitions and picture-editors for 'country' magazines. She also discusses a recent project of images and voices, 'Changing Rural Devon', which focused on the experiences of farm women in the county. Through a combination of still photographs and oral histories, her exhibition has been able to uncover some of the more hidden elements of farm life, for example, the interior spaces of the farm, and the varied aspects of individual women's lives. Sarsby suggests that such exhibitions of image and sound provide an important interactive medium for her work, with photographs allowing time for contemplation and the recorded voices highlighting that these images belong to people who hold on to different world views.

In Chapter 9, Annie Hughes explores what she terms the 'hidden geographies' of women in the countryside. Drawing on feminist critiques of social science, she suggests that rural studies generally have tended to neglect the voices of women as a research subject. Moreover, cultural constructions of rurality tend to draw on highly gendered images of home and community, appropriating women to the domestic sphere. Based on recent qualitative research in a mid-Wales village, the chapter explores women's experiences of 'community' - real and imagined, their perceived roles as community linchpins, and different reactions to dominant gender positions within the village. As such, the chapter highlights the ways in which dominant discourses of rurality are bound up with women's everyday experiences of rural living.

In the final chapter, David Crouch examines the ways in which certain leisure uses of rural space are marginalized within English culture. Focusing on two alternative leisure practices in rural areas - caravanning and small-holding - he explores the processes involved in the constructions of geographical knowledge at a local level. The chapter tells a story of contested country, disputed landscape claims, unstable identities and power within contemporary culture and the academy. Crouch suggests that both leisure activities can be viewed as 'other' within dominant discourses of rurality because they opt out of 'consumer citizenship' and create their own versions of the rural. These creations involve negotiation between individual and collective identities, drawing on metaphors of different values and ideologies. The chapter also highlights how positions of 'otherness' are maintained by associations of caravanning with 'low culture' and small-holding with economic and political marginality. However, Crouch concludes by arguing that it is the signs of commodified country that should be seen as 'other', out of touch with the ways in which the rural is worked and reworked within people's lives.

Notes

1. Quoted in ACRE's Rural Digest, Issue 23, 30 November 1995; see also the Movement's charter (Countryside Movement, 1995).
2. The word English rather than British is used deliberately here since it can be suggested that associations between dominant culture, power structures and rurality are different in Wales and Scotland.
3. Many sociologists and social anthropologists working in rural areas have long engaged in these subject areas. Cohen (1982), for example, highlights this rich vein of study within British rural social anthropology.
4. See Crouch (1992) for a notable exception.

References

Bell, D. and Valentine, G. (1995) Queer country: rural lesbian and gay lives. *Journal of Rural Studies*, 11 (2), 113–22.

Bennetto, J. (1994) Howard backs hunters with new laws. *Independent on Sunday*, 7 November.

Cohen, A. (1982) *Belonging: Identity and Social Organisation in British Rural Cultures*. Manchester: Manchester University Press.

Countryside Movement (1995) *Our Charter*. London: Countryside Movement.
Crouch, D. (1992) Popular culture and what we make of the rural: the case of village allotments. *Journal of Rural Studies*, 8 (3), 229–40.
Duncan, J. and Ley, D. (1993) (eds) *Writing Worlds*. London: Routledge.
Etzioni, A. (1993) *The Spirit of Community*. New York: Crown.
Jones, N. (1993) *Living in Rural Wales*. Llandysul: Gomer.
Keeble, J. (1995) Hunt, shoot, fish ... kill. *Guardian* (Society section), 15 November.
Midgley, S. (1995) Tim Hughes wants to expand his farm. His neighbours have objected. It will smell, they claim. But, he says what on earth do they expect in the countryside? *Independent*, (Country section), 26 August.
Murdoch, J. and Pratt, A. (1993) Rural studies: modernism, post-modernism and the 'post-rural'. *Journal of Rural Studies*, 9 (4), 411–27.
Murdoch, J. and Pratt, A. (1994) Rural studies of power and the power of rural studies: a reply to Philo. *Journal of Rural Studies*, 10 (1), 411–27.
Philo, C. (1992) Neglected rural geographies. *Journal of Rural Studies*, 8 (2), 193–207.
Philo, C. (1993) Post-modern rural geography? a reply to Murdoch and Pratt. *Journal of Rural Studies*, 9 (4), 429–36.
Sibley, D. (1992) Outsiders in society and space. In K. Anderson and F. Gale (eds) *Inventing Places: Studies in Cultural Geography*. Melbourne: Longman, 107–22.
Sibley, D. (1994) Putting people in their place: stereotypes and landscapes. Paper presented to a conference of the Rural Economy and Society Study Group, University of Manchester.
Stokes, P. (1993) Corky the cock gagged by court. *Daily Telegraph*, 20 March.
Whatmore, S. (1993) On doing rural research (or breaking the boundaries). *Environment and Planning A*, 25 (4), 605–7.

1

Re-negotiating the Boundaries of Race and Citizenship: The Black Environment Network and Environmental and Conservation Bodies

PHIL KINSMAN

Introduction: Landscape, Race and National Identity

This chapter briefly introduces the work and ideas of an organization called the Black Environment Network (BEN) which since 1988 has played a pivotal role in bringing the issues of multiculturalism and the representation of ethnic minorities on to the agendas of countryside and environmental organizations. Its activities are best seen in the context of a specific argument about the concurrence of three ideas: race,[1] nation and landscape. This argument, which can only be briefly sketched here, turns mainly upon the continuing centrality of the idea of race to British nationhood, as argued by Paul Gilroy (Gilroy, 1987). Recently, new attention has been given to landscapes within cultural geography in terms of their power as signifiers of national identity (Daniels, 1993), and this has been argued as especially pertinent in Britain (Lowenthal, 1991, p. 213). This argument can be taken one stage further, that ideas of race form an implicit part of the articulation of national identity through landscape imagery and ideology.

The contemporary articulation of these ideas springs from a historical tradition which is reworked and re-configured within the present social and cultural context. However, they have not gone uncontested, as a number of black[2] people in Britain have responded to the exclusivity articulated through landscape imagery and ideology, and ideas of race and nation are currently being socially reconstructed and spatially reconstituted within a variety of media and situations, from detective and post-colonial fiction to landscape photography. BEN is one such creative response which translates ideas contesting the dominant conceptions of national identity as articulated through landscape imagery into some form of political action.

Methods and Sources

This analysis of BEN is based on a variety of sources. First, it explores a range of material which the organization has produced in the context of its operations. This material takes a number of forms, from educational, academic and journalistic writings to television programmes. It therefore addresses a number of different audiences, and its messages are tailored accordingly.

Second, there is the organization itself, in the form of the individuals who comprise it and their accounts of its work. There has already been a sociological account of BEN which describes it in the context of the British environmental movement and the growing environmental concerns of the United States' black and ethnic minority population (Taylor, 1993). This chapter does not attempt to reproduce Taylor's analysis. Rather it looks at BEN in terms of its wider contexts and ideological goals. The material presented in this chapter was gathered from two conversational interviews conducted with Julian Agyeman during 1992 and 1993,[3] an interview with three members of BEN within the radical development journal *Third World First* (BEN, 1990) and Taylor's account which emerged while the research was under way.

Third, there is corroborative evidence from the other individuals and organizations with which BEN has engaged, which does offer an indication of the reliability of the informants' responses, and places them within the wider context of the organizations and ideas they are seeking to influence. Although problems exist with the use of these sources they do nevertheless provide a critical portrayal of BEN that is accurate up to January 1995.

The Black Environment Network

BEN represents a means by which the ideological discontents found within the landscapes of Britain have been translated into some form of political action. This is not meant to be a misrepresentation of the activities of BEN so that it appears to be the cutting edge of contemporary black radicalism, but it will perhaps show how changes in both the conditions of existence of a section of the black population and in wider society are resulting in a new area of political activism for black people and perhaps a shift in the agenda which shapes the politics of race in Britain. BEN is not the only organization to emerge from the late 1980s around a growing sense of ethnic minorities' environmental concerns. There are also the Karibbean Ecology Trust, the Overstone Project, the Association for Black People in Planning, the National Alliance of Women of African Descent (Taylor, 1993, pp. 271–3) and the Black Environmental Action Group[4], all of which have broadly environmental concerns as their focus. However, BEN seems to be the only one which specifically links them to issues of national identity.

The Story of the Black Environment Network

BEN was founded in 1988 after a conference called 'Ethnic minorities and the environment' sponsored and organized by Friends of the Earth and the London Wildlife Trust, although it was originally suggested by black activists (Agyeman 1990a, p. 235; Agyeman *et al.*, 1991, p. 7). BEN was seen as something of a break-away group and was formed around the felt need for a 'statement of ethnic minority environmental viewpoints and expression of needs' and began to establish a network of ethnic minority groups with environmental interests (Agyeman *et al.*, 1991, p. 7).

In April 1990, BEN merged with the Ethnic Minorities Award Scheme (EMAS), a body which had existed since 1987 with the goal of 'enabling ethnic minority groups to participate within the mainstream environmental movement' (Agyeman *et al.*, 1991, p. 6) through funding small projects, forming partnerships with the mainstream environmental movement, contributing expertise and providing a network of individuals and organizations to support its aims and objectives. Funding for EMAS came primarily from the Inner Cities Unit and later the Environmental Unit of the National Council for Voluntary Organisations[5] (NCVO), together with charitable organizations. EMAS is now fully incorporated within BEN to fulfil specific functions in terms of the execution of projects.

Much of BEN's political strategy and ideology is the work of a single individual, Julian Agyeman. The context of his personal biography and career trajectory are, therefore, important. He was born in East Yorkshire in 1958, his mother was English and white, his father Ghanaian and black. He grew up in Yorkshire, attending a comprehensive school with his brother where he experienced no overt racial hostility, and he enjoyed outdoor activities such as bird watching. He graduated from Durham University with a BSc in Botany and Geography in 1980 and then trained to be a teacher at Newcastle during 1981–2.[6] For several years he taught geography and environmental studies in Carlisle, leading field trips to the Lake District where on a number of occasions he experienced the attention of other walkers and feelings of heightened visibility, despite feeling comfortable with that environment and being appropriately equipped (Agyeman, 1990b). In 1985 he moved to London to be the Senior Environmental Education Officer in the Borough of Lambeth, and after working in another position with Islington Borough Council until 1992 is now a freelance environmental consultant and writer. He also teaches part time at the University of the South Bank, London, where he is co-director and environmental consultant of the Centre for Local Environmental Policies and Strategies (CLEPS), and a member of the editorial board of *Local Environment*, a journal it is launching.[7]

He has recently published a Keystage 2 book based upon his PhD research called *People, Plants and Places* (Agyeman, 1995) and has published widely on various aspects of his perception of the relationship of environmental and countryside organizations to Britain's ethnic minority population as well as more generally within the area of environmental policy (see Appendix). He resigned the Chair of BEN in September 1994 due to his expressed desire to democratize its management and is now less involved in BEN's activities, although he has done some consultancy work for the organization in his freelance role. He was followed as Chair by Vijay Krishnarayan, another founder member, who has subsequently been replaced by Claire Taylor of the British Trust for Conservation Volunteers.[8]

BEN's Basic Structure, Goals and Strategy

BEN defines itself as 'a multi-racial organization which works to enable the missing contribution of black and ethnic minority communities to come forward in environmental work' (Agyeman *et al.*, 1991, p. 1). It is not easy to define as an organization, as it is not merely a facilitator of ethnic minority involvement in environmental issues. Much of its stated purpose consists of being a channel for the exchange of information, networking various groups that have not connected so far (BEN, 1990; Agyeman *et al.*, 1991). Then again, it has also been a useful institutional platform for Agyeman to mount a political critique which has applied pressure to environmental and countryside organizations to both recognize the presence of ethnic minorities and to take account of their needs.

It sees itself as among the first organizations to connect environmental and social issues, and argues for this to be remedied because the lack of ethnic minority involvement in environmental issues is 'an enormous waste of potential' (Agyeman *et al.*, 1991, p. 1). One of BEN's key ideas is that 'everyone is part of the environment, and the environment affects everyone. But environmental issues and action have become the domain of a narrow section of society' (Agyeman *et al.*, 1991, p. 3). Moreover, 'black and ethnic minority communities offer a unique perspective on environmental issues' given that the 'environmental movement is enriched by including and celebrating alternative visions of nature and the environment' (Agyeman *et al.*, 1991, p. 1). The two main thrusts of its vision are summarized in quotations from two key workers: 'There will only be environmental quality when there is human equality' - Julian Agyeman (he refers to this as his epitaph, and this idea appears frequently in his writing), and 'We must make use of the knowledge of the world within Britain' - Judy Ling Wong, BEN's director and only full-time employee (Agyeman *et al.*, 1991).

BEN employs the term 'black' in a specific and inclusive way, to describe:

> the common experience of all ethnic minority communities including the less visible white minority communities such as the Polish, Greek Cypriots or the Irish. BEN's award scheme, EMAS (the Ethnic Minority Awards Scheme for environmental projects), is the spearhead of our contact with the public, and for that we chose to use the term 'ethnic minorities' to ensure that we did not exclude the Chinese, Latin American and other groups we welcome but who do not often consider themselves black. (Agyeman *et al.*, 1991)

This shows an awareness of the slippery nature of the terminology of classifying groups according to ethnic criteria and the linguistic pitfalls to which its type of work is so prone.[9] Although the inclusive thrust which has caused it to define 'black' so broadly that it could lose much of its meaning has opened up BEN to criticism, it was obviously of concern to the organization to find a name which would be credible with the groups it sought to represent but which would not be exclusive, and it is committed to a constant review of its terminology in the light of shifting meanings (Agyeman *et al.*, 1991, p. 4).

Around BEN's metropolitan headquarters are local groups, formerly called local forums, which is how BEN is trying to develop grass roots support and become a national organization (Agyeman *et al.*, 1991, p. 8). They are not based on a single model, but aim to link up ethnic minorities with environmental groups in their local areas, offer advice to local groups, facilitate access to EMAS grants, provide support to existing organizations to develop 'a multi-racial environmental movement at grass roots level' and to 'enable BEN to develop nationally with a clear understanding of the needs of individuals and groups at a local level' (Agyeman *et al.*, 1991). They have taken on an extended role in some areas, working to involve local community groups in environmental issues and twinning inner city groups with countryside organizations and sites. More recently there have been some difficulties between the local groups and the headquarters, with some seceding from BEN to become independent organizations themselves. However, this is not necessarily seen as a problem as BEN considers itself to be a temporary group which will no longer need to exist when ethnic minority groups and the environmental movement have been linked up, and the local groups going out on their own may be a part of this process.[10]

The BEN Report (Agyeman *et al.*, 1991) lists 74 EMAS awards for the period 1990–91, divided into four areas: London, Birmingham and Black Country, Bristol, and Other (which includes places such as Bolton, Leicester, Liverpool, Leeds, Edinburgh, Sheffield, Ashton-under-Lyme, and Nottingham). This is a strategy based around what Julian Agyeman has called 'the multicultural community',[11] which in Britain is largely, but not exclusively, in the urban areas of England (Owen, 1992, p. 6). Thirty-five of the EMAS awards were in the London area; 6 in the Birmingham and Black Country area; 11 in the Bristol area; and 22 in other areas. The type of groups involved varied from the Bengali Workers Action Group and Hackney Black People's Association to the Kilburn Irish Young Mothers Group and the Centre for Armenian Information and Advice.

A number of points of contact have been important in tapping into local ethnic minority communities, such as schools, community centres, and theatre and arts groups. Another important point of contact was through religious groups, such as the Railton Road Methodist Youth Club and the Muslim Community Centre, Stockport, as most of the ethnic groups contacted had mobilized around the focus of cultural identity which was religious, rather than political (Agyeman *et al.*, 1991, pp. 22–6).

In describing its relationships with other organizations, BEN uses the language of partnership. It clearly sees itself as a pressure group, but its language is conciliatory. This involvement is seen as a process of negotiation, but one which involves the real transfer of power and not tokenism. Actual relationships are more problematic than this, but this seems to be inherent in pressure politics, and BEN seems as happy to live with, and even make use of, contradictions as to try to resolve them all neatly.

BEN is aware of the implications of being involved with established and powerful organizations within the environmental movement, and often stresses its recent beginnings and relatively small resources, although this perhaps does some injustice to the political leverage it is able to exert over its partners. Taylor stresses BEN's financial reliance on a small number of institutionally powerful funders, resulting in a process of accommodation and de-radicalization through being drawn into the network of government sponsored environmental organizations, which means that only Agyeman as a private individual and not BEN itself is critical of its funders (Taylor, 1993, p. 289). However, the majority of articles he has published have declared his affiliation to BEN while at the same time being critical of the bodies which fund it. Thus, it is not the case that BEN is being simply and unproblematically institutionalized. Also, BEN does not necessarily see itself as a confrontational and radical organization, although Agyeman is concerned that it should not lose its radical edge. It should be seen instead as involved in a process of negotiation within the defined boundaries of a civil society, even if its greater goals run, at times, contrary to this dominant, orthodox political vision.

BEN's Ideological Project

BEN exists, therefore, as a political organization facilitating the involvement of ethnic minority groups in environmental issues and the environmental movement, but it operates at levels other than the purely pragmatic. All its EMAS projects reflect the strands of what is described here as its ideological project. These include not only the perceived narrow agenda of the environmental movement, but also wider issues of social justice and equality (Agyeman *et al.*, 1991, p. 1). There are, however, other issues which are an implicit part of BEN's critique and reconstruction, namely, national identity, ideas of race and cultural identity, and black identities. The projects that BEN organizes, funds or encourages are themselves used in a series of articles, papers, reports and television programmes, along with what is seen as evidence of the exclusivity of the landscape as a national icon, to build a complex critique which has varied immediate goals, but a consistent central concern. The projects and the articles are a two-edged sword able to address the achievement of several seemingly disparate goals simultaneously.

There are six discernible strands to BEN's ideological project:

1. Urban Conservation, Local Communities and the London Wildlife Trust

Julian Agyeman's critique of the environmental movement began in 1988 with a very urban concern, that of the preservation of urban green space. In an article in *Town and Country Planning* about the London Wildlife

Trust's (LWT) efforts to preserve a now wooded goods yard on Shakespeare Road, Brixton (Agyeman, 1988a, p. 50) he criticized environmental organizations for being prone to what he called the 'process or product syndrome' (Agyeman, 1988a, p. 51). That is, they overlook the *process* of involving a representative cross-section of the community in trying to attain a particular *product*, in this case the preservation of the Shakespeare Road woodland. He used data from a postal questionnaire to make his case (see Table 1.1). From a sample of 97 people who attended a public meeting shortly after a developer pre-emptively bulldozed the site, he showed that compared to national and borough averages, the sample contained higher proportions of owner-occupiers and co-operative dwellers, people with further education qualifications, and in A or B employment groups. He argued that the views of the 'real community' were not properly sought, nor were their needs, such as for housing or employment, taken into account. The consultation was in fact a process of negotiation between elite groups.

Table 1.1 Shakespeare Road sidings gets the bulldozer treatment: what did the locals really want?

Housing	Participants at meeting %	Herne Hill %	LB Lambeth %
Owner-occupier	63	35	26.6
Housing Association rented	11	19.1	6.7
Private rented	7.5	22.6	23.5
Local authority	7.5	23.1	43.1
Other	11*	0.2	0.1
Education	Participants at meeting %	National %	
CSE/O Level/O Grade	11	26.2	
A Level/Highers/B.Tech	13	15	
Degree/HND/Higher Degree	62	6	
Student (full-time)	3	5	
No qualification/response	11 (nr)	48 (nq)	
Employment	Participants at meeting %	LB Lambeth %	National %
Managerial/Professional (A/B)	65	13	14
Technical/Clerical (C1)	35	37	22
Skilled Manual (C2)	5	23	31
Unskilled Manual (DE)	0	27	33

Note: *Exclusively Co-op dwellers
Source: Agyeman (1988b, p. 51)

Although the issue of race is not explicitly mentioned in the article, the location of the community in question – Brixton – identifies it as one of Britain's most important black communities, which was, therefore, being excluded from the process of consultation and the use of power in the making of decisions affecting their lives. The term 'inner city', which he uses, is also synonymous with the nexus of race, poverty and violence in the discourse of recent British society. This chapter is, therefore, a first step for Agyeman in building a critique of environmentalism involving the category of race, which had so far remained unaddressed by environmental organizations.

2. Access to the Countryside and the Countryside Commission[12]

In 1987 the Countryside Commission produced a policy document called *Policies for Enjoying the Countryside* (Countryside Commission, 1987) which tried to shape the future direction of the Commission's role in encouraging conservation but also encouraging greater visitor access. It recognized that 'the countryside is changing – and so is society' (Countryside Commission, 1987a, p. 3), and among the social trends the Commission discerned was 'the greater ethnic diversity of our society' which will 'make new and changing demands on the countryside' (Countryside Commission, 1987a, p. 6).

From its own research the Countryside Commission found that the 25 per cent of the population who visit the countryside rarely or not at all 'include the elderly, those on low incomes, the unemployed and ethnic minorities' (Countryside Commission, 1987a, p. 3). However, despite this recognition of the under-representation of ethnic minority groups among countryside visitors and the barriers they face (Countryside Commission, 1987a, p. 13), it offered no policy suggestions specifically targeted at meeting their needs, and also categorized them among groups regularly perceived as a problem. This opened up space for Agyeman to focus his developing critique on the Countryside Commission, at first in print (Agyeman, 1989a, 1989b, 1990a, 1990b, Agyeman and Hare, 1988), but later also in the mass media.

The publications Agyeman produced in 1988–90 asked questions rather than directing accusations:

> In Britain, how much research has been done by the Countryside Commission specifically on black access to the countryside; how much has been done by environmental organizations on the campaign participation of black people; how much has been done by the Department of Environment on the environmental quality of life enjoyed [*sic*] by black people? …

> Official alarm only occurs when there is empirical evidence. Owing to a lack of research, the evidence here is largely circumstantial.
>
> How much of the Countryside Commission's £20 million grant is spent on increasing black access to the countryside? Certainly not the proportion of £20 million made up by black people's taxes. Perhaps this is why they held their first think-tank in May [*1989*] on 'ethnic minorities and the countryside' ...
>
> Did the Commission involve black people in these deliberations and does it plan to act upon them? (Agyeman, 1989b, p. 337; also in different forms in 1989a and 1990a)

BEN was by this point one of the Countryside Commission's partners, and was one of the 457 organizations consulted by the Commission through its consultation paper, *Visitors to the Countryside* (Countryside Commission, 1991).[13] The paper specifically mentions the special difficulties faced by ethnic minorities in gaining access to the countryside (Countryside Commission, 1991, p. 3) and four of its proposals for comment addressed their concerns directly.[14] Moreover, the Commission set itself and other countryside agencies specific proposed targets, one of which was '1 per cent of countryside staff employed in front-line recreation provision to be of ethnic minority origin by 1995, rising to 2 per cent by the year 2000' (Countryside Commission, 1991, p. 15). Despite these positive steps, BEN took the opportunity of the launch of this document to place more pressure on the Commission, as Julian Agyeman describes:

> ... one of the things we did was we criticized a press launch that they had on *Visitors to the Countryside*, the latest policy document, which actually was very good and put forward some positive statements, ones that we have made and there was no thanks to us in that, but they *didn't* invite us to the press launch, consequently, the *Telegraph* picked it up, and came up with the headline something like, you know, 'Blacks to be taught countryside crafts ...'[15,16]

This interest from print media, and the particular interpretation by the *Daily Telegraph* led to other opportunities for BEN to air its concerns. During 1991 and 1992 Julian Agyeman and Judy Ling Wong appeared in a number of regional and national television programmes in which they represented BEN, and in which the Countryside Commission was often the object of specific criticism, in the light of the launch of *Visitors to the Countryside*. These programmes brought together issues which are not normally seen as related within what are well-defined boundaries in the medium of television. In one of them, *Countryfile*, Agyeman is able to further articulate his understanding of the exclusiveness of the English countryside. While walking round a gymkhana, a 'white event' as he puts it, he describes the countryside as 'a cultural club with its own rules, etiquette and traditions'. His final words, over the strains of Jerusalem, are interesting as an imperative for access to the countryside:

> Britain prides itself on being a multi-cultural society, yet out here in the countryside that's far from the truth. I believe that being British means more than owning a British passport. We need to feel confident that we can explore every corner of it, but until then, we'll continue to feel like strangers in our own land.

Citizenship is not enough; some kind of belonging born of personal knowledge of Britain is required to avoid estrangement from the nation.

In an edition of *Birthrights*, a component of the BBC's minority programming, Jeremy Worth, Head of the Recreation and Access Branch of the Countryside Commission, repeated the target of 40 out of 2000 countryside staff being drawn from ethnic minority groups by the year 2000, although he anticipated that this would be difficult, as although competition for such jobs is intense, black people did not tend to apply for them. The goal was subsequently withdrawn on the grounds that it was impossible to monitor.[17]

Alongside this application of pressure through mass media, BEN has also developed a co-operative relationship with the Countryside Commission. In the BEN Report, the Commission is described as one of BEN's major national partners, funding EMAS projects to enable ethnic minority groups to go on visits to the countryside, and in turn 'the Countryside Commission has been pleased with the results in encouraging a wider range of people to understand and value the countryside, and to use it more for recreation' (Agyeman *et al.*, 1991, p. 17). This is part of BEN's strategy 'to link ethnic minority groups interested in environmental issues with existing environmental organizations, and to help those organizations be more responsive to the needs and wishes of ethnic minority groups' (Agyeman *et al.*, 1991), rather than set up another environmental group competing for a specific niche market of support. Countryside trips to promote ethnic minority access to the countryside have been an important component of BEN's work, with 31 per cent of its award money going on such trips between 1987 and 1989 (Taylor, 1993, p. 277).

In engaging with the Commission, BEN was able to access a wide range of countryside and environmental organizations which the Commission oversees and advises, as well as bringing their concerns to the attention of a wider public. Although the achievement of specific employment targets was eventually withdrawn, the Commission still has the issue of ethnic minority access on its agenda due to its relationship with BEN, seen in the publication of a report on the use of community forests by ethnic minority groups (Thakrar, 1994).

3. The Native/Alien Debate and Partnership with English Nature

The story of BEN's involvement with English Nature began, as with the Countryside Commission, with an initial engagement with an individual at the middle management level of its organization - in this case George Barker, director of Urban Ecology - followed by an exchange of ideas and securing of funding. Then came a period of public exposure of criticisms and the interpretation of their ideas by the media. With English Nature, however, BEN approached ideas of national identity more explicitly through the anthropomorphism perceptible within a scientific discourse; that of ecology.

Agyeman's basic argument is that the use of the terms native and alien for plant species is inappropriate in the context of urban ecology in schools. This is for two reasons: first, the ecology of cities is greatly influenced by human activity which has constantly introduced new species of plants and animals, so they are scientifically inaccurate terms; second, they might be a barrier to learning for ethnic minority children in urban schools.

Agyeman goes on to use this as a means to implicitly criticize English national identity, arguing that black people are somehow perceived as polluting the English countryside. Furthermore, the non-participation of black people in the countryside and environmental movement is a concomitant of this: 'There would appear to be no place in this rural idyll for black people, even as visitors, let alone residents. In this respect, black people are human aliens' (Agyeman and Hare, 1988, p. 39). Also, he places the native/alien dichotomy alongside that of country/city, to argue that black people in Britain 'occupy some of the most run-down, ill-serviced, and environmentally impoverished areas of Britain's cities and are repeatedly portrayed as doing so' (Agyeman and Hare, 1988).

In addressing anthropomorphism in ecology, Agyeman is tapping into a powerful and established critique of scientific practice. The naming of the natural world is not objectively scientific, and the collection and naming of flora and fauna across much of the world, just like the naming of places, has been substantially influenced by the history of European imperial expansion (Crosby, 1986; MacKenzie, 1988).

It was this issue of the naming of the natural world which attracted the most intense media interest for BEN upon the misreporting of some comments made by George Barker to a local journalist. This resulted in some ripples in environmental and forestry publications (Marren, 1992;

Garthwaite, 1993), but it was again in the *Daily Telegraph* that it was given special attention as an issue of national identity. A brief article called 'Rooting Out Racism in Trees' begins: 'The native oak will, in future, simply be an oak tree to English Nature, which has decided the prefix causes offence to ethnic groups and is irrelevant' (Moore, 1992, p. 2).

This led to a longer piece in the *Weekend Telegraph* by Bill Deedes, which consisted of a conversation he had with Julian Agyeman, while walking in Finsbury Park. Having picked up on BEN through a specific scientific issue, the *Daily Telegraph* translated and located it almost from the outset within a discourse of national identity. The piece is called 'Another Country'[18] and Deedes feels able to speak for an undefined but confidently perceived constituency of rural Britons. After some time discussing Agyeman's ideas, with reference to a number of historical case studies he often uses, the conversation ends with this rather bizarre exchange:

> I decide this is a bridge too far. 'If I made my house over to the National Trust, and they wanted to put up a plaque declaring that my grandfather was a slave driver … I would hesitate … well, I wouldn't give it to them'. Agyeman concedes with a laugh. 'All I'm asking for is some honesty. As a teacher in Carlisle, I'm not aware that the kids up there were told there was a black Roman …' We're back on Hadrian's Wall again and I am determined to make a point of my own.
>
> 'The countryside,' I say, 'it's the last fort, and it's under fire. The British feel a lot has been taken from it in recent years. Our people in the countryside feel that things are going away from them. Now we're to be Europeanised … There are two sides to this, nervousness on both sides …'
>
> 'Exactly.' Agyeman accepts my point, which pleases me. I feel I should say something helpful by way of conclusion.
>
> As we part, I say to him, 'What about Black Environment Network coming out in favour of field sports … "Blacks for Fox hunting!" That would win them a lot of marks in the countryside just now. Come on!' There is no reply, but Julian Agyeman has a thoughtful look as he leaves. (Deedes, 1992)

He is not concerned to rectify Agyeman's interpretation of the historical record or offer an alternative one. Instead he personalizes this hidden history as an affront to his personal and family sense of identity and claims the countryside as the last refuge of national identity.

This is not to say that at the last Deedes retreats fully into a ready-prepared reactionary position. His article displays an even-handedness with these issues and Agyeman's ideas, which might normally be thought to be anathema to the *Daily Telegraph*. Agyeman is also convinced that he made an impression on Deedes, whose parting comments he recalls as

'You've lit a candle here Julian, not a bonfire, but a candle.' His encounter with Deedes was also more positive in some ways than with other journalists, as Deedes, for instance, was the only journalist Agyeman has been interviewed by who sent him finished copy for him to read prior to publication. He considered the article to be good publicity for BEN and a reaching of a new audience for these ideas, although he recognized that it was re-cast within a certain language he called 'Telegraphese'.[19]

4. The Black Diaspora and a Global Environmentalism

The fourth strand of BEN's ideological project has not been as highly developed as the preceding two, partly because it has not had the qualities which have been able to attract the media, but also because it is the aspect of BEN's critique of the environmental movement which is most radical and demands greater changes in the structures of thought which govern it.

Agyeman has also chosen to relate it specifically to the concerns of black people in Britain as a means of popularizing environmental issues among them by showing that they have a relevance to their everyday lives. In a number of articles in the black and other specialist political and environmental press, and eventually in the national press, he has sought to address issues of international, environmental and social concern, which have a specificity for the lives of black people in Britain.

In 1988 he argued in *The Voice*, Britain's largest circulation black newspaper, that environmental problems like the disposal of toxic waste, desertification and deforestation affect black people disproportionately, and that in Britain black people are 'the inhabitants of some of the most environmentally impoverished areas in the land' (Agyeman, 1988b, p. 2). He sees a link between these problems that might routinely be perceived as Third World and First World respectively. As well as there being a commonality of the experience of environmental problems for black people, there is also a commonality in the responsibility for these problems: they are all 'directly or indirectly the result of human decisions and actions. Being more specific, they are largely the work of white people, either through the legacies of colonialism, or through debt-induced policies created by lending nations' (Agyeman, 1988b; see also Agyeman, 1992b).

In *Black Briton*, (Agyeman, 1992a) he argued that in Britain black people do not participate in the environmental movement because the issues the movement focus around are irrelevant to ethnic minorities. As an example of this he hypothesizes that the African and Caribbean fresh produce which can be found in food stores in areas of concentrated ethnic minority population, as well as certain other niche markets in Britain, are probably treated with agricultural chemicals which are banned in Europe, but are still sold to countries where there are not such tight restrictions on their use, yet none of this is of interest to the environmental movement (Agyeman, 1992a).

He builds an argument around the global nature of the community of black diaspora to demonstrate why environmental issues should be of concern to black people in Britain. The community of diaspora here becomes a global community inhabiting a single world, which must put aside its differences to ensure some form of continued collective existence.

5. Heritage, the Presentation of History and the Presence of a Black Population in the British Countryside

An article in the *Guardian* in March 1993 provided Agyeman with an opportunity to develop an aspect of BEN's ideological project which had already begun to emerge elsewhere (Coster, 1991; Deedes, 1992). It concerned the contemporary conflict over the burial site and former country seat of Duleep Singh, the last Sikh Maharajah and a favourite of Queen Victoria (Bunting, 1993, pp. 1–2). He owned Elveden, an estate in Suffolk, where he hosted George V for a shooting weekend, and was one of the most prominent individuals in developing driven shooting in Britain in the 1850s and 1860s (Ruffer, 1977, pp. 54–6). The article explores the contradictory meanings of his burial site for England's Sikh community and local villagers, and identifies a rural brand of racism. It takes the story, quite appropriately, as an engagement over national identity, and 'a tale for our times' (Bunting, 1993, p. 1). The article provided an opportunity for Agyeman to have a letter published in the *Guardian*, where he was able to use it as a spring-board to raise 'the general lack of interest from anti-racist organizations' in this aspect of racism, and 'the undefined notion of heritage in a supposedly multicultural society' (Agyeman, 1993a). It led to another publication in *Museums Journal* where he turned his attention to issues of heritage.[20]

Here, he uses the 'heritage clash between the villagers of Elveden and members of the Sikh community in Britain' (Agyeman, 1993b, p. 22) to criticize parochial presentations of heritage which exclude black people. He offers a number of sites as evidence to affirm their historical presence in a multicultural history of Britain, such as Abavalla, near Carlisle, where a division of North African legionaries were stationed in the third century AD, and Race Down Lodge, where Wordsworth lived for some time under the patronage of John Kinney, 'one of Bristol's biggest sugar planters and slave owners' (Agyeman, 1993b). He also uses a picture of Ingrid

Pollard's[21] to highlight another hidden history, this time of Knole, former home of the Sackvilles and now a National Trust property, where the black page 'had always been called John Morocco regardless of what his true name might be' (Agyeman, 1993b, p. 23, quoting Sackville-West, 1958). He points to the few examples of museum presentations concerning slavery as a way forward, and calls for a 'multicultural task force' to change attitudes within the bodies which control the presentation of heritage (Agyeman, 1993b). He recognizes the power of notions of heritage, in their ability to inculcate a sense of belonging, but also their potential exclusiveness:

> There is a growing sense of anger and urgency surrounding the lack of any substantial, mainstream representation of black British heritage. Heritage is not for fun; it is not an abstraction, a 'take it or leave it' process that can be swept under the carpet. Its popular importance goes far deeper. It is fundamental to black people's visions of themselves and their self-esteem in the context of British culture and society. It is also about the right to obtain some form of control, ownership, belonging and a sense of place. Until the practitioners recognize this, heritage sites, exhibits and museums will continue to be visited by a white middle-class mirror image of those gatekeepers who manage such resources. (Agyeman, 1993b)

Heritage is here seen as vital to the development of black identities in Britain, one dimension of which is distinctly geographical: sense of place. These new arguments about what are normally seen as historical, cultural and political issues are overlain by the repetition of his argument about the terms 'native' and 'alien', to which he adds additional details of history, in the form of eighteenth and nineteenth century plant hunters.

6. BEN's Alternatives: 'The Multicultural City Ecosystem'

Agyeman offers not only a critique of established ideas, but the beginnings of alternatives to them (Agyeman, 1991b). The title of a research project he was then completing encapsulates the ideas as he has developed them so far. It is called 'The multicultural city ecosystem as a new approach in environmental education and urban ecology'. The idea of cultural ecology was present in one of his earliest publications, in which he argued that 'there is a fundamental *cultural* link between people and nature' (Agyeman and Hare, 1988, p. 40) which the environmental movement was ignoring at its peril.

These ideas were presented in two similar articles in publications aimed at the secondary educational sector in which Agyeman was then working as Environmental Education Co-ordinator in Islington (Agyeman, 1991a, 1991b). They begin by asking the reader to imagine what, as an 'Asian or African-Caribbean pupil', their own feelings would be if they were told in the course of an exercise in urban ecology that '"native" British plants should be used in preference to "alien" or foreign ones, implying that they are "better"' (Agyeman, 1991b, p. 21). Agyeman then argues that alien species are always assumed to be highly invasive, like rhododendron, but this fear 'may be justified in the case of special (and predominantly rural) habitats such as Sites of Special Scientific Interest' but not in 'the context of the diverse ecology of urban areas, where 85 per cent of the population lives' (Agyeman, 1991b). He was concerned that rural planting policies were being applied unthinkingly to urban ecological projects, and that this rural model was being applied as universal in ecology. His more multicultural vision can be seen in the following section of text from one of his articles where he describes cities as systems:

> [Cities] are not static, isolated physical and living structures, cut off from local, national and global influences. They are dynamic open systems involving inputs of energy and different forms of matter, and outputs such as manufacturing products and waste. In this respect they are similar to ecological systems, except that ecosystems recycle waste. Just as an ecosystem depends on the sun's energy, towns and cities need power. If the power supply to a city stops, the system slows down. If it were never returned, the city would finally change form, or die. Moreover, improved global communications mean that urban areas are increasingly heterogeneous and cosmopolitan; they receive inputs from all over the planet. This means greater diversity, not only in human, but in ecological terms. (Agyeman, 1991b, p. 21)

This is not just a recognition of a cultural dimension to environmental issues. It is also a naturalization of the social world. This is not a new occurrence, but Agyeman takes multiculturalism, a concept which was specifically developed as an educational strategy to combat racism, as a metaphor for the natural world. For him nature is constituted as much by co-operation and co-existence as by competition, and this notion is applied to the history of Britain which is recast in a more thoroughgoing multiculturalism which sees the human population of the British Isles as essentially hybrid. (Agyeman, 1993b). This is also translated into action. He has written a book for Key Stage 2 (Agyeman, 1995) called *People, Plants and Places* and, from his PhD, intends to produce resources for teachers based on these ideas. It is very much a deliberate strategy. Although it is not a term which he necessarily developed himself, Agyeman is keen to pursue the movement he sees within environmental education from the cognitive to the affective.

Conclusion

It is interesting that through BEN, ideas of race, landscape and national identity are beginning to achieve a degree of circulation, and that the connections between these categories are being explored by people who in part live out their daily lives through them. BEN is reinventing these ideas within a new context, which is not unproblematic, but which also seems to offer opportunities for personal and collective meaning for those involved, as well as providing an unexpected challenge to dominant categories of identity.

It would have been easy to appropriate BEN and its work into the language of postmodernism, to construct a particular and highly historically specific critique of the nation and the rural as categories of study. To find in BEN's work a rural 'other' would perhaps be to impose what is a very metropolitan vision on the notion of the countryside. Moreover, BEN does not define itself as a countryside organization and in trying to serve the environmental needs of ethnic minorities it has tried to focus on issues which impinge upon the environments in which they mostly live on a day to day basis; that is, cities. Agyeman's intuitions about the environmental issues which concern ethnic minorities have been validated by recent research (Jeffcote and Keamey, 1994), and they are indeed focused around the quality of urban living environments and not conservation at a regional, national or global level, around which much of the environmental movement is organized.

However, BEN's urban concerns have not received the same degree of attention from the media. This is partly due to it being on the boundaries of the categories normally mobilized to deal with the issues it draws together, but is also because the more urban issues do not speak directly to one of the key foci of national identity in Britain - the countryside - and so excite the interest of the media. Through the notion of access in particular, BEN has been able to mobilize the categories of the rural and the countryside to address notions of citizenship, national identity and black identities.

Part of BEN's work has recently come to focus on revealing the hidden or erased historical presence of black people within rural environments, but it does not claim to speak for a contemporary rural black population, which is still very small. Instead BEN has engaged in what are primarily ideological issues, such as national identity, in order to address what it perceives to be a neglected but central aspect of the lives of ethnic minority groups in Britain. BEN is in fact a metropolitan group both in terms of the location of its organization, the focus of its activities and in the political values which inform its work. However, the aspect of BEN's work which has generated the most interest has been that which could be called rural, because in Britain the rural is an ideological terrain where notions of identity are hotly contested.

Notes

1. Race is a concept fraught with conceptual difficulties and will be treated here as an 'essentially contested concept' (Gallie, 1962). It is now widely held to be a meaningless category, a second order abstraction which uses phenotypical variation to ascribe status and roles rather than allow their achievement (Banton, 1983, p. 8). This does not mean, however, that it can simply be dismissed, as it is an elaborately constructed ideology which releases powerful political forces, and it is the very emptiness of racial signifiers which makes them vulnerable to appropriation, and their contradictions which give them power (Gilroy, 1987, pp. 38–40). As a concept it has a particular history and geography (Banton, 1977, 1983; Livingstone, 1992a, 1992b) which is mutable and connected within specific locations and times (Poliakov, 1971; MacDougall, 1982; Barkan, 1992). It seems to bear close relation to nationalism, even springing from it (Balibar, 1991), as another imagined community which configures identity at a number of scales (Anderson, 1983). It is emphasized here that race is a relative and negotiated process which takes black people outside history, constructing them as problems or victims, paradoxically by reworking past images and ideas within a new context (Gilroy, 1987, pp. 27 and 44–69).
2. The term 'black' is used here to denote people of indigenous African, Afro-Caribbean and Asian descent, and, therefore, as a political grouping rather than as a racial signifier (Miles, 1989).
3. These interviews are cited below when a statement is directly based upon their content and not on the following published reference.
4. Conversation with Julian Agyeman, 25 January 1995.
5. NCVO is a quasi-autonomous governmental organization providing information, support and advice for voluntary groups, especially during an initial launching period building up to independence. This is the process through which BEN is currently going, and has been published within the magazine of NEST, the NCVO Environmental Support Team, several times. BEN uses NCVO's address, was initially provided with rent-free accommodation, operated under the financial umbrella of NCVO, and was in fact drawn in part from an initiative of NEST's in which Judy Ling Wong was already involved (Agyeman *et al.*, 1991, pp. 6–9 and 22).
6. Conversation with Julian Agyeman, 8 May 1992.
7. Conversation with Julian Agyeman, 11 February 1994.
8. Conversation with Julian Agyeman, 25 January 1995.
9. This research faces the same kind of problems, and in this chapter the use of the term 'ethnic minorities' is used in a similar way to that of BEN, as it identifies a particular constituency of shared experience without actually using racial signifiers to classify people.
10. Interview with Julian Agyeman, 20 May 1993.

[11] Interview with Julian Agyeman, 20 May 1993.
[12] For a more detailed discussion of this strand of BEN's ideological project see Kinsman (1996).
[13] Personal communication with Peter Ashcroft of the Countryside Commission's Recreation and Access Branch, 8 January 1993.
[14] Among the proposals for comment which the paper offers are:

> 13. Basic training for countryside staff should include customer care, and ensure that it gives recognition to the *cultural and social diversity for modern society*.
> 14. Colleges, career counsellors, employers and trainers of countryside staff should *enhance the representation of ethnic minority people among front-line countryside staff*, through the positive promotion of accessible training opportunities.
> 15. Would an 'equal recreation opportunities charter' - an award scheme to recognize local authorities who take positive steps to develop confidence across their entire population - encourage action on this front?
> 16. All originators of countryside leaflets and information should *encourage a greater presence of, and reference to, minority groups*. (Countryside Commission, 1991, p. 14; emphasis added).

[15] See Moore (1991) Countryside 'must welcome blacks'.
[16] Interview with Julian Agyeman, 26 June 1992.
[17] Personal communication with Peter Ashcroft of the Countryside Commission's Recreation and Access Branch, 8 January 1993.
[18] A title which has become an obstacle to negotiate for people choosing to write about these issues, as it has been used on at least three occasions already (Coster, 1991; Deedes, 1992; Derounian, 1993). Although it is unclear, it seems more likely that its resonance for authors comes from the film of public school intrigue starring Rupert Everett rather than from James Baldwin's jazz novel, although both contain a notable sexual tension.
[19] Personal communication with Julian Agyeman, 8 May 1992.
[20] Issues of environment, heritage and cultural diversity are explored more fully in Agyeman and Kinsman (1997).
[21] A black photographer who has explored her relationship to the English landscape in her work (Kinsman, 1993, 1995).

Appendix: BEN's Discursive Environment: Publications and Locations

The following references, under headings of the type of publications in which they appear, are included to give an indication of the discursive locations in which BEN has published and so the types of audiences and organizations it has reached. Not all of them are referred to in the text.

Academic Journals

Agyeman, J. (1988a) A pressing question for green organizations. *Town and Country Planning*, 57 (2), 50–1.

Agyeman, J. (1989b) Black people, white landscape. *Town and Country Planning*, 58 (12), 336–8.

Agyeman, J. (1990a) Black people in a white landscape: social and environmental justice. *Built Environment*, 16 (3), 232–6.
Agyeman, J. (1991b) The multicultural city ecosystem. *Streetwise: The Magazine of Urban Studies*, 7, Summer, 21–4.
Agyeman, J. (1993b) Alien species. *Museums Journal*, 93 (12), 22–3.

Mainstream Press

Agyeman, J. (1989a) A snail's pace. *New Statesman and Society*, 2 (35), 30–1.
Agyeman, J. (1993a) Rural racism. Letter to the *Guardian*, 8 March 1993.
Agyeman, J. (1993c) Please go away, we're saving the world. *Independent*, 21 June, 20.
Coster, G. (1991) Another country. *Guardian* (Weekend section), 1–2 June, 4–6.
Deedes, W.F. (1992) Another country. *Daily Telegraph Weekend*, 18 April, 1.
Moore, T. (1991) Countryside 'must welcome blacks'. *Daily Telegraph*, 26 April, 2.
Moore, T. (1992) Rooting out racism in trees. *Daily Telegraph*, 18 March, 2.

Black and Other Specialist Press

Agyeman, J. (1988b) Viewpoint: whose world is it? *The Voice*, 6 September, 3.
Agyeman, J. (1991a) Black people exposed to pollutants. *The Socialist*, 1 June.
Agyeman, J. (1992a) When black means green. *Black Briton*, 20 March, 6.
Agyeman, J. (1992b) World, face up to the real issues. *Black Briton*, 12 June 1992, 61.

Educational Publications

Agyeman, J. (1991c) Hardy perennials. *Times Educational Supplement*, 21 June.
Agyeman, J. (1994) The wild side of town. *Times Educational Supplement*, (Extra: Environment) 10 June, viii.
Agyeman, J. (1995) *People, Plants and Places*. Crediton: Southgate Publishers.

Countryside/Environmental Publications

Agyeman, J. (1988c) Ethnic minorities - an environmental issue? *ECOS*, 9 (3), 2–5.
Agyeman, J. (1990b) A positive image. *Countryside Commission News*, 45, 3.
Agyeman, J. (1990c) Mind your language. *New Ground*, Summer.
Agyeman, J. (1990d) Into the 1990s: quality and equality. *AREE* Third Issue, 3, 23–5.
Agyeman, J. (1990e) Ecological patchwork. *PSLG*, July/August, 22–24.
Agyeman, J. (1993c) Life on the margins. Letter to *The Ecologist*, 23 February, 77.
Agyeman, J. and Evans, B. (1994) *Local Environmental Policies and Strategies*. London: Longman.
Agyeman, J. and Hare, T. (1988) Towards a cultural ecology. *Urban Wildlife*, June, 39–40.
Black Environment Network (1990) Fighting for environmental justice. In N. Druce (ed.) *Links 38. Green Globalism: Perspectives on Environment and Development*. Oxford: Third World First, 15–20.

BEN Publications

Agyeman, J., Warburton, D. and Wong, J.L. (1991) *The Black Environment Network Report: Working for Ethnic Minority Participation in the Environment*. London: BEN.
Black Environment Network (1991) *A Transformed View of People and Landscape*. Pamphlet produced by the Black Environment Network.

Television Programmes

Birthrights, 1992, BBC2, Narrator and Producer - Stella Orakue.
Countryfile, June 1990, BBC1, Presenter - Michael Cullen.
Countrywide, 1 August 1992, BBC2, Presenter - Michael Jordan.
First Take, 4 December 1992, ITV Anglia: Producer and Director - Celia Tait, based on research by Julian Agyeman and Tony Hare.
In Our Back Yard, May 1993, Channel 4.

References

Agyeman, J. (1988a) A pressing question for green organizations. *Town and Country Planning*, 57 (2), 50-1.
Agyeman, J. (1988b) Viewpoint: whose world is it? *The Voice*, 6 September, 3.
Agyeman, J. (1989a) A snail's pace. *New Statesman and Society*, 2 (35), 30-1.
Agyeman, J. (1989b) Black people, white landscape. *Town and Country Planning*, 58 (12), 336-8.
Agyeman, J. (1990a) Black people in a white landscape: social and environmental justice. *Built Environment*, 16 (3), 232-6.
Agyeman, J. (1990b) A positive image. *Countryside Commission News*, 45, 3.
Agyeman, J. (1991a) Black people exposed to pollutants, *The Socialist*, 1 June.
Agyeman, J. (1991b) The multicultural city ecosystem. *Streetwise: The Magazine of Urban Studies*, 7, Summer, 21-4.
Agyeman, J. (1992a) When black means green. *Black Briton*, 20 March, 6.
Agyeman, J. (1992b) World, face up to the real issues. *Black Briton*, 12 June, 61.
Agyeman, J. (1993a) Rural racism. Letter to the *Guardian*, 8 March 1993.
Agyeman, J. (1993b) Alien species. *Museums Journal*, 93 (12), 22-3.
Agyeman, J. (1995) *People, Plants and Places*. Crediton: Southgate Publishers.
Agyeman, J. and Hare, T. (1988) Towards a cultural ecology. *Urban Wildlife*, June, 39-40.
Agyeman, J. and Kinsman, P. (1997) Analysing macro- and microenvironments from a multicultural perspective. In E. Hooper-Greenhill (ed.) *Cultural Diversity: Developing Museum Audiences in Britain*. London: Leicester University Press.
Agyeman, J., Warburton, D. and Wong, J.L. (1991) *The Black Environment Network Report: Working for Ethnic Minority Participation in the Environment*. London: BEN.
Anderson, B. (1983) *Imagined Communities: Reflections on the Origins and Spread of Nationalism*. London: Verso.
Balibar, E. (1991) Racism and nationalism. In E. Balibar and I. Wallerstein (1991) *Race, Nation, Class: Ambiguous Identities*. London: Verso.
Banton, M. (1977) *The Idea of Race*. London: Tavistock.
Banton, M. (1983) *Racial and Ethnic Competition*. Cambridge: Cambridge University Press.
Barkan, E. (1992) *The Retreat of Scientific Racism: Changing Concepts of Race in Britain and the United States Between the World Wars*. Cambridge: Cambridge University Press.
Black Environment Network (BEN) (1990) Fighting for environmental justice. In N. Druce (ed.) *Links 38. Green Globalism: Perspectives on Environment and Development*. Oxford: Third World First, 15-20.

Bunting, M. (1993) In pursuit of the Suffolk Maharajah. *Guardian* (Tabloid section), 3 March, 2–3.

Coster, G. (1991) Another country. *Guardian* (Weekend section), 1–2 June, 4–6.

Countryside Commission (1987) *Policies for Enjoying the Countryside*. CCP 234. Cheltenham: The Countryside Commission.

Countryside Commission (1991) *Visitors to the Countryside*. CCP 341. Cheltenham: The Countryside Commission.

Crosby, A.W. (1986) *Ecological Imperialism: The Biological Expansion of Europe, 900–1900*. Cambridge: Cambridge University Press.

Daniels, S. (1993) *Fields of Vision: Landscape Imagery and National Identity in England and the United States*. Cambridge: Polity Press.

Deedes, W.F. (1992) Another country. *Daily Telegraph Weekend*, 18 April, 1.

Derounian, J. (1993) *Another Country: Real Life Beyond the Rose Cottage*. London: NCVO Publications.

Gallie, W.B. (1962) Essentially contested concepts. In M. Black *The Importance of Language*. Englewood Cliffs: Prentice-Hall, 121–46.

Garthwaite, P.F. (1993) End to term 'Native'. Letter dated 25 October 1992 in the *Quarterly Journal of Forestry: the official publication of the Royal Forestry Society of England, Wales and Northern Ireland*, 87 (1), 59-60.

Gilroy, P. (1987) *There Ain't No Black in the Union Jack: The Cultural Politics of Race and Nation*. London: Hutchinson.

Jeffcote, M. and Kearney, D. (1994) *The Asian Community and the Environment: Towards a Communications Strategy*. Environ Research Report 16, produced by Environ, Leicestershire County Council and Leicester City Council.

Kinsman, P. (1993) Landscapes of national non-identity: the landscape photography of Ingrid Pollard. *Working Paper 17*, University of Nottingham, Department of Geography.

Kinsman, P. (1995) Landscape, race and national identity: the photography of Ingrid Pollard. *Area*, 27 (4), 300–10.

Kinsman, P. (1996) Conflict and co-operation over ethnic minority access to the countryside: the Black Environment Network and the Countryside Commission. In C. Watkins (ed.) *Rights of Way: Policy, Culture and Management*. London: Pinter, 162–78.

Livingstone, D.N. (1992a) 'Never shall ye make the crab walk straight': an inquiry into the scientific sources of racial geography. In F. Driver and G. Rose (eds) *Nature and Science: Essays in the History of Geographical Knowledge*. Historical Geography Research Group Series, 28, 37–48.

Livingstone, D.N. (1992b) *The Geographical Tradition*. Oxford: Blackwell.

Lowenthal, D. (1991) British national identity and the English landscape. *Rural History*, 2 (2), 205–30.

MacDougall, H.A. (1982) *Racial Myth in English History: Trojans, Teutons and Anglo-Saxons*. Montreal: Harvest House.

MacKenzie, J.M. (1988) *The Empire of Nature: Hunting, Conservation and British Imperialism*. Manchester: Manchester University Press.

Marren, P. (1992) Twitcher in the swamp: groaning in the gloaming from Peter Marren. *British Wildlife*, 3 (5), 321.

Miles, R. (1989) *Racism*. London: Routledge.

Moore, T. (1991) Countryside 'must welcome blacks'. *Daily Telegraph*, 26 April, 2.

Moore, T. (1992) Rooting out racism in trees. *Daily Telegraph*, 18 March, 2.

Owen, D. (1992) *Ethnic minorities in Great Britain: settlement patterns, 1991*. Census Statistical Paper No. 1, Centre for Research in Ethnic Relations, Warwick.

Poliakov, L. (1971 *The Aryan Myth: A History of Racist and Nationalist Ideas in Europe* (tr. Edmund Howard). London: Chatto/Heinemann.

Ruffer, J.G. (1977) *The Big Shots: Edwardian Shooting Parties*. London: Debrett-Viking Press.

Taylor, D.E. (1993) Minority environmental activism in Britain: from Brixton to the Lake District. *Qualitative Sociology*, 16 (3), 263–95.

Thakrar, N. (1994) *Ethnic Minority Participation in Community Forest Activities*. Cheltenham: The Countryside Commission.

2

The March of the Earth Dragon: A New Radical Challenge to Traditional Land Rights in Britain?

NICK FIDDES

> The past two years have seen a coming together of many ideologies, a unification of many issues and people, and the realisation of a common trend. You could call it a heightening of consciousness, or also that the Earth Dragon, awoken at Twyford, is now at large in the land. (Alexandra Plows, activist)

Environmental protest in Britain has recently taken on a new character. Within the movement, once-radical organizations such as Greenpeace are widely perceived to have repositioned themselves towards the conventional structures of political and economic organization. Their erstwhile political and social space has been filled not just by equivalent configurations, but by an eruption of grassroots activism bound by ideas more than by formal associations.

This new breed of protesters rose to public prominence in 1992 at Twyford Down, beside Winchester, England - a historic site of ancient field systems and legendary reputation. A few, mainly young, protesters arrived to camp near the construction site for a new road, carrying little more than canvas, blankets, pots, and handtools. Over the months their number swelled to dozens or hundreds, and at times thousands, of fellow travellers in loose alliance with other local campaigns against the development. Local pathways, the Dongas, lent the most prominent 'tribe' their chosen name. They deployed a range of predominantly non-violent direct action (NVDA) tactics to delay building work: often simply standing in front of, or on, the machines.

That road has now been built, but similar episodes have followed at a dozen or more significant locations up and down the UK, each developing its own character and refining tactics on the basis of experience and the authorities' responses. The approach to protest first distilled at Twyford has provided an example and inspiration for countless freelance crusaders, in both environmental and other 'progressive' campaigns. NVDA tactics have included occupying the Annual General Meetings of banks or construction companies, the 'ethical shoplifting' of mahogany to highlight its probable theft from indigenous people's lands, and disabled activists padlocking their wheelchairs to buses in busy London thoroughfares. The environmental battleground has spread to supermarkets, showhouses, and local authority planning department offices. But road construction projects remain the key domain.

This chapter describes the backgrounds, beliefs, and evolving ways of life characteristic of the new road protest movement in Britain.[1] In particular, it outlines a range of ways in which power is negotiated, and reveals contested conceptions of rights and ownership with respect to property and to the land.

The pattern, to date, has been for a few ardent protesters to take up spontaneous residence on or near the site of a proposed road development, usually (for pragmatic reasons of accessibility) near an urban settlement. They commonly select a Site of Special Scientific Interest, an Area of Outstanding Natural Beauty, or a place with particular social, historic, or spiritual importance (new roads in Britain commonly affect such places, since conservation regulations restricting development, ironically, make them cheap for the authorities to obtain by compulsory purchase). Urban locations also allow the impacts of road development on the social environment to be emphasized. Three examples from 1994 are Solsbury Hill, near Bath, where a by-pass was run through water meadows below an ancient hilltop fort, 'Pollok Free State' on the outskirts of Glasgow, where the local authority intends a major road to transect one of Europe's largest urban open spaces, and the M11 development where a Victorian London terrace, Claremont Road, became the site of the nation's most expensive ever eviction.

The more seasoned activists bring a wealth of experience from other environmental, anti-nuclear, and peace movements. But it is difficult to distinguish clearly those who are present primarily to protest, from the 'New Age Travellers', squatters, or others who may share the space in return for their occasional weight of bodies. Thus, disillusioned ex-soldiers and urban refugees from the streets or 'sink' housing schemes mingle with idealistic middle-class school or university students. It would be wrong to characterize the protesters only as the marginalized underemployed with little else to do; many have given up well-paid jobs, or could work if they wished, and even 'celebrities' and aristocracy augment the numbers.

The majority share anti-consumerist styles of self-presentation, including deliberately tatty clothing and unkempt hair, which earn them the general appellation of 'crusties' (this style has an element of making a virtue of necessity, occasioned by the inevitable hardships of living outdoors in all seasons). Most stem from the cities and, despite their central concern for conserving and living in closer proximity to 'nature', many have little prior experience of living on, or off, the land.

The camps quickly become functional communities, relying on their own resources so far as possible. Much of the life is communal, with tasks, possessions, and problems shared, and participants typically tapping whatever personal assets they possess to further the cause. The many vegetarians or vegans might gather edible vegetation to supplement bought, brought, or begged produce, while others might hunt rabbits. Donations do come, sometimes from surprising sources, and are as likely to be in the form of banjos, bagels, or bicycle locks, as in direct financial support.

For inspiration, participants tend to cite other political or environmental movements involving NVDA. Favourites include Ghandian philosophy, the Himalayan Chipko 'tree-huggers' (Weber, 1988), or the Australian and North American campaigns to protect remaining ancient forests, which perhaps reached their most spectacular form in 1993 when almost a thousand people were convicted through a legal process devised specially for the purpose at the behest of the logging company, after peacefully blockading the clearcutting of Clayoquot Sound in British Columbia (Berman *et al.*, 1994).

Most protesters would subscribe to what may be termed a 'deep ecology' environmental philosophy or agenda (Devall, 1988, pp. 32–4), stressing the intrinsic, as opposed to utilitarian, value of natural diversity. Their words commonly evoke a utopian and somewhat mythical bygone age. Their ideas spring from anarchism, but also from romanticism; they compound individualism and communism and tribalism; they select freely from New Age, Deep Green, and non-industrial cultural sources; their tastes include organic or biodynamic growing or husbandry organized on permacultural principles; they prefer homeopathic or shamanistic or naturopathic healing; they favour animistic or eastern-influenced or occult spirituality; and their political views are united only by distance from those of 'fucking Tories' (as Conservatives are customarily termed), although representative politics, hierarchy, and leadership are commonly rejected entirely. The way of life appears disorganized, as often it is, because 'organization', as a synonym for power relationships, is anathema.

These protests develop and promote a diversity of alternative ways of living, for the long term, but there are usually two main immediate aims. The first is to raise people's awareness of environmental damage and other arguments against particular developments, both directly and through the media. The second is to add to project costs through delays and expensive security: for example, the few days it took to evict protesters at Claremont Road is estimated to have cost £2 million alone, added to perhaps £4 million in security and delays over the course of the campaign.

Tactics have included climbing on to, or 'locking on' to bulldozers, occupying buildings, fields, and (famously) a copse of trees, for weeks or months on end, or simply invading worksites without protective clothing so that, by law, work should stop. From early dependence on simple devices such as hardened steel bicycle locks for 'locking on', the protesters have created increasingly inventive methods of retarding their removal. (Workshops in NVDA techniques and philosophy are regular events at local, national, and international 'green gatherings' just as their antagonists disseminate their own tactical information.) A sophisticated battle of wits ensues, with protesters needing continually to evolve new stratagems as the developers or authorities find ways to combat the old ones:

> The bailiffs brought a new tool to Claremont Road last week. It was a bladed hook about two foot long, cleverly designed to extract arms embedded in barrels of concrete without tearing too much flesh. At first it was devastatingly effective, and people who had expected to spend three hours being dug out with pneumatic drills and angle grinders were freed in just five minutes. But as news of the device spread along the rooftops, the protesters started binding their arms with tape and plastic hosepipe, plugging the holes down which the arm extractor could be pushed. (Monbiot, 1994a, p. 5)

And they have not been alone. Although the mainstream environmental groups have largely preferred to maintain their distance, the protesters have found willing patrons among their local communities. Sets of plans are mysteriously 'found' in skips behind planning departments; bakers drop off fresh supplies in the dead of night; trucks divert an hour or two from their rounds to help shift heavy loads; end-of-date stock from the local supermarket (as well as from its skips) finds its way to their kitchens. And, at weekends, women in white silk and gold chains and their husbands in Pringle knitwear come with boxes of chocolates, and perhaps to lend a hand with the others.

It is, perhaps, this latter factor which has given this movement its greatest impact: the hitherto improbable alliances that have been springing up with more conventional community groups, and the deep roots of public sympathy from which the protesters have sprung. Many of the activists proclaim allegiance to loose groupings such as Earth First! but, unruly appearance notwithstanding, their support and influence go much wider than a single campaigning organization. They have been notably successful in distilling and promoting a groundswell of public disapproval at the Government's £23 billion road building programme, and have scored clear victories such as the 1993 decision to abandon plans to build a road through London's last surviving fragment of ancient woodland at Oxleas Wood, which was dropped in the face of a 5000-strong NVDA pledge drawn mainly from the local community.

However, to focus exclusively on the direct aims and impacts of this protest would be to misunderstand the movement entirely. The activism is about more than just public resistance to the construction of a few undesirable transport projects. For most of those at the heart of the protests, developing a way of living is at least as important, with progress and well-being measured by radically different criteria to those championed by the political authorities of the day. Road construction projects which the protesters hold to be destroying some of the most valued remnants of an older and better social landscape while promoting increasingly harmful economic and cultural behaviour, provide an exemplary backdrop against which this contest of ideas can be waged.

The mainstream media rarely cover more than the most dramatic clashes, when protesters invade or are invaded. But the true meaning about what is going on in these places is not revealed only, or even mainly, at the showpiece conflicts. Rather, it is the sub-society which sustains the protest which is of singular significance, continually developing as a consciously, unconsciously, or self-consciously lived expression of shared ideals. It is not just an activity, but an all-encompassing way of life. At one action, a protester, being berated by a well-to-do 'Suit' to 'get a job', instantly retorted: 'This is my job – the only difference between you and me is that you're overpaid for yours!' As a relatively self-sufficient community, the protest attracts a wide fellowship of individuals who feel they had little place in conventional society, and are attracted by the marginality, as well as the potential for community and creativity.

The body of people at least sympathetic to this way of life has been swelling by the year, and developing into not just a culture, but a society within wider society, the scope and meaning of which remains largely impenetrable to those who have no direct contact with it. Attempting to quantify the movement depends substantially on questions of definition, and it can be hard to draw firm lines between these protesters and other (mainly, but by no means exclusively, youthful) subcultures who may or may not congregate in the vicinity and co-operate in their activities – particularly since many individuals drift in and out of active involvement in protest. Certainly, firm links have developed with other like-minded groups: particularly travellers, but also squatters, the rave scene, and radical politics, all of whom have an interest in redefining society, and reinventing culture. Moreover, significant numbers decline to register on central censuses, partly out of a generalized distrust of, or simple lack of interest in, centralized organizations, and particularly since the abortive Community Charge or 'Poll Tax' for which the British Electoral Register was deployed as an instrument of fiscal leverage. While the number of protesters active nationwide at any one time is probably in the order of a few thousand, the company from which they spring measures at least in the hundreds of thousands.

Whatever an individual's background, most joining road protest camps soon adopt the mannerisms, conventions, and styles of a recognizable but eclectic culture, characterized by general devaluation of material attachments. Sahlins (1973) pointed out many years ago that human societies can pursue two alternative routes to affluence: to have much, or to desire little. And Maslow (1943) suggested over 50 years ago that once humans' basic material needs are satisfied, further growth in well-being was unlikely to come from more material goods but rather from such areas as love and belongingness, self-esteem, and self-actualization. During this period, however, the influential Trinity of industry, politicians, and the mass-media has continued to form policy on the basis that more money is the root of real happiness. This is a message the protesters resist. But their rejection of consumerism has come to mean more than 'living lightly on the land' as an act of selfless virtue, or rebellion against authority. Rather, the placing of little value on material things is taken to represent a route to fuller and more meaningful relationships, with other people and with the natural world.

Consumerist 'goods' are interpreted as impeding, rather than promoting, welfare in this context. On the other hand, items produced creatively would be highly valued for their relational history (as, of course, would entities with their own existence, such as animals and trees, as well as some inanimate subjects or spaces). Thus, the deliberate despoliation of a small sculpture, say, would be regarded with outrage, but the accidental loss of an expensive camera as merely unfortunate. A large communal storage 'bender' (a sort of makeshift tent, often tarpaulin covered) on Solsbury Hill bore a sign above its entrance saying 'People's tat, not tatable tat', to indicate it should not be used as a rubbish tip. Tat can be roughly translated as junk or garbage. Even useful property is junk and the resolutely anti-consumerist 'crusty' image in clothing and hairstyles, therefore, a positive statement.

Likewise, acts that in the wider world might be construed as theft, or at least rudeness, are commonplace, with the most habituated group members routinely 'borrowing' or lending each others' sleeping bags, beer, or other utilitarian goods as needs arise. Possessions with personal value would be exempt, as would those in known regular use - and sometimes the property of those known to be possessive about their 'tat', or peripheral members of the community. Moral standing, crucially, lies in non-attached attitudes to one's own property, rather than in disrespect towards others. Even then, however, disposition towards property is commonly more flexible than is normal elsewhere in contemporary Britain. A television cameraman who had the good idea of letting the 'tree-hangers' at Solsbury Hill take a shot for him from the perspective of their permanent camp fifty feet above took many days to regain his equipment, apparently from mischief rather than a desire to steal. There was a feeling abroad that he needed to learn to be less hung up about his 'tat' (although it was unclear whether this aim was achieved).

Similarly, carvings, crafts, drawings and paintings, poetry, installations, performance, and any art form imaginable are seldom far away, reflecting the emphasis on individual creativity. 'Pollok Free State' resembles a sculpture park as much as a protest site, and the impromptu art gallery in Claremont Road drew international attention. The subject matter commonly combines ancient icons with contemporary issues. It eschews the morals and mores of a decadent dominant culture which is perceived to have lost touch both with its relationship with nature and with itself, as described by a Twyford veteran:

> We all felt that people had been ripped from their roots. We felt people had been de-sensitized, did not know how they depended on the earth for survival, were not aware of their arrogance over nature.... At the same time we discovered an alternative to what we saw as the self-destructive society - a way of life in tune with the earth. We picked herbs for medicines and food, carried firewood and water, lived communally in simple structures. We learned old crafts. We chose to express our ethics and beliefs in symbols and ancient archetypes. It was empowering and it was fun. We danced and

sang at night and charged out to meet the machines in the day. (Plows, 1994, p. 5)

The life can indeed be fun, with food and relaxants, conversation, spiritualism, emotional bonding in various forms, tolerance, a liberal capacity for decadence, and above all a sense of belonging ... all are in abundance. Recorded music comes only from security guards' radios, and not only for want of batteries; the rest is inexorably live, made up mainly of rhythmic drumming and chanting, with a dash of folk themes, simultaneously evoking tribalism and traditional ways on the one hand, and rejecting even the melodic principles of mass-marketed music on the other. Attitudes to drugs are also revealing, with drink and 'soft' drugs such as cannabis widely accepted and celebrated recreationally, but individual dependence on alcohol or harder drugs typically regretted as a symptom rather than blamed as a cause of wider social problems. Compared with the censorious alternatives, it is not hard to see why this self-help and proactive culture has proved a magnet to thousands disillusioned by what they feel to be the sterility, personal devaluation, and regimentation of a mass-consumerist culture to which they may or may not be admitted. Indeed, one abiding, if unintended, legacy of the 'Thatcherite revolution' could be that many of 'her children' are choosing to take responsibility for their own destinies, to shape their future, and to re-invent their own purposeful, participatory, and mythopoetic culture.

The emphasis on pleasure, artistic and tactical creativity and involvement which characterizes these communities serves several purposes, all of which, to some extent, subvert the authorities' perceived advantages. The real battle, in many ways, takes place not on the ground, nor even necessarily in the media, but in the hearts and minds of participants and witnesses. Thus, however chaotic the sites and scenes may seem, the conflict is waged with a relatively sophisticated and pragmatic appreciation of the contestation of power. Most activists recognize that to attempt to wage war on the authorities' own terms would be futile, both practically and philosophically. Meeting force with force would fail, and not only because the State controls immeasurably greater substantive resources. More importantly, to the protesters, perceiving power only as the ability to coerce by weight of might would be to fall into the trap of accepting an analysis which is abhorred, since attempts to exert dominance over others are uniformly considered morally reprehensible. Therefore, the protesters' task is to shift the ground to marginalize the authorities' strengths, while shifting their own agenda to centre stage. They set about this in a number of ways.

Pragmatically, people are more likely to spend their time supporting a cause if it is actively enjoyable and rewarding. Although to outsiders the way of life may appear austere, and potentially fruitless or even dangerous, those involved find it enjoyable and fulfilling, with plentiful sociability and support. This helps to attract volunteers who encounter a spirit of community that in turn engenders levels of mutual assistance and trust which can be crucial to effective NVDA.

Emphasizing the simple pleasures of human interaction and creativity can help to 'free' individuals from what are seen as the alienated alternatives which tie so many people to the materialist realm, and so liberate them from the propaganda of consumerism. This is characteristic not only of the protest movement, but also of much of the associated subcultures, such as travellers or squatters, from which fresh activists may be drawn.

Involvement and proactivity counters deep-rooted feelings of disempowerment, which many activists believe the Government instil purposefully to quell dissent. In the face of a powerful confederacy of business and politicians, each small performance, whether artistic or resistive, is felt to empower those who originate and indeed those who may witness. Individuals report discovering a heady rush of self-belief on learning that a bulldozer can be stopped in its tracks simply by standing in front of it. Such fulfilment may be a rare commodity in the overwhelmingly powerless life choices conventionally open to many protesters, and is also a potent antidote to the hopelessness engendered by an excess of environmental doom-mongering. This quest for autonomy is formalized in the declarations of independence, complete with passports, constitutions, and appeals to the United Nations for recognition, made at places like 'Pollok Free State' and 'Wanstonia'.

A prevailing mood of fun can also be vitally protective in disarming the more aggressive elements in the security forces sent to police the protests. Despite near-universal insistence on non-violence by the activists, there are many alleged incidents involving hostility, sexual abuse, and physical brutality by contractors, security guards, and the police force, as well as unsympathetic vigilantes. Fear of violence is ubiquitous, and can indeed frighten individuals off from becoming involved. Befriending or entertaining these opponents, and generally keeping the mood 'fluffy' through lighthearted banter and songs, can be the protesters' best defence against such aggression.

Protest is often heavy with symbolic statements, independently of practical efficacy. To the sceptical observer, the sheer obscurity or minimal scope of such personal artistic or obstructive acts of conscientious objection can sometimes seem hopeless to the point of perversity.

Such performances bid to inspire as well as inform, and to counter destruction with creativity (at least until their works are 'trashed' before the cameras in their final stands). However, their possible power should be gauged not necessarily by direct impact, but by their potential for iconoclastic impact in contesting entrenched ideas, whereby the apparent futility can convey part of the message. A dramatic example of this principle might be that nameless figure facing down the tanks in Tiananmen Square, whose lone act of defiance wrought world-wide influence out of proportion to its delay to the military operation.

By using poetry, music, and dance, as well as often highly personal and emotional statements of opposition to the environmental destruction, the protesters are able to introduce a discourse that denies the sovereignty of 'rational' material and economic arguments to which the authorities prefer to restrict discussion in public debate.

At least as important as the ends (or 'product'), of protecting a particular site, are the means (or 'process'), of developing relationships with each other and with the place. By attempting to put into daily practice a cosmology which includes non-violence and the rejection of hierarchical relationships, and which values spontaneity over orthodoxy, and creativity over entertainment, the protesters hope to demonstrate the abusive and 'life-denying' relationships which are considered characteristic of organizations where power is concentrated. Accordingly, the authorities' perceived abuses of power (including routine police and court bias) is seen only as further evidence of a political system wildly out of democratic balance.

The use of ancient iconography is effective on several levels, affirming for the participant as well as the watching world the posited superiority of 'older ways' over those of contemporary consumerism. At Solsbury Hill, for example, a small shrine was laid below the brow of the hill, combining a sun-figure with an assortment of natural icons and incantations in verse, in homage to the ancients, and as a reminder to the moderns. The often-eclectic selection of pre-modern imagery does more, however, than simply symbolize rejection of technocratic society's excesses; it also shrewdly outflanks the aristocratic or political establishment's own iconographic claims to the authority of tradition, by evoking even older principles and practices.

All in all, while non-violence is, for the vast majority, either a deeply-held philosophy or at least a pragmatic tactic maintained by group pressure, awareness of issues of power and its negotiation is a multi-faceted fixation among the protesters. However, the operant opposition (at least from the point of view of the activists) is not always, as it seems on the surface, between developers and Dongas. The contest is between powerful and powerless, with violence - against people, or animals, or the land - ubiquitously stamped as a hallmark of the abuse of power. But the powerless in each case is the land and its occupants 'under attack', whose interests are reckoned to go unrepresented in our contemporary economic and political system, without the advocacy and intervention of voluntary human agents. The activists' self-appointed task, therefore, is not so much to fight for their own interests, as to win back power on behalf of disempowered people, animals, or biosphere. This generates an asymmetry in the conflict, since the developers tend to view themselves as under siege by the protesters, but the protesters see the developers 'waging war' on the land and its occupants which it is their intent to protect.

In principle, most of the protesters have little respect for laws which conflict with the pursuit of their purposes, since to their conception they are obeying a 'higher' law. The authorities' claims that the protesters seek to impose their views without the legitimacy of democratic (or regal) authority are normally met with one of two responses. One mockingly disdains the notion that business or government observes either the spirit or the letter of democratic procedures in pursuing their interests, and so forfeits the right to respect. For example, it is axiomatic within the protest movement that the Government's enthusiasm for road building is deeply conditioned by the construction and haulage companies' substantial donations of political funding to the governing party. This partiality is perceived to be manifest in countless artifices such as the Solsbury Hill development being officially designated a 'by-pass' (in spite of its evident destiny to form one section of an arterial 'Euroroute') to limit the scope of the public enquiry. The second probable response points out that badgers, or trees, or future generations, or whatever, do not have a vote, and so hardly enter into democratic consideration. This returns us to the notion of higher laws, and a duty for the 'aware' to act as their agents. Along with appeals to teleological or consequentialist considerations, this is one of two basic arguments used to justify civil disobedience, both of which:

> rely upon some intelligent weighing of consequences of the disobedient act. The protester here argues, in effect, that his [*sic*] particular disobedience of a particular law, at a particular time, under given circumstances ... is likely to lead in the long run to a better or more just society than would his [*sic*] compliance, under those circumstances, with the law in question. (Cohen, 1971, p. 120)

These justifications precipitate questions such as the following:

> How great is the expense incurred by the community as a consequence of the disobedience? ... Is any violence entailed or threatened by the disobedient act? And if so, to property or to persons? ... Has a bad example been set, a spirit of defiance or hooliganism been encouraged? Has respect for law been decreased in the community, or the fundamental order to society disturbed? (Cohen, 1971, pp. 125–6)

Thus, their reluctance to obey, unquestioningly, the laws of the land is not to say (as their more populist detractors do) that these activists are devoid of ethical standards. The more anarchistically inclined might object to rule by law on principle, but principle is none the less present. Debates on topics such as the above are rarely far from the surface among the road protesters, with a view to desired long-term effects at least as much as to immediate outcomes. Indeed, with the possible exception of certain purposefully religious communities, few groups can be underpinned by more definite moral assumptions, with members characteristically putting principles into personal practice on a daily basis with greater rigour. True, their moral judgements are *different* to many of those prevailing in the dominant society which either they have rejected, or which has rejected them. But ethical, they certainly are.

And there remains a tension between a need for effective organization and a widespread presumption of personal autonomy. In practice, many of the codes by which the protesters operate (mainly involving the proper conduct of relationships) remain tacit, or communicated through indirect discourses such as the discussion of their protagonists' evils. An individual who transgresses even unwritten codes might find that he or she is subject to appropriate sanctions ranging from a ragging, or a kicking, to (worse) the withdrawal of community, such as happened to one drunken traveller who had 'the windows of his car smashed for driving 30 miles an hour through the site where there were kids' (Lowe and Shaw, 1993, pp. 178–9).

The protesters' attitudes towards property, relationship, and the law, may help to illuminate their understanding of the land, and access to the land. What happens to personal possessions might be of little importance, but land is not in the same category. Rather, land is a unique entity with both its own intrinsic worth, and also its value to all of its human and non-human occupants. Thus, decisions perceived to be taken by and for a powerful few, without due consideration of the legitimate interests of all that would suffer by such actions, are clearly to be resisted as a matter of principle. So, a protester at Solsbury Hill explained how she could justify occupying other people's land, simply and directly: 'The land invited me on ... I'm doing what it's asked me to do.' She was acting, to her mind, as the agent for a powerless entity, under a system of ethics which overrode those statutes which the powers-that-be are perceived to have enacted largely to protect and enhance the interests of the already powerful, to the neglect of the powerless (whether that be human, other animals, plants, the environment, or posterity).

From the point of view of the protesters, the protest is not just a matter of being willing to break the law to prevent road-building from destroying water meadows and ancient badger setts; it is even more than declining to recognize the legitimacy of traditional land ownership, that 'source of power throughout British history' to which concepts of 'freedom' have been closely allied (Norton-Taylor, 1982, p. 17). Rather, it is a simple and direct statement of a self-referentially logical world view in which the self-interested actions of a few powerful individuals in business and government are self-evidently criminal or insane. It is not just that the land does not and cannot belong to anyone to treat with such apparent disrespect, but rather that we all belong to the land. Whereas attachment to material possessions is a spiritual perversion, attachment to one's habitat is a fundamental relationship.

Needless to say, the world view by which a few crusty protesters justify their actions also appears self-evidently criminal or insane, to those individuals in business and government with an established presumption of land-as-commodity. David Pepper (1993, p. 236) relates a comparable example from Australia in the 1970s, when campaigners successfully used the occupation of buildings and other tactics to oppose a high-rise speculative office development. Perhaps most interesting was the Lord Mayor of Sydney's disdainful comment, that: 'What's now coming is a new type of personal property in which you have some "rights" just living in a place' (Bolton, 1981). It is just such an approach which the protesters would defend. Indeed, they would be unlikely to restrict it to humans' rights. To many, such views are clearly anathema and deeply threatening. For example, the legal adviser to the Country Landowners' Association, interviewed for a BBC television *Heart of the Matter* programme on 'New Age Travellers', called the statutory tolerance of any form of access to privately owned land 'a very dangerous precedent indeed'. Certainly, the debate opens up a Pandora's box of issues concerning the democratic legitimacy of the use of 'private' land when it impacts upon other people's interests or concerns, and, according to the protesters, upon non-human interests.

Of course, we are used to recognizing that an Englishman's (or woman's, or Scot's) home is not necessarily his or her castle in every circumstance. Whether it be constraints on private sexual behaviour, or laws governing the humane treatment of pets or farm animals, conservation regulations, or Prince Charles's or indeed public authorities' interventions on behalf of the architecturally concerned public, there are many ways in which we already impose ethical or aesthetic norms upon each other, even when out of the public eye. Land-use planning already imposes far stricter controls on how the land itself may be disposed of than for other types of personal 'property'. But to dispute the possibility of rights to land ownership not just in degree, but in principle, strikes at the very heart of capitalist ideology, policy, and practice.

Few, if any, of these ideas are entirely new. Were this activity confined only to a radical fringe, the Government might tolerate the limited expenses and irritations of such protests as something which many influential people in British society undoubtedly find objectionable, but which, as legitimate democratic dissent, is one of the costs of sustaining a free society. Indeed, some members of the legislature might even agree with Thomas Jefferson's statement of over two centuries ago that 'a little rebellion now and then is a good thing .... It is a medicine necessary for the sound health of government ... God forbid that we should ever be 20 years without such a rebellion' (Letter to James Madison, 30 January 1787).

However, the current administration is responding otherwise. These, and many other related activities, are now being prosecuted under the terms of the 1994 Criminal Justice Act - a wide-ranging piece of legislation which is either an overdue attempt to restore the rule of law in environmental disputes, or draconian authoritarianism, depending on your perspective. The Criminal Justice and Public Order Act effectively criminalizes not only the actions but the entire way of life of this sub-society of people - the road protesters, foxhunt saboteurs, squatters, travellers, festival-goers, and people who enjoy (rave) music 'wholly or predominantly characterized by the emission of a succession of repetitive beats', in the words of the Act. The civil rights organization Liberty has called this law 'one of the most wide-ranging attacks on domestic human rights' and claims that 'rather than tackling crime, the Bill seeks to outlaw diversity and dissent' (Liberty, 1994).

The introduction of the Criminal Justice Act seems set to precipitate a showdown between those believing in the legitimacy of NVDA and other forms of extra-ordinary environmental activism, and traditional possessors of authority. It is too early to achieve a reliable picture, but so far at least the Government's attempt to arbitrate this civil dispute through new legal processes has been unsuccessful, if the aim was to diminish the level of combat and costs. The Act is widely understood to have been introduced exclusively on behalf of the developers, without equivalent measures to address the protesters' environmental and social agenda. And so, far from quelling dissent, it serves only to fuel the prevailing sense of injustice and martyrdom.

But, as the previous discussion of contestations of power suggested, the battle-lines may not be as clear cut as the legislators seem to assume. Belying their social and economic disadvantages, the protesters possess an apparently infinite capacity for imaginative demonstration, coupled with a little-to-lose contempt for authoritarian sanctions, which bestows real potential for subverting each attempted crackdown into a propaganda coup of their own. For example, a recent front page of a national morning newspaper carried a photograph of a 'trial' of politicians held before a jury of 250 protesters in the garden of the Home Secretary's own home, while six others scaled his roof (*Guardian*, 21 November 1994, p. 1). That occasion recalled another event some weeks previously when protesters occupied the roof of the Houses of Parliament on the date of the Act's introduction. And that, in turn, evoked another protest some months before when anti-roads protesters occupied the Transport Secretary's roof, unfurling a banner designed to resemble a motorway driven through the politician's home. Repeatedly taking to the rooftops, to occupy the physical as well as the moral high ground, aims to drive home the message of politicians' personal involvement in harmful processes from which they are accused of being unreasonably detached. When such actions cease to prove newsworthy, similarly thought-catching events will follow.

It is easy to dismiss the movement as little more than the latest in a long and illustrious line of rebellious fringes, such as the Levellers, the Diggers, or the New Model Army, which have dared to challenge the British establishment, yet accomplished only minor progress in challenging prevailing patterns of privilege. Indeed, as George Monbiot (1994b) has pointed out, there are startling parallels between the modern Criminal Justice Act and some earlier statutes. In 1662, for example, the ruling aristocracy drew up laws which punished Quakers with a fine or three months imprisonment for 'ecstatic gatherings' (precisely the same penalty as faces contemporary ravers, with their chemical Ecstasy). That was soon followed by another law prohibiting 'Rogues, Vagabonds and Sturdy Beggars' from travelling around the countryside or settling in makeshift dwellings – as, again, does the Criminal Justice Act. In 1714 'filthy ruffians' were squatting and sabotaging road-development sites, objecting to environmental damage and economic inequity. The Riot Act of 1715 made provisions to outlaw public protest gatherings in very similar ways to the new law. And hunt sabotage can arguably be traced back to the time of the Black Act of 1723 which made frightening-off deer to disrupt the hunt a hanging offence, although the 'saboteurs' motive then was to protest Royalty's expropriation of land for the chase.

Just as it would be naive to assume any contemporary movement, however active, will inevitably prevail, so it would be an error to presuppose that our current social organization and assumptions will inevitably endure. Certainly, modern Western society is very different in its activities and values to any culture that existed 50, 500, or 5000 years ago, and there is little cause to suppose we have achieved a stable state. Many believe that the time is ripe for deep-rooted cultural change with global implications, such as it was when Christianity rose to prominence, or during the Enlightenment and the Scientific and Industrial Revolutions. And the protesters' own often makeshift cosmologies are informed and reinforced by those of a rapidly swelling corpus of cultural analysts (e.g. Capra, 1982; Russell, 1992; Swimme and Berry, 1992; Elgin, 1993), who in turn draw their inspiration partly from the flourishing of such movements world-wide. If these, and other commentators, are even half-correct in their analyses, such blunt instruments as the new social-control measures will do little more than anoint martyrs and divert the energies of protest into alternative channels. It is to be hoped the activity retains its creative and non-violent doctrine, and that a frustrated minority, denied civil expression, does not turn to more socially pernicious forms of dissent.

The asperity of the 1994 Criminal Justice Act is perhaps most usefully viewed as testimony to the perceived seriousness of the clear and present danger, which these new protest movements, and ways of life, may yet present, not so much to the economic activities as to the central belief on which contemporary British power structures are founded. As previously stated, the way of life and the associated cosmology is proving so attractive - not just economically as an escape from difficult alternatives, but in a positive social and spiritual sense also - compared with the options offered by conventional society, that tens (if not hundreds) of thousands are now subscribing to at least elements of its philosophy, and children are growing up who have known no other culture. In this way the situation is probably comparable to that of the 20,000 to 100,000 or so (depending on season) New Age travellers - who might, at times, also be protesters. One study reported that, without exception, respondents found the way of life positive, constructive, and preferable to their previous ways of living (Davis *et al.*, 1994, pp. 3–4). Furthermore, the numbers of protests and protesters appear to be continuing to rise, providing new alliances, partnerships, and role models, all of which serve to affirm and reinforce the participants' sense of ideological validity. Such empowerment, once tasted, may be only reluctantly given up.

The threat to the establishment - and this does not just mean the current Government, since a wide range of traditional authorities may be challenged by such developments - seems to be that of the 'good example' which the way of life may set. It is not just that large numbers of people may be losing respect for the agency of law. More seriously than that, there is a real possibility of a critical mass developing of those who do not accept the fundamental premises on which those laws have been framed, and who perceive themselves not as law breakers but as moral upholders of a higher law. Many of the protesters do indeed perceive themselves to be akin to a fifth column, spreading the socially destabilizing notion that you can in fact enjoy a full and satisfying life - indeed at least in some ways a fuller and more satisfying life - beyond the ramparts of industrial consumerism. They will quickly point out that the authorities would not care what was happening to them if they were homeless or reduced to drug dependency in high-rise squalor. But, as one protester put it:

> What they can't accept is that we're having a good time, and learning to do for ourselves. So long as we're sleeping in doorways, we're no threat. But now I'm waking up to a brilliant view, and learning new skills, and making sound friends. And I'm not costing them a thing. But they're scared cos I'm having a good time.

The NVDA movement's ultimate success will be measured not by whether or not the protesters succeed or are defeated on particular campaigns, but by the extent to which the values, beliefs, and assumptions which inform their actions continue to inculcate and inform a broader public (or perhaps, to put it another way, the extent to which the public at large, out of which this movement has sprung and found support, continues to move). Contrary to a newspaper correspondent's assertion that to 'identify the anti-roads movement as the embodiment of a burgeoning counter culture [portrays it] as an unrepresentative bunch of old crusties' (Harkell, 1994), the presence at such protests of teachers, young mums, and elderly residents confirms the progress already made in disputing the direct equation of industrial development with human welfare. The numbers of 'ordinary decent citizens' turning up to support this singularly radical form of environmental protest, to the growing unpopularity of the British government's policy of investing in roads at the expense of public transport, to features on 'benders' appearing in 'home fashion' magazines, all testify to the growing normality of ideas which would once have been much too radical for common acceptability. And repression might yet add to the communities' 'glamour'.

The movement could continue to grow, in activity or in influence. A reservoir of individuals apparently surplus to the needs of the conventional economic and cultural system is sufficiently large to sustain for some time the recent expansion of the groups described. And ever-wider economic differentials between the 'haves' and 'have nots' leaves more people feeling they have little to lose by jettisoning materialist culture. That in itself would be significant. But if the values this cosmology and way of life represent gain wider acceptance still, beyond the ideological ghettos of the 'dispossessed', to inflect the culture of the consumption-satiated, the consequences for the future of our prevailing economic system are socially, and politically, incalculable.

Note

1. Based on research work in progress, funded by the UK Economic and Social Research Council, grant ref: R000235050: 'Environmental Activism: an ethnography of ecological "direct action"'.

References

Berman, T., Ingram, G., Gibbons, M., Hatch, R., Maingon, L. and Hatch, C. (1994) *Clayoquot & Dissent*. Vancouver: Ronsdale Press Ltd.

Bolton, G. (1981) *Spoils and Spoilers: Australians make their Environment*. Sydney: Allen & Unwin.

Capra, F. (1982) *The Turning Point*. London: Fontana.

Cohen, C. (1971) *Civil Disobedience: Conscience, Tactics and the Law*. New York: Columbia University Press.

Davis, J., Grant, R. and Locke, A. (1994) *Out of Site, Out of Mind: New Age Travellers and the Criminal Justice and Public Order Bill*. London: The Children's Society.

Devall, B. (1988) *Simple in Means, Rich in Ends: Practising Deep Ecology*. Layton UT: Gibbs Smith.

Elgin, D. (1993) *Awakening Earth: Exploring the Evolution of Human Culture and Consciousness*. New York: Morrow.

Harkell, G. (1994) Road to hell, *Guardian* (letters), 12 December, 19.

HSA (1994) *News Release*, 19 November, PO Box 1, Nottingham NG4 2JY: Hunt Saboteurs Association.

Liberty (1994) *Defending Diversity and Dissent: What's wrong with the Criminal Justice and Public Order Bill* – copied 14 June 1994 from WWW pages: http://www.bath.ac.uk/~bs2ajs/Lib1.html.

Lowe, R. and Shaw, W. (1993) *Travellers: Voices of the New Age Nomads*. London: Fourth Estate.

Maslow, A.H. (1943) A theory of human motivation, *Psychological Review*, 50, 370–96.
Monbiot, G. (1994a) Defiant culture, *Guardian* (Society section), 7 December, 5.
Monbiot, G. (1994b) Heavy hand of history, *Guardian* (Society section), 26 October, 4–5.
Norton-Taylor, R. (1982) *Whose Land is it Anyway?* Wellingborough: Turnstone.
Pepper, D. (1993) *Eco-Socialism: From Deep Ecology to Social Justice*. London: Routledge.
Plows, A. (1994) Ground cover, *Guardian* (Society section), 7 December, 4–5.
Russell, P. (1992) *The White Hole in Time: Our Future Evolution and the Meaning of Now*. New York: Harper Collins.
Sahlins, M. (1973) *The Original Affluent Society*. London: Routledge.
Swimme, B. and Berry, T. (1992) *The Universe Story: From the Primordial Flaring Forth to the Ecozoic Era – A Celebration of the Unfolding of the Cosmos*. New York: Harper Collins.
Weber, T. (1988) *Hugging the Trees: The Story of the Chipko Movement*. New York: Viking.

3

Environmental 'Others' and 'Elites': Rural Pollution and Changing Power Relations in the Countryside

SUSANNE SEYMOUR, PHILIP LOWE, NEIL WARD
AND JUDY CLARK

Introduction

Recent debates in rural studies have highlighted the need to reconsider power relations in the countryside by allowing 'other' voices to be heard (see especially the exchange between Philo (1992, 1993) and Murdoch and Pratt (1993, 1994)). The 'others' referred to in these debates are those marginalized not just in terms of class and property (well-established ways of assessing power relations in the countryside, see Newby *et al.*, 1978), but those considered marginal from a much broader perspective in terms of gender, race, lifestyle, health and sexuality; in Philo's (1992) words 'the "otherness" of sickness, physical disability and mental disability ... the social relations of sexuality ... [and] a multitude of other "others": gypsies and travellers of all sorts ... "New Age hippies" and companion seekers of "alternative lifestyles", homeless peoples and tramps' (pp. 201–2). In the light of the obvious power of farmers in terms of property and traditional cultural standing, to add them to the list of rural 'others' might seem to be deliberately provocative. But there are on-going changes in contemporary society which involve a questioning of farmers' cultural authority and landowning power. This is particularly so in debates over the natural environment where farmers are increasingly labelled as 'others'. In a context of increasing service sector employment and consequent detachment from personal dilemmas of economic and environmental welfare, farmers, with their intimate involvement in the processing of natural resources, remain outsiders to an emerging social consensus which regards damage to the environment as morally wrong (Grove-White, 1993). On the other hand, groups conventionally marginalized in the countryside and rural decision making, such as the public and environmental pressure groups, have grown in power and standing.

Farmers have long regarded themselves as somehow different to the rest of modern, predominantly urban society, but fundamental to its existence. Historically viewed as a central emblem of English national identity, heralded as the backbone of the nation through the figure of the 'sturdy yeoman', farmers today promote an image of themselves as patriotic food producers and the guardians of the countryside who know best how to protect it.

Conversely for many years those with environmental interests have been considered as 'others' in a British countryside dominated by production 'elites'. Various studies have related how environmental groups have been excluded by policy makers from the consultative process in which, by contrast, agricultural interests were firmly embedded (Cox *et al.*, 1986; Lowe *et al.*, 1986). Mounting evidence of wildlife decline, landscape change and habitat loss in the 1960s and 1970s signalled the changing nature of agriculture and aroused public unease (Shoard, 1980). But arguably it has been the indictment, since the early 1980s, of a range of farmers and farming processes as polluters of rivers and water sources that has presented the greatest challenge to the image of farmers as natural guardians of the countryside. Agricultural pollution long remained a submerged issue, precisely because farming was seen as the antithesis of industry. It is likely that it needed the romantic image of farming to be attacked from other sources (for example, over wildlife, habitat and landscape destruction and animal welfare problems) before agricultural pollution could even be recognized. Yet, because of breaches of the law and court appearances, water pollution caused by agriculture presented a legal indictment of intensive agriculture in a way in which previous environmental issues had not. This was especially so as it became clear that it was not just a small deviant minority of farmers who were causing pollution but a larger number including Justices of the Peace and National Farmers' Union (NFU) officials. Condemnation of intensive practices was further strengthened in the context of curbs on agricultural production, highlighting surpluses and undermining the strength of the agricultural policy community.

In this chapter we explore the changing power relations between the rural 'others' and 'elites' through debates over the environment and specifically over water pollution from dairy farming in Devon. In doing this we draw on work carried out on an ESRC-funded programme on

Pollution, Agriculture and Technology Change in 1990–92 which explored constructions of farm pollution by various rural groupings. While we used ideas of policy communities, work cultures, class, property ownership and localness to inform our analysis, the research was premised on the notion that society is not a fixed entity but that social relationships are constantly being made. Thus, our approach, informed by the work of Callon *et al.* (1986), was to 'follow the actors' (p. 4), and to study the worlds they constructed in their own terms (see also Marsden *et al.*, 1993). Various stories about pollution and the rural environment were told, some wielding more power than others. In our analysis here we will assess how far debates over pollution have challenged existing power relations in the countryside and consider some of the implications of these challenges for the rural environment and broader society.

Traditional 'Elites' and 'Others' of the Post-War Countryside

Food production was the dominant concern of the post-war countryside. From the 1940s to the early 1980s there was an overriding policy commitment from successive governments to expanding and promoting the efficiency (in terms of labour and capital in a neo-classical micro-economic model) of food production. Even as late as 1975 the Government White Paper, *Food From Our Own Resources*, outlined a target expansion of 2 per cent a year. Farmers, through the NFU, developed corporatist relations with policy makers and a special status for agriculture with regard to government subsidy and exclusions from many environmental regulations. An agricultural view of the countryside prevailed in which farmers were depicted as its natural guardians and any challenges to this view were regarded as either unscientific or as revealing a deep misunderstanding of the ways of the countryside. Farmers, the argument went, had created the British countryside; they had always looked after it and would continue to do so. The policy of increased domestic self-sufficiency in food production cast farmers in a patriotic role as the nation's food providers, from which position any harmful consequences of intensive farming could be dismissed as the unfortunate but unavoidable side-effects of pursuing an important national goal.

In this context, the debate over the environmental impacts of agricultural change focused either on special safeguards for important landscapes and habitats (mainly but not always in agriculturally marginal areas) or on remedial measures of an essentially aesthetic or cosmetic character (Cox *et al.*, 1990). Fundamental critiques of production policy were sidelined (Clunies-Ross and Cox, 1994). Underlying problems that would have challenged mainstream production policies but which did not visibly resonate with the aesthetic and wildlife preoccupations of the British conservation lobby, itself regarded as a narrowly focused elite grouping by Newby and his colleagues (1978, pp. 239–40), tended to remain submerged. This was particularly so with most aspects of farm pollution.[1] Indeed, the dominant view was that pollution was not a rural problem but an urban and industrial one.

Although water pollution from any source has historically been covered by the common law of nuisance, statutory law, originating in the mid-nineteenth century, was devised to control urban and industrial pollution. Post-war changes to this legislation formally incorporated agriculture but with little practical consequence. Thus, the 1951 and 1961 Rivers (Prevention of Pollution) Acts made it an offence to use rivers and streams for the disposal of any polluting matter and required all effluents discharged from trade premises – including from farms – to have the consent of the water authorities. But these catch-all provisions were inoperable in relation to farming, not least because they did not recognize at all the distinctive nature of farm pollution. A major obstacle was the number of farm discharges with which water authority staff potentially had to deal. By mid-1969 131,171 discharges from farm to river had been recorded but only 2.7 per cent were under consent. Both the mammoth task involved in monitoring a myriad of widely scattered and sporadic discharges and the problem in ensuring that very variable but occasionally potent farm effluents complied with the normal standard limits for industrial effluents (20 ppm for BOD; 30 ppm for suspended solids), discouraged the registration of farm discharges. In any case, assumptions about the cleanliness of rural rivers and the dominant perception that the real problems lay in urban industrial areas ensured that regulatory and monitoring efforts were not focused on the countryside (Gowan, 1972; Weller and Willetts, 1977).

Nevertheless, agricultural interests became concerned at the threat of controls over farming practices, particularly as pollution in general became a public issue in the late 1960s and early 1970s, illustrated by the appointment of a new Royal Commission on Environmental Pollution in February 1970. In the 1974 Control of Pollution Act, they secured an exemption from prosecution for causing water pollution for farmers pursuing 'good agricultural practice' as determined by the Ministry of Agriculture, Fisheries and Food (MAFF). This can be seen as the high point of the dominance of agricultural production concerns over pollution regulation.

Whereas previous legislation had equipped water authorities with ineffective regulatory controls over farm pollution, the 1974 Act strongly discouraged them from prosecuting farmers. There was little incentive even to address the problem. Water authorities were inclined to acquiesce in the priority given by government to the expansion of food production and to allow the agricultural view to dominate. Farm effluents were seen as a minor technical matter best left to the industry itself to resolve. Indeed, water authority staff were wary of any dealings with farmers. Keith Hawkins, in his work with pollution control staff in the 1970s, reported that dealing with farmers was seen to demand particular tact and diplomacy and that officers from rural areas learnt early on, as one put it, 'to avoid getting their backs up'. The same officer continued, 'You get their backs up and you'll get nowhere.' Too ready a reference to the law was considered to be counter-productive and field staff were inclined to turn a 'blind eye' to problems of farm pollution as long as there were no wider implications. One area supervisor said he would bend the rules on farms because 'farmers are one of the most intractable problems you can get. You can't treat farm effluent satisfactorily .... So far as I'm concerned the farmers can continue until someone squeals' (quoted in Hawkins, 1984, pp. 134, 217).

Challenges to Traditional Rural 'Elites': The Creation of the Farm Pollution Issue from the mid-1980s

The view of the agricultural policy community that farm pollution was not an issue continued to dominate until the mid-1980s and, with it, farmers upheld their position as a traditional rural 'elite'. Then farm pollution began to be discovered and publicized by groups traditionally dismissed by the farming elite as 'outsiders'. These included pollution regulatory officials, environmental pressure groups and a growing rural public of middle-class residents, many from urban backgrounds. Their opportunity to play a part in defining the issue arose because established policy communities had been thrown into disarray: the agricultural policy community by curbs on production, most notably the sudden imposition of milk quotas in 1984; and the water policy community by Conservative Government plans, issued in 1986, to privatize the water industry. On the one hand, the official recognition of massive surplus capacity in agriculture effectively demolished the case that environmental losses had to be accepted in the cause of increased productivity. On the other hand, the assumption that the new private water companies would simply assume the regulatory duties of the former Regional Water Authorities caused widespread outrage and led to strong demands for greater public recognition and control over all sources of water pollution. These demands led ultimately to the creation of the National Rivers Authority (NRA), self-styled as Europe's largest environmental protection agency and one of the great anomalies of the Thatcher era.[2]

Mobilized to some extent by earlier debates over agricultural intensification (such as those over landscape change and habitat loss), a number of environmental groups (who had grown in strength and number) turned their attention in the 1980s to farm pollution. In particular, Friends of the Earth (FoE) with its general orientation to combatting environmental pollution, played a key role in generating adverse publicity and debate about nitrates in water and later about farm effluents (Friends of the Earth, 1991; Seymour *et al.*, 1992). The recognition of farm pollution also needed the countryside to become more widely viewed as a place of consumption, not just of agricultural production. Such a view has been strengthened by the increased migration of predominantly middle-class residents into the countryside, as well as by policy moves to combat agricultural surpluses and the increased recognition, particularly since privatization, of water as a valuable and marketable resource (Champion and Watkins, 1991; Marsden *et al.*, 1993). Under the microscope of media attention and the direct experience of new rural dwellers, dairy farming came to be redefined as a polluting and highly industrialized activity and the role of the farmer further questioned.

Three key publications, issued in the mid-1980s, played an important role in this process by publicizing the polluted nature of rural rivers and streams. Perhaps most crucially from 1986 water pollution incidents caused by agriculture were publicized by the water authorities and allowed some measure to be made of the problem. The definition and use of pollution incident statistics, essentially records of reported gross pollution events, was doubly significant as they gave increased importance to the person on the ground doing the reporting (Ward *et al.*, 1995). Not just water authority staff but any member of the general public could report such incidents, a feature which environmental groups and the rural public have exploited and water authorities have subsequently encouraged. The prominence given to farm pollution by the publication of this incident data was augmented by the findings of the 1985 *River Quality Survey* (issued in 1986 by the Department of the Environment and Welsh Office). This was the first of the national five-yearly surveys conducted since the late 1950s to indicate a net decline in the quality of the country's rivers. This was largely due to a deterioration in previously high quality rural stretches. Furthermore, agriculture was highlighted as a major culprit. Finally, a local report issued by South West Water Authority in 1986 on the River Torridge catchment proved highly influential. This detailed account associated sharply declining salmon catches from the River Torridge with the intensification of dairy livestock production in its catchment. Not only was this the first report of its kind examining such changes and their impact on a single catchment, but the choice of a celebrated salmon river in a pastoral setting, popular with tourists and retired people and with its cultural associations with the literary landscape of *Tarka the Otter*, contributed greatly to its symbolic impact. In the highly charged political context following the proposal to privatize the water industry, rural rivers and streams were subjected to even closer public scrutiny.

The establishment of the National Rivers Authority (NRA) as a national regulatory body, cast by itself and the environmental lobby in the role of pollution watchdog, also injected a new morally charged discourse into the proceedings. The creation of the NRA not only gave institutional expression to increased popular concern over the environment and introduced a tougher regulatory rhetoric but also significantly altered the balance of expert opinion in the definition of farm pollution and its prevention. The former water authorities were dominated by chemists and engineers, most of whom moved over to the water companies at privatization. The NRA, in contrast, inherited and appointed many biologists and environmental scientists. Thus a concern with efficient and clean water supply was superseded, or at least supplemented, by a rising concern with the ecological integrity of the whole water environment. This holistic view is increasingly broadening the definition of pollution and advocating a lowering of tolerance thresholds.

The policy-making structure of the NRA also accommodated environmental interests in ways that its predecessors, the Regional Water Authorities, did not. At the national level, the NRA Board membership covered a broad range of expertise, although MAFF still appointed two of its members and representation from the former water authorities was notable. A key committee at the regional level, the Regional Rivers Advisory Committee, which commented on draft national policy as well as regional regulatory and management matters, also typically included representatives of a number of environmental organizations, notably FoE, the Royal Society for Nature Conservation (RSNC), the Council for the Protection of Rural England (CPRE) and the Royal Society for the

Protection of Birds (RSPB), as well as more traditional interest groups, such as the NFU, Country Landowners' Association (CLA), the Confederation of British Industry (CBI) and water companies. These meetings were also open to members of the public and the press (NRA, 1990a).

Yet, there remained an ambivalence in the regulatory attitude of the NRA towards farmers and farm pollution. This is well represented in a reworking of the First World War recruiting poster featuring General Kitchener which was used in anti-pollution literature for farmers (see Figure 3.1). In the caption, Kitchener questions 'Do you have pollution problems?' The use of the military imagery suggests that the NRA saw itself as engaged in a war on pollution. This was the new patriotic and morally charged cause. Kitchener attempts to enlist farmers in this new war against pollution. Just as the boundaries between persuasion and compulsion were frequently blurred in wartime troop conscription, so they were in the regulatory strategies suggested by this image. There is both an appeal to the farmer's patriotic sensibilities to volunteer to prevent pollution and also the threat of military discipline if this call is ignored. Indeed within the NRA itself there was evidence of a more compelling style of conscription. For example, in 1992, the South West region, renowned for a conciliatory stance in dealing with farmers, moved from its established policy of 'information and persuasion' to the deployment of special task forces which 'blitzed' problem catchment areas (Water Authorities Association, 1986: 10; NRA South West, 1992). Yet, past conciliatory approaches were not completely abandoned - the appeal, conveyed by the poster, was to potential polluters to join in the battle against the enemy, pollution. The identification of pollution and not the farmer as the real threat to environmental security is highlighted in another piece of anti-pollution literature issued to farmers which features the slogan 'Silage liquor can kill'. In the light of this, it is unsurprising that in 1992 the NRA confirmed how it would continue to have a special approach when dealing with agricultural pollution. 'Protection of the water environment from the various sources of agricultural pollution', it declared, 'requires a broader approach than court action' (NRA, 1992a, p. 33). This middle ground position which the NRA appears to have adopted, of condemning pollution but courting farmers, will be further explored in our case study as we consider the way in which power relations in the Devon countryside have been challenged by struggles over water pollution from dairy farming.

Do YOU have
POLLUTION PROBLEMS?
FOR INFORMATION ON PREVENTION CONTACT THE:
NATIONAL RIVERS AUTHORITY
AT THE FOLLOWING ADDRESS:

Figure 3.1 NRA anti-pollution material aimed at farmers

Struggles over Farm Pollution in Devon

The public outcry against farm pollution has been particularly strong in Devon, partly because of a high density of dairy farming there, partly because of social changes in the Devon countryside and its status as a prime tourist area. Devon has experienced the influx of new people into the countryside to a marked degree. During the 1970s while the rate of national population growth was 0.5 per cent, that of Devon was 6.7 per cent, followed by a further 5.9 per cent in the 1980s. This growth has not just been in the market towns but also in villages and hamlets with a substantial development of new houses on former agricultural land and conversions of redundant farm buildings (Devon County Council, 1983, 1990).

The increasing numbers of articulate, middle-class people who have moved into rural Devon in the past 20 years have taken with them ideas about how the resources of the countryside should be managed which differ considerably from those of traditional agricultural production interests. These new rural dwellers in particular have complained about previously undiscovered or unreported pollution. Since the mid-1980s, their views have had a growing influence on the water authorities, especially since pollution itself is increasingly defined by members of the public reporting what they consider to be pollution incidents to the water authorities. Under the NRA in particular, this has become a reciprocal arrangement, with every encouragement given to the public to report any water pollution they encounter. Many rural parish noticeboards in Devon carry a poster informing members of the public of the dangers of pollution and urging them to be vigilant and to call the NRA on its free Pollution Hotline if their suspicions are aroused.

A local network of newspapers, environmental groups and activists has also enhanced the high public profile of farm pollution issues in Devon. The regional newspaper, the *Western Morning News*, has played a key role, and its coverage of South West Water Authority's report on pollution in the River Torridge helped make farm pollution a public issue not just in the region but also nationally. Since that time press activity has been persistent, with numerous articles publicizing both pollution and the fate of polluters and regular press interest in the activities of farmers and the NRA. Press representatives were invariably present at the South West NRA's Regional Rivers Advisory Committee meetings, the main regional forum at which water quality issues were debated. Campaigns, linked to the region's popularity with tourists and new residents, to preserve fisheries and re-establish otters, have identified intensive dairy farming as a major reason for declining water quality. A notable example is the Tarka Project which drew very obviously on a literary view of the countryside, that of Henry Williamson's novel, *Tarka the Otter*, popular especially with a middle-class readership and (often in an abridged version) their children.

The dependence of the NRA on public reporting of pollution incidents also drew it into a close relationship with two groups with a strong interest in river quality - anglers and riparian owners. For example, in East Devon, the River Otter Association, a riparian and conservation organization, has around 100 members who regularly feed in reports of the state of the river through its River Watch. These were used both to inform and lobby the NRA. The group is in a very influential position because it appears to be better informed on the state of the river and the threats to its water quality and fisheries than any other organization, including the NRA itself.

The efficiency of some environmental organizations in indicting farming has been phenomenal, the most notable case being the record of Friends of the Earth. In 1989–90, the national organization and the growing local membership funded a six-month campaign in the South West and paid for two full-time workers whose activities focused on farm pollution. The main aims of the campaign were to publicize the farm pollution problem, to bring pressure to bear on the NRA to be tougher in making prosecutions and to draw up a manual to assist other local groups to combat farm pollution. The campaigners patrolled rivers looking for farm pollution and taking water samples. If pollution was found, the NRA was alerted and sometimes the media, so as to maximize adverse publicity. In particular, they targeted prominent farmers and a 'victory' for this strategy came when the farm of the Vice-Chairman of the Devon county branch of the NFU was found to be polluting. He was subsequently successfully prosecuted, receiving a £1,240 fine, events which received television coverage from the BBC. In its activities, however, FoE has not only been critical of farmers but also of the NRA. In fact, its campaign was geared as much to monitoring regulatory action as to locating pollution in the first place. Criticism was levied against the 'together we can beat it' ethos at the time still prominent among the authorities in the South West and FoE made it clear it wanted NRA officials to 'sharpen up their act'. Both to assess NRA performance and to encourage public participation in monitoring water pollution, FoE also produced leaflets which were distributed to local members and displayed on parish noticeboards. These asked people who discovered farm pollution not only to report it to the NRA, but also to contact FoE's Farm Pollution Monitoring Unit (personal interview, FoE campaigner).

Key actors promoting the strict regulation of pollution most often come from the new rural groups. For example, both the secretary of the

River Otter Association and the FoE campaigner for Devon had migrated from the South East. Our field survey work suggests the views of such groups contrast markedly with those of the majority of Devon farmers.

For many years farmers and their representatives across the country denied that there was a farm pollution problem and their views prevailed. Changes to farmers' views probably began to take place in Devon in the mid-1980s, although as late as September 1986 the county magazine of the NFU, *The Devon Farmer*, complained that 'Hardly a month goes by without some fuss about "environmental pollution" or in our terms run-off into water of slurry and silage effluent' (p. 2). In 1991 we undertook a semi-structured survey of 60 dairy farmers in East Devon from which we have distinguished three main attitudes to agricultural pollution (for further details see Ward and Lowe, 1994).

About a sixth of the farmers (10 or 17 per cent) still really questioned whether there was a farm pollution problem at all. These 'sceptical' farmers felt that the pollution problem had been 'blown up out of all proportion' and that regulation itself had 'gone too far' in restricting what farmers could do. All of them felt that agricultural pollution was far less of a problem than industrial pollution, and suspected that farmers were being more strictly regulated. Most questioned whether farm effluents were 'serious' pollutants at all. For example, one said:

> I feel that chemical waste [from industry] is much more serious compared to farm waste. I know it kills fish, but I can't see what's wrong with brown water – it's natural. I know silage effluent is bad, but it's only like juice from grass. It's not like a liquid from industry.

A further 62 per cent, most of the farmers surveyed, were more ambivalent about farm pollution. While they readily acknowledged that farm pollution was a problem and that measures had to be taken to address it, they seemed motivated more from a sense that it was unacceptable to break laws and regulations than a strong belief that the pollution itself was morally wrong. Pollution was a problem for these farmers in the sense that, as one said, it 'can get you into trouble'. Although they did acknowledge there was an environmental threat, they defined much farm pollution as 'accidental' and argued for the lenient treatment of farmers who they regarded as the 'victims' of such 'accidents'. Furthermore, they were keen to distinguish this majority of 'accidental' pollution incidents from what they perceived as 'much more serious' deliberate pollution incidents, perpetrated by an irresponsible minority. Such judgements focus on the moral responsibility of the actor rather than the consequence of the action. This is a discourse that farmers' leaders have helped to structure. It is one which, incidentally, happily sees them translated as instruments of government policy - any responsibility for pollution when farmers are conforming to policy is thus displaced (see Seymour *et al.*, 1992). Critically, these farmers saw pollution as a problem *for* farming, rather than a problem *of* farming.

Only 22 per cent of those interviewed, a group of mainly younger farmers with more diverse contacts with rural society, appeared to regard farm pollution as something reprehensible in itself. They also generally felt it to be the responsibility of the individual farmer to ensure that pollution is adequately prevented and so tended not to differentiate between accidental and deliberate pollution incidents. In addition, a number questioned the initial production of so much potentially polluting effluent on modern dairy farms and were more willing to consider means to remedy this, such as covering collecting yards and using straw-based rather than slurry systems.

So, for the majority of farmers, the problem of farm pollution meant new regulatory threats to their businesses and reputations: river quality was not the prime concern. The substantially unchanged productivist stance of most of the farmers surveyed contrasts markedly with the heightened environmental awareness of many rural dwellers and takes us some way towards understanding why many farmers are experiencing conflicts in their own backyards. Of the 60 dairy farmers we interviewed in Devon, ten had experienced direct pressure to change their farming practices from neighbours and local people. Farmers themselves perceived that social change in the countryside was diminishing their authority and, although increasing regulation from Whitehall or Brussels has engendered a general air of fatalism and bitterness, farmers have perhaps been most affected by this loss of local authority and support.

Prompted in part by the efforts of local activists as well as the increased moral imperatives of its new environmental ethos, the NRA in the South West adopted a high profile campaign against farm pollution. An important element of this was the establishment, in 1990, of a 24-hour, free Pollution Hotline to facilitate the reporting of farm pollution incidents in particular. Hotline cards could be found in local libraries, on parish noticeboards, in police stations and even in local branches of the NFU. The aim was both to draw on a reservoir of concerned public opinion and to spread the responsibility for pollution control. Clem Davis, Environmental Protection Manager for the region, summed up the NRA view, declaring, 'Everyone has a role to play in caring for our rivers ... the public are our ears and eyes too' (NRA, 1990b, p. 3).

Among Pollution Inspectors in the field there was evidence of a gradually changing view of pollution, between the 1970s and the 1990s, from seeing it as an infringement of the rules to seeing it as an environmental crime. Alongside this there has been a lowering of the threshold of seriousness at which enforcement action is triggered. Compared to the relative judgements of former water authority staff and ADAS (Agricultural Development and Advisory Service) advisors, Pollution Inspectors' assessments of pollution (as revealed in our ethnographic study conducted in 1991) were framed by absolutes. To Inspectors pollution was a 'dirty' stream or river and 'seeing a once dirty stream made clean' was the ultimate goal. In principle nothing less can be condoned.

In practice, however, Pollution Inspectors needed and had more workable definitions and these were very much shaped by their practical experience and the problems they regularly encountered in the field and with administrative and legal processes. On the one hand, the public stance of the NRA as an environmental guardian and the public reporting and definition of pollution incidents encouraged Inspectors to take an absolute view of pollution as wrong-doing deserving of punishment. On the other hand, ambivalence over the deterrent value of prosecution, particularly in light of still generally low levels of fines when compared to pollution prevention costs, inexperience in gathering evidence for prosecutions and an appreciation of the problems farmers face, and the perceived need not to alienate them, encouraged more flexibility.

Inspectors' interpretations of pollution also tended to be influenced by the types of problems they encountered. What counts as pollution on a day-to-day basis is often dictated by the succession of incidents reported by the public or water users. From the mid-1980s to 1991, any such report, whether substantiated or not, was considered to constitute a pollution incident. In contrast, working assessments of pollution took little account of the hidden problems of groundwater contamination or more diffuse pollutants such as nitrates. However, Inspectors were much less influenced than previously by the attitude of the farmer and much more by the state of the river.

Yet, as the activities of FoE suggest, the NRA was caught between pressures from environmental groups, public demands and its own environmental imperatives on the one hand and, on the other, a legacy of regulatory leniency coupled with a desire not to alienate farmers who are regarded as crucial figures in the prevention of farm pollution since they are the ones actually managing potentially polluting practices. Pollution Inspectors realized that without the co-operation of the large majority of farmers, their task would be impossible. While they obviously cannot be everywhere 24 hours a day, farmers are on the spot and their action or inertia often makes the crucial difference between either a clean or a polluted river. In order not to alienate farmers, Pollution Inspectors also realized they had to act in a way that the farming community regarded as reasonable. Yet being confronted by a majority of farmers who had not accepted a moral imperative in pollution prevention made the Pollution Inspectors' task more difficult and countered their heightened sensitivity to pollution as an environmental crime. Thus, although in the South West there was a move to a tougher regulatory image, through the running down of the high profile and overtly conciliatory 'Together we can beat it' Farm Campaign and the adoption of catchment task forces, work at the farm level was still regarded as crucial and, in practice, persuasion was still preferred to prosecution.

Conclusions

There are signs that power relations in the countryside are beginning to shift, primarily because of the growing role of the countryside as a place of consumption and a decline in agricultural production imperatives. It is through environmental debates, which reflect substantially consumer rather than producer views, that traditional rural 'elites' have come to be challenged by 'others' and are themselves increasingly seen as 'environmental others'. The new rural residents have challenged traditional agricultural interests over several different aspects of the quality of life they look for in the countryside: clean surroundings, quiet, beauty, natural scenery and wildlife. Their ideal of country living has frequently been shattered by experience of the practices of modern industrial farming, and their traditional image of farming has been shattered too.

On the other hand, many farmers continue to regard their modern farming practices as part of a traditional way of life and fail to recognize or acknowledge the industrial nature of many of them. At the local level, many farmers have seen their standing decline: their practices are increasingly challenged by their neighbours; the press condemn them; environmental groups launch campaigns to patrol the rivers passing through their property; water regulators may ask them to spend thousands of pounds upgrading effluent facilities; a number have been convicted in court as polluters; their produce is no longer so highly valued (indeed they are paid not to produce); and they face more regulation of their practices. Farmers, so long allowed to engage in practices which caused damage to the environment, are having as much difficulty in adopting an environmentally sensitive perspective as they are in coming to terms with less intensive farming practices. The increase in the level of public criticism has left a minority feeling 'embattled' and alienated to a considerable and potentially dangerous degree. However, most agree that certain of their former practices - principally those condemned by regulatory or legal action, such as the disposal of large amounts of slurry or silage liquor into rivers and streams - are no longer acceptable and acquiesce in moves to prevent them from continuing.

Yet while farmers may be regarded as 'others' of the countryside from an environmental point of view, they remain, in many respects, a powerful group. As owners of land and managers of potentially polluting practices, farmers obviously have a great deal of direct influence over the state of the rural environment. Furthermore, they still form a part of a powerful grouping because of their continued alliance (albeit less close than in previous decades) with MAFF, and the Ministry's own success in keeping much of the environmental policy which relates to agriculture under its control. For example, MAFF officials manage the policies relating to Environmentally Sensitive Areas and Nitrate Sensitive Areas and MAFF's advisory arm, the Agricultural Development and Advisory Service (ADAS), polices them on the ground. In relation to farm effluent problems, in 1989–94 MAFF controlled the grant scheme whereby farmers received up to 50 per cent of costs to invest in a range of anti-pollution measures, and it commissions anti-pollution advice from ADAS (see Lowe *et al.*, 1992). Both farmers and MAFF sought to enrol the NRA into a technical 'agricultural' definition of the farm pollution problem. The Authority made attempts to resist this by introducing broader issues into the debate (such as the catchment-wide environmental implications of farm pollution) which challenged the fundamental ethos of intensive farming practices (NRA, 1992b). But despite obvious public support the NRA still seemed to be fighting a rearguard action. While traditional production interests in MAFF continue to have so much influence over agri-environmental policy and continue to send productivist signals to farmers, problems are likely to continue. Farmers will be left in a dilemma over their role in the modern countryside and alienated from the growing moral imperative to protect the environment.

Notes

1. There were two major exceptions. Agricultural pesticides had been recognized as a public problem, in terms of their impact on wildlife, since the publication of Rachel Carson's *Silent Spring* (1962) but the 'bad guys' identified in this case were the agrochemical companies, while farmers were often portrayed as the reluctant victims of the so-called pesticide treadmill. The other exception was intensive livestock units (generally pigs and poultry) which were acknowledged to produce localized pollution, but here the problem was frequently presented as an aesthetic one (of odour) rather than an ecological or public

health issue (see Royal Commission on Environmental Pollution, 1979).

2. On 1 April 1996 the NRA ceased to exist after it was incorporated into the new Environment Agency.

References

Callon, M., Law, J. and Rip, A. (1986) How to study the force of science. In M. Callon, J. Law and A. Rip (eds) *Mapping the Dynamics of Science and Technology*. London: Macmillan Press, 3-17.

Carson, R. (1962) *Silent Spring*. London: Hamish Hamilton.

Champion, A. and Watkins, C. (eds) (1991) *People in the Countryside: Studies of Social Change in Rural Britain*. London: Paul Chapman Publishing.

Clunies-Ross, T. and Cox, G. (1994) Challenging the productivist paradigm. In P. Lowe, T. Marsden and S. Whatmore (eds) *Regulating Agriculture*. London: David Fulton, 53-74.

Cox, G., Lowe, P. and Winter, M. (1986) Agriculture and conservation in Britain: a policy community under seige. In G. Cox, P. Lowe and M. Winter (eds) *Agriculture, People and Policies*. London: Allen & Unwin, 181-215.

Cox, G., Lowe, P. and Winter, M. (1990) *The Voluntary Principle in Conservation*. Chichester: Parkard.

Department of the Environment/Welsh Office (1986) *River Quality in England and Wales 1985. A Report of the 1985 Survey*. London: HMSO.

Devon County Council (1983) *County Structure Plan First Alteration 1981 Data Base*. Exeter: Devon County Council Planning Department.

Devon County Council (1990) *Devon into the Next Century*. Devon County Structure Plan - third alteration - explanatory memorandum. Exeter: Devon County Council Planning Department.

Friends of the Earth (1991) *The Water Campaigner's Guide to Farm Pollution*. London: FoE.

Gowan, D. (1972) *Slurry and Farm Waste Disposal*. Ipswich: Farming Press.

Grove-White, R. (1993) Environmentalism: a new moral discourse for technological society? In K. Milton (ed.) *Environmentalism: The View from Anthropology*. London: Routledge, 18-30.

Hawkins, K. (1984) *Environment and Enforcement: Regulation and the Social Definition of Pollution*. Oxford: Clarendon Press.

Lowe, P., Cox, G., MacEwen, M., O'Riordan, T. and Winter, M. (1986) *Countryside Conflicts: The Politics of Farming, Forestry and Conservation*. Aldershot: Gower.

Lowe, P., Clark, J., Seymour, S. and Ward, N. (1992) *Pollution Control on Dairy Farms: An Evaluation of Current Policy and Practice*. London: SAFE Alliance.

Marsden, T., Murdoch, J., Lowe, P., Munton, R. and Flynn, A. (1993) *Constructing the Countryside*. London: UCL Press.

Murdoch, J. and Pratt, A.C. (1993) Rural Studies: modernism, post-modernism and the 'post-rural'. *Journal of Rural Studies*, 9 (4), 411-27.

Murdoch, J. and Pratt, A.C. (1994) Rural studies of power and the power of Rural Studies: a reply to Philo. *Journal of Rural Studies*, 10 (1), 83-7.

National Farmers' Union (NFU), Devon County Branch (1986) *The Devon Farmer*. September, Exeter: NFU.

NRA (1990a) *Annual Report and Accounts 1989/90.* Bristol: NRA.
NRA (1990b) *The Water Guardians.* No. 7, Bristol: NRA.
NRA (1992a) *Water Pollution Incidents in England and Wales - 1991.* Water Quality Series No. 9, Bristol: NRA.
NRA (1992b) *The Influence of Agriculture on the Quality of Natural Waters in England and Wales.* Water Quality Series No. 6, Bristol: NRA.
NRA South West (1992) NRA in the New Year pollution blitz. News Release. Exeter: NRA South West.
Newby, H., Bell, C., Rose, D. and Saunders, P. (1978) *Property, Paternalism and Power.* London: Hutchinson.
Philo, C. (1992) Neglected rural geographies: a review. *Journal of Rural Studies*, 8 (2), 193–207.
Philo, C. (1993) Post-modern rural geography? a reply to Murdoch and Pratt, *Journal of Rural Studies*, 9 (4), 429–36.
Royal Commission on Environmental Pollution (1979) *Agriculture and Pollution* 7th Report. Cmnd 7644, London: HMSO.
Seymour, S., Cox, G. and Lowe, P. (1992) Nitrates in water: the politics of the Polluter-Pays-Principle. *Sociologia Ruralis*, 32 (1), 82–103.
Shoard, M. (1980) *The Theft of the Countryside.* London: Temple Smith.
South West Water Authority (1986) *Environmental Investigation of the River Torridge.* Exeter: Department of Environmental Services, South West Water Authority.
Ward, N. and Lowe, P. (1994) Shifting values in agriculture: the farm family and pollution regulation. *Journal of Rural Studies*, 10 (2), 173–84.
Ward, N., Lowe, P., Seymour, S. and Clark, J. (1995) Rural restructuring and the regulation of farm pollution. *Environment and Planning A*, 27 (8), 193–211.
Water Authorities Association/Ministry of Agriculture, Fisheries & Food (1986) *Water Pollution from Farm Waste, 1985, England and Wales.* London: WAA.
Weller, J.B. and Willetts, S.L. (1977) *Farm Wastes Management.* London: Crosby Lockwood Staples.
Williamson, H. (1927) *Tarka the Otter.* London: G.P. Putnam and Sons.

4

The Beleaguered 'Other': Hunt Followers in the Countryside

GRAHAM COX AND MICHAEL WINTER

Introduction

'If you're born a countryman you're harassed.' Those words capture precisely the sense in which the field sports community can so readily feel itself beleaguered. They were spoken during Radio 4's *Farming Today* programme on 25 February 1995 shortly before the vote on the Labour MP John McFall's Private Member's Bill seeking to make it illegal to cause a dog to kill, injure, pursue or attack a mammal. But the speaker neither hunts nor shoots. Robin Page lives and works on a small family farm in Cambridgeshire where he was born. He is a member of his local Wildlife Trust and the Duchy of Cornwall's Wildlife and Landscape Advisory Group and he was among those responsible for the establishment of the Conservation Committee on South Cambridgeshire District Council on which he served since 1970. A writer and broadcaster, he published *The Fox and the Orchid* in 1987. With a foreword from Sir Derek Barber, then Chairman of the Countryside Commission, it explores the connections which, for him, bind country sports, natural history and conservation in a single logic.

But for many, more than ever before, that logic is beyond the bounds of the morally acceptable. Though engaged in lawful pursuits, there is increasingly a presumption that the activities of the field sports community are, at best, untoward and, at worst, reprehensible. A recently published introductory text on ethics, for instance, concludes its short section on foxhunting as follows: 'An activity which necessarily involves the fearful chasing, painful maiming and final destruction of a non-human animal arguably disqualifies itself as a sport or an entertaining pastime' (Vardy and Grosch, 1994, p. 210).

Vardy and Grosch's preceding discussion assesses three arguments for hunting: the need for culling, the value of tradition, and the sport and entertainment it provides. At no point do they attempt to assess the evidence on the pain or suffering endured by the fox. That is a taken-for-granted assumption brought in to clinch the ethical argument.

It is hardly surprising, therefore, that the minority who find the logic of hunting neither impenetrable nor morally questionable should seek to draw a contrast between true country people and what they consider an uncomprehending urban majority. In this scenario country dwellers present themselves as a misunderstood and oppressed cultural minority.

Certainly there is no questioning their minority status, nor the accompanying sense of paradox, given that hunting has been, perhaps, the most emblematic of the elements which have together made up an anglo-centric and essentially anti-urban dominant culture in Britain (Lowe, Murdoch and Cox, 1995). Putting numbers to such shifting centres of moral gravity is a notoriously fraught activity. The League Against Cruel Sports and others in the anti-hunt lobby have been remarkably successful in focusing arguments on issues of animal rights and cruelty so that far less attention has been paid, for instance, to the implications of hunting for the rural landscape. They have long felt able to claim that an overwhelming majority of the British population wishes to see hunting stopped and, recently, that 'public opinion opposing all forms of hunting with hounds is at an all-time high' (League Against Cruel Sports, 1994). The 1992 British Social Attitudes Survey reported that, in response to a question asking whether foxhunting should be banned by law, 45 per cent agreed, 26 per cent disagreed and some 27 per cent had no view (Clark *et al.*, 1994). Following the publicity in the run up to the McFall Bill, and shortly before the Bill was presented to Parliament, a *Mail on Sunday/Mori* poll showed 70 per cent to be in favour of banning foxhunting and hare coursing, 82 per cent opposed to staghunting and even 53 per cent favouring the banning of shooting (*Guardian*, 3 March 1995).

The figure relating to staghunting is noteworthy: for it reveals that, even within the context of a very general opposition to hunting, it is an activity which attracts special opprobrium. If field sports are beleaguered, the staghunting community can count itself particularly embattled. But the struggle is enjoined on a number of distinct - albeit closely connected - terrains, and staghunters are not without considerable resources which they can mobilize. Recent developments on the legal terrain - the failure of Somerset County Council to maintain a ban on hunting over land owned by the local authority itself - have, in particular, substantially modified the overall balance of forces in a direction favourable to the supporters of staghunting.

This chapter draws on research undertaken in 1992 (Winter *et al.*, 1993) to examine the character of this beleaguered 'rural' institution: 'rural' because, while those engaged in the activity would certainly embrace such a description, the concept of the 'rural', no less than the term 'countryman', can be as analytically deceptive as it is descriptively beguiling. Our examination necessarily includes much contextual description for in the presentation of our results to academic audiences, at conferences and seminars, we have been struck by the generally low level of knowledge about how hunting is organized and who is involved. Part of the purpose of this chapter, therefore, is to provide some basic information on hunting as an economic and social activity. We then return to a discussion of some of the legal developments and of the issue of whether hunting can truly be said to be beleaguered.

The DSSH and QSH

The study of two geographically adjacent Hunts in the south-west of England, the Devon and Somerset Staghounds (DSSH) and the Quantock Staghounds (QSH), was carried out for the National Trust which had come under increasing pressure from sections of its membership to ban hunting on its land. The Trust owns large tracts of countryside on Exmoor and any such ban would have had devastating implications for the Hunts in these two areas (unlike a third deerhunt, the Tiverton, which was not included in the survey since it does not hunt over land owned by the National Trust). It is not, however, the purpose of this chapter to consider the interpretation put upon our research by the Trust Working Party which subsequently recommended that hunting should be permitted to continue on Trust lands (National Trust, 1993) not least because, subsequently, the governing body of the Trust resolved to set up a working party to study suffering as a factor in the management of wild red deer on Exmoor and the Quantock Hills and that inquiry is continuing.

The principal aim of our study was to examine the economic impact of hunting. But the varying sources of data on which we drew made it possible to give close consideration also to its social aspects. A postal survey of a sample of DSSH and QSH Hunt subscribers resulted in 326 responses: a response rate of 63 per cent and a sample representing 31 per cent of the total population of subscribers. In addition we surveyed 24 non-subscribing visitors and Riding Club members and conducted key interviews with a sub-sample of twelve subscribers. Two seminars with key informants were held and separate seminars were held with representatives of the two Hunts and with representatives of groups opposed to staghunting. These seminars resulted in numerous follow-up informal interviews and conversations with key informants from the two Hunts.

Although hunting is associated with an extensive and colourful literature and has been the subject of social histories (Itzkowitz, 1977) and political assessments (Garner, 1993; R. Thomas, 1983), this study represents the only one of its kind. There have, however, been attempts to quantify the importance of hunting to the rural economy and to nature conservation (Cobham Resource Consultants 1982, 1992) and such studies have claimed that hunting is a regular leisure pastime for close on a quarter of a million people, with some 4500 of those involved with staghunting. Those who hunt red deer on Exmoor and the Quantocks are, within that more general context, highly distinctive. The elaborate rituals, customs and practices characteristic of hunting generally are, if anything, more pronounced (Cox *et al.*, 1994) and they help constitute a form of life whose members are strongly conscious of an essentially separate identity.

Those who hunt occupy clearly differentiated positions within a highly ritualized organizational hierarchy. It is the Hunt Committee which owns the hounds and is responsible for paying fixed costs such as rent and maintenance on buildings. Hunt membership, conferred on subscribers and others who have demonstrated a high level of commitment to the Hunt, is by invitation of the Committee and it is members who can vote at its Annual General Meeting. Not all members subscribe, however, so that, for instance, whereas some 872 individuals in 538 households were registered as members of the DSSH, no fewer than 156 did not subscribe.

It is the Masters who employ the Hunt servants and kennel staff and, normally, one of them, acting as Fieldmaster, takes charge of the followers who make up the Field on a hunting day. The Field will typically comprise subscribers, farmers, visitors and guests. Subscribers (many of whom are members) pay an annual subscription set by the Committee which varies according to how many of their family, if any, wish to hunt. But the Committee also approves exemptions and many farmers, for example, pay no subscription. Indeed, in 1990–91 some 21 per cent paid less than the rate of £70 for car followers' subscriptions although 7 per cent paid £350 or more. The maximum rate of subscription, meanwhile, was £765 for 'the subscriber, family and guests hunting from the house (guest's days limited to three)'.

Those who are neither guests nor pay a subscription are expected to pay a cap on a daily basis. The level of the cap varies according to the time of year and is reduced if the follower is a subscriber to an adjacent hunt. Mounted followers with the DSSH, though not with the QSH, also pay field money, fixed, when we carried out our study, at £2 per day. The cap, inclusive of field money, for the DSSH was £25 for subscribers to adjacent hunts, otherwise £40 for autumn staghunting and hindhunting and £50 for spring staghunting. Children pay much reduced rates and guests pay neither subscription nor cap, but their days are strictly limited in number. Car followers are also technically part of the Field and they too either subscribe or pay a car cap.

The hindhunting season runs from 1 November until the end of February. Hindhunting is farmer oriented and the size of the Field is usually smaller than for staghunting, although there can be some big turnouts on Saturdays and over the Christmas and New Year holidays. The season concludes with spring staghunting which starts at or near the beginning of March and runs until the end of April and it is during late March and April that very considerable numbers of visitors come to hunt with both the DSSH and the QSH as, by that time, foxhunting has ceased.

The hunting economy centres, more than anything else, around the horse and we took particular interest in patterns of equine use and expenditure. Subscribers were asked to provide, from a list of 16 horse associated activities, the principal reason for keeping each of their horses. Horses kept as a business activity were excluded from the analysis and the information provided for 621 horses represented 87 per cent of all horses kept by subscribers. Hunting (47 per cent) was the dominant reason for keeping horses and was a part reason in a further 7 per cent of cases. The large minority (46 per cent) of horses not kept principally for hunting were, most frequently, being used for breeding, hacking and for point-to-pointing. Some horses, needless to say, were kept for more than one purpose and again hunting, breeding and hacking were the most significant both in terms of numbers of horses involved and numbers of days' usage.

The information on numbers of hunting days showed that no fewer than 43 per cent of the subscriber households recording mounted hunting also recorded car following and, indeed, a higher proportion of the subscribers were car followers (70 per cent) than were mounted (58 per cent). But while the significance of car following should not be underestimated it is horse-related economic activities which are at the core of the hunting economy. Although just over a quarter of DSSH subscribers had no horse, some 29 per cent of them kept two or three, and as many as 24 per cent had between four and nine with 5 per cent having ten or more.

Many of the subscriber households spent £100 or less per annum on their hunting, while at the other end of the scale 7 per cent spent between £11,000 and £30,000 per year. The majority of respondents (66 per cent), meanwhile, estimated an annual expenditure of between £500 and £5000. Such figures, along with the location of the expenditure, have to be treated with great caution. Interviews with 12 subscribers showed that one had slightly overestimated expenditure, but that the remaining 11 had, if anything, underestimated it, with five doing so significantly because they had neglected to include large one-off items of expenditure such as new stables, a new horse or a vehicle.

Such figures are indicative of the broad levels of economic resources to which the Hunts have access and we found that economic vigour was underpinned and accompanied by a no less pronounced level of social involvement. Proponents of hunting have always been anxious to claim that it is an activity enjoyed by a wide cross-section of people and is not confined to the rural upper classes. In fact some 40 per cent of the total sample of subscribers from Exmoor and the Quantocks proved to be farmers with a further 21 per cent having professional or managerial occupations. Moreover, many of the retired 23 per cent were from those two categories as well. At 53 per cent, farmers, in fact, made up over half of the economically active subscribers whereas nationally they constitute just 1 per cent of the economically active population.

Manual workers, by contrast, accounted for just 8 per cent of that sample. Among this group, which could be considered part of the indigenous rural working class, were farm and estate workers, a lorry driver, a coach driver, a postman, a stone mason and a taniliser operator at a sawmill. The self-employed, including representatives of a number of local trades such as builders and shopkeepers, were another small category. A miscellaneous group making up just 5 per cent of the sample included three housewives (about whom we had too little information to be able to categorize elsewhere), two unemployed people and a small group of people with other occupations encompassing a wide range of middle class and service sector occupations.

Turning to consider the place of residence of the subscribers we found that although a minority lived in other parts of Devon and Somerset, or even further afield, the majority lived within the hunt countries, neither of which contains a major town. Indeed, the areas hunted are wholly rural in character and are relatively thinly populated: so while it is notable that the majority of Hunt followers live within them it is equally important to appreciate that we estimated that only 4.1 per cent of the total population of the DSSH and QSH country are resident in households where one or more members subscribe to either Hunt, although that is a figure which rises to 7.6 per cent when non-subscribing followers are taken into account.

It is hardly surprising, perhaps, that those taking part in an activity which the overwhelming majority of the British people find ethically unacceptable, and which casts them as a minority even within their own rural locations, should be especially conscious of their status as a distinct community. They are no less conscious that its internal cohesion is one vital precondition for its continued viability. The socialization of the very young, every bit as much as the involvement of the elderly, has its place.

Social activities associated with the DSSH and QSH have a significance at a number of levels that go well beyond the basic necessities of fund raising. The spread of events encompasses all age ranges within the relevant community. Degrees of involvement and expenditure suggest that high levels of commitment and cohesion are sustained. The Hunt Ball, for instance, which is the one social event associated with hunting of which the general public is aware, is really only the apex of a pyramid whose broad base reaches into all areas of the hunted country, providing a focus for social activity irrespective of age or gender. This is quite literally the case in the Quantocks, where the topography effectively divides the country in two and where hunt activities are - as one respondent put it - the occasions when 'folk from over the hill get to meet'.

It is notoriously the case that clubs, societies and voluntary organizations are often highly dependent on the very considerable efforts of a few officers and members. We therefore considered that one measure of the level of commitment of the subscribers to the hunts, and of the importance of the hunts to the social life of the area, would be the number of people actively involved in organizing social events of various sorts. Consequently, in addition to general questions seeking information about attendance at hunt functions we asked whether subscribers, or any member of their household, had been 'involved in organizing or running' any of the events listed 'including clearing up afterwards'.

The responses to this question revealed that no fewer than half of all respondents had been involved in helping in some way at these functions. The figure is an impressively high one which indicates a distinctive cohesiveness among the hunting community in Exmoor and on the Quantocks. Many respondents took the opportunity to emphasize the significance of hunting as a social experience, commenting on its ability to provide a framework for their lives and meaning to the term 'community' in a remote and very rural area. There was, in that sense, a strong impression created by the comments of a community based on shared activities as well as shared values.

Beleaguered or Privileged?

Economically and socially, therefore, the deerhunting community exhibits a vigour which might be thought to give the lie to the claim that they constitute a beleaguered 'other' in the countryside. They have strong traditions on which they can draw and such narratives of identity make the presupposition of continuity, of the present as a living embodiment of the past, an unquestioned absolute. And yet it is no less obvious that the social cohesion is also powerfully cemented by the siege mentality which almost inevitably accompanies their inability to occupy the 'high ground' in a society in which 'the boundary encircling the area of the moral' (K. Thomas, 1983) is, to their disadvantage, progressively being enlarged. They are convinced of their own rectitude. But they cannot, at the same time, be unaware that for a great many people their activities place them beyond the bounds of the acceptable.

For many years, the proponents of hunting could draw some comfort from the fact that opinion polls, on their own, may do little to shift political opinion. Moreover, the unreliability of opinion polling as a guide to the sorts of views that people might express in response to differently contextualized questions is well-known. But less readily discounted has been the ideological impact of sustained political pressure at the country, district and borough level. The succession of votes on whether hunting should be allowed to take place on land owned by local authorities received a fillip with the rise of the Liberal Democrats in many formerly Conservative rural areas. Although bans, when enacted, are important in terms of public consciousness of the hunting debate, they usually have little practical effect on the practice of hunting in the short term as local authorities own relatively little land. Much local authority land is, moreover, let to agricultural tenants who may allow hunting to continue over their farms; although new tenancy clauses could be inserted when farms become vacant and are re-let.

In the wake of the local council elections in May 1993, in which the Conservatives lost control of all but one county council, the League Against Cruel Sports claimed that over 150 local councils had implemented a ban. Many such bans, however, had been enacted in Labour controlled inner-city authorities like Brent and Haringey and were, to that extent, firmly within the ambit of the politics of gesture. By the end of the year, however, the League could reasonably expect that by April 1994 at least half the county councils and regional authorities would have voted to ban hunting on their land. By September 1993 they included among their number Leicestershire; home of the Quorn, Belvoir and Pytchley packs and arguably - certainly in terms of its traditions - the quintessential hunting county. But of the 10,000 acres covered by the ban only 58 would have been used by hunts.

The previous month Somerset County Council voted by 26 votes to 22 to ban staghunting on its lands because the sport was 'morally repugnant' and, in contrast, and as if to confirm the especially embattled status of the staghunting community, here was a vote which promised to have a significant practical impact on the viability of a hunt. While the Council is only one of several landowners within the extensive Quantock Staghounds country, its 140 acres at Over Stowey Customs Common effectively bisect the 38 square mile Quantock Hill range and are, therefore, critical to the chase.

The QSH resolved to mount a legal challenge to the local authority's decision on the basis that there might have been procedural irregularities in the decision-making process and a fighting fund was promptly established with more than £3000 (towards anticipated initial costs of £15,000) raised at a joint meet with the DSSH at Honeymead, near Exford, Somerset, at the beginning of October 1993. They were given leave by Mr Justice Brooke a month later to bring judicial review proceeding against the Liberal Democrat controlled council, although their application for an immediate suspension was refused because the ban had already been in force for three months and he deemed that the council should be given a three-week period in which to provide evidence in support of its ban.

The Queen's Bench decision on 9 February 1994 (*Regina* v *Somerset County Council Ex parte Fewings and Others*, *The Times*, 10 February 1994) proved a daunting challenge to the ambitions of the anti-hunting lobby. In the case brought by Mr William Fewings, the Master of the Quantock Staghounds, Somerset County Council's ban was declared unlawful and quashed in a ruling which provided a basis for field sports supporters to challenge all county council bans. Mr Justice Laws said that the law conferred no entitlement on a local authority to impose its opinions about the morals of hunting on the neighbourhood. He ruled that public bodies such as the Liberal Democrat controlled council enjoyed no such thing as 'unfettered discretion' so that, whereas under common law individuals could do what they liked as long as it was not prohibited, any action by public bodies 'had to be justified by positive law'.

In a judgment reminiscent of the Council of the National Trust, which has consistently sought to argue that the ethics of hunting are a matter for Parliament, he explained that under the rules of judicial review it was not his task to consider moral and ethical questions, but rather simply to consider whether the ban was lawfully imposed. The passion and sincerity of the majority of councillors who had voted for the ban was unquestioned: but he had to consider whether this 'engine of their decision' justified the prohibition as a measure conducive to 'the benefit, improvement or development' of the land in line with the council's obligations under the 1972 Local Government Act.

Mr Justice Laws ruled that the language of the relevant section of the Act was not wide enough to 'permit the council to take a decision about activities carried out on its land which is based on free-standing moral perceptions as opposed to an objective judgement about what will conduce to the better management of the estate'. In this instance it was the best means of managing the deer herd that was in question and while justifiable arguments relating, for instance, to the need to protect rare flora or the amenity of the area could perhaps have been mounted 'the view that hunting is morally repulsive, however pressing its merits, has nothing whatever to do with such questions'. In his view the council had been given no authority by Parliament to translate such views into public action and whether hunting should be banned or limited was 'pre-eminently a matter for the national legislature'. A second count on which the ban was quashed was the failure of the council to consider the future management of the deer herd when imposing its immediate ban. The council was ordered to pay the legal costs of the case, estimated at £50,000, and was given leave to go to the Court of Appeal.

But the appeal failed, considerable further costs were incurred, and the Audit Commission subsequently advised that contributions by other local authorities to the costs to be paid by Somerset County Council to the Quantock Staghounds 'could be illegal and would not be being used for a proper purpose and would therefore be *ultra vires*': a judgement covering contributions already made as well as future pledges. On the legal terrain, at least for the present, the staghunting community is presently anything but beleaguered. In other ways too, the balance of forces has been substantially modified by changes within the legal sphere which bear on broader political struggles.

In November 1994 the Criminal Justice and Public Order Bill became law. Attended by intense controversy it included among its provisions the offence of aggravated trespass. It is an offence which can be deemed to have been committed if a person 'trespasses on land in the open air and, in relation to any lawful activity which persons are engaging in or are about to engage in on that or adjoining land in the open air, does there any thing which is intended by him to have the effect: (a) of intimidating those persons or any of them so as to deter them or any of them from engaging in that activity, (b) of obstructing that activity, or (c) of disrupting the activity'.

The essence of the offence lies in the intention of the accused to intimidate, obstruct or disrupt. These are precisely the intentions of field sport saboteurs, whereas they are not among the intentions of recreational users of the countryside, even where such people behave thoughtlessly or unreasonably. While the DSSH and QSH have not, by the standards of some foxhunts, been particularly subjected to the attentions of hunt saboteurs, their activities are under constant scrutiny from an attentive local and national press and, more often than not, from video filming by anti-hunt activists. It is not that the new provisions of the Act are likely to be invoked, but rather that their very existence signals a change in the framework assumptions that partly constitute the context of the activity.

The fact that hunting is, at present, an entirely legal activity has been affirmed in recent judgments and to that extent the economic and social strengths of the hunting community have been buttressed by a clarification of the nature of the legal terrain. These are considerable resources on which they are able to draw. But politically, and in terms of the broad public opinion indicated by polling and routinely claimed by those opposed to hunting, the staghunting community remains the most obviously beleaguered: paradoxically cast in the role of a rural 'other' despite being a defining element within a still prevalent conception of the 'rural'. In his social history of foxhunting, Itzkowitz (1977) talks of the sport as a peculiar privilege, at once open to all and uniquely aristocratic and English. The privilege, as this section has demonstrated, persists. Its peculiarity now, however, is that it is a beleaguered privilege.

Conclusions

Politically and ideologically, the national area remains critical for the hunting community. The free vote in February 1992 on Kevin McNamara's Wild Mammals (Protection) Bill, whose main provision sought to ban the use of dogs in hunting wild animals, resulted in a defeat by only 12 votes. Parliamentary changes and other developments encouraged the expectation that a similar bill introduced three years later would have a very strong chance of success. In the event, competing claims about the numbers of Conservative MPs likely to support the aims of such a Bill proved difficult to substantiate as pro-field sports MPs united in a tactic to abstain or vote in favour of the Bill which was carried by 253 votes to nil.

John McFall's Bill, designed to abolish hunting with hounds and coursing and to restrict seriously certain forms of pest control sought, also, through its first clause to outlaw the 'kicking, beating or torture' of wild animals. MPs who support country sports abstained in order to express their support for the principle of this clause and to emphasize that a Bill stripped of anti-country sports provisions in committee would be almost certain to be successful. Tactics in the House suggested that any sense of victory might prove entirely Pyrrhic since the Bill had done much to produce, in the words of the acting Director of the British Field Sports Society, 'an unprecedented alliance in the countryside against urban interference in the country way of life ...' (*Shooting Times & Country Magazine*, 9–15 March 1995).

Certainly, though predictable, the range of groups asserting the right of individuals to choose their country sport was broad and they were joined by the National Farmers Union and the Farmers Union of Wales who attacked the Bill's interference in methods of pest control and the Country Landowners' Association which reiterated its view that country sports should not be a matter for legislation. Meanwhile, on the day that the McFall Bill was debated, attended by weather which made travel difficult, an estimated 40,000 country sports supporters gathered at eight rallies around the country.

Among those addressing them was the broadcaster Robin Page, who in his *Farming Today* interview had followed his comment about the harassment suffered by 'born countrymen' by expressing the hope that if the Bill were to be passed it would be disobeyed. The prospect was acknowledged by the *Independent* in a leading article after the day of rallies. 'Until a convincing and sustained majority against hunting arises', it commented, 'no sensible legislator should want to hazard the creation of a law which risks the contempt of a significant section of the citizenry. Animal idealists will disagree. But there is something else that matters here: the ends, however honourable, do not justify the means, namely riding roughshod over the views of a minority.'

At the level of ideology the battle lines, never obscure, are now drawn with a clarity which demonstrates just how pivotal they are to the still emergent conception of a post-productivist countryside (Marsden *et al.*, 1993). In such a context simplistic contrasts between the urban and the rural carry less and less conviction. The 'countryman' card is an obvious one to play, but if the hunting community is to add a greater ideological and political security to its economic and social strengths, then alliances with those who cannot, or do not wish to identify themselves with that ever more elusive category, will have to be forged. The supporters of hunting need to return their sport to the category of a peculiar rather than a beleaguered privilege.

References

British Social Attitudes Survey (1992) *Social and Community Planning Research*. London: HMSO.

Clark, G., Durrall, J., Grove-White, R., Macnaghten, P. and Urry, J. (1994) *Leisure Landscapes*. London: CPRE.

Cobham Resource Consultants (1982) *Countryside Sports: Their Economic Significance*. Oxford.

Cobham Resource Consultants (1992) *Countryside Sports: Their Economic and Conservation Significance*. The Standing Conference on Countryside Sports, Reading.

Cox, G., Hallett, J. and Winter, M. (1994) Hunting the wild red deer: the social organization and ritual of a 'rural' institution. *Sociologia Ruralis*, 34 (2–3), 190–205.

Garner, R. (1993) Political animals: a survey of the animal protection movement in Britain. *Parliamentary Affairs*, 46, 333–52.

Itzkowitz, D. (1977) *Peculiar Privilege: A Social History of English Foxhunting 1753–1885*. Sussex: Harvester Press.

League Against Cruel Sports (1993) *Before the Hunt*. London: LACS.

Lowe, P., Murdoch, J. and Cox, G. (1995) A civilised retreat?: anti-urbanism, rurality and the making of an Anglo-centric culture. In P. Healey *et al.* (eds) *Managing Cities*. Chichester: John Wiley, 63–83.

Marsden, T., Murdoch, J., Lowe, P., Munton, R. and Flynn, A. (1993) *Constructing the Countryside*. London: UCL Press.

National Trust (1993) *The Conservation and Management of Red Deer on Exmoor and the Quantocks*. Report to Council by Deer Hunting Working Party.

Page, R. (1987) *The Fox and the Orchid*. London: Allen Lane.

Thomas, K. (1983) *Man and the Natural World*. London: Allen Lane.

Thomas, R. (1983) *The Politics of Hunting*. Aldershot: Gower.

Vardy, P. and Grosch, P. (1994) *The Puzzle of Ethics*. London: HarperCollins.

Winter, M., Hallett, J., Nixon, J., Watkins, C., Cox, G. and Glanfield, P. (1993) *Economic and Social Aspects of Deer Hunting on Exmoor and the Quantocks*. Cirencester: Centre for Rural Studies Occasional Paper 20.

5

Hidden from View: Poverty and Marginalization in Rural Britain

PAUL MILBOURNE

'It probably does exist but we don't see that much.'[1]

Introduction

Issues of poverty in the British countryside can be seen as neglected parts of research in human geography and the social sciences in two important ways: first, a growing interest in issues of post-modernism and the so-called 'cultural turn' has acted to deflect attention away from what has been referred to as the 'politics of inequality' towards the 'politics of identity' (Leyshon, 1995) in both rural and urban arenas; and second, it is possible to view 'the rural' as a generally neglected critical research area within human geography and social science (Whatmore, 1993), and this is particularly the case when this research has concerned poverty, where academic discourses of poverty are located predominantly within urban spaces.

This chapter sets out to reclaim 'the rural' from such an urban research stranglehold on poverty, arguing that rural poverty represents an important area of study once the cloak of prosperity is removed from dominant images of the British countryside. The chapter also positions the subject of rural poverty within recent debates on representation, power and identity within rural research and writing (see Philo, 1992, 1993; Murdoch and Pratt, 1993, 1994). It is suggested that encounters with the experiences of being poor or marginalized in rural areas need to be seen as complementary to research on broader issues of power and inequality which may act to produce such situations within rural society. As such, the chapter proposes a multi-method approach to (rural) poverty research; one that engages with issues of 'identity' alongside those of 'inequality'.

The chapter begins with a review of some key recent debates within poverty research in (mainly urban areas of) Britain, focusing on shifting and conflicting definitions of poverty and deprivation, and wider notions of exclusion and marginalization. In the second part of the chapter attention is given to some key previous studies which have addressed issues of poverty and deprivation in rural Britain and America. Here emphasis is placed on the hidden nature of problems in rural areas, which can be seen as linked to physical settlement patterns and dominant discourses of rurality which present these areas as healthy, problem-free idyll-ized environments in which to live. The chapter finishes by drawing on one particular recent study of rural poverty and deprivation - the Rural Lifestyles project (Cloke *et al.*, 1994a, 1994b) - which involved interviews with 4000 households in 16 rural areas in England and Wales. In this section of the chapter attention is focused on both material and experiential components of poverty, deprivation and marginalization in these areas of the British countryside.

Searching for Definition: The Dynamics of Poverty in Britain

> Poverty is a difficult question from both a methodological and a theoretical point of view. Furthermore, it is a very ambiguous political issue. Many difficulties derive from the irreducible distance between the abstract concept and the findings of research. The concept is based on the idea that, for various reasons and for variable periods of time, a part of the population lacks access to sufficient resources to enable it to survive at a historically or geographically determined minimum standard of life and that this leads to serious consequences in terms of behaviour and social relations. (Mingione, 1993)

This quotation, taken from a special issue of the International Journal of Urban and Regional Research on 'new' forms of urban poverty in Britain and the USA, illustrates something of the confusion and complexities associated with poverty research in 'affluent' societies. Little consensus exists surrounding any standard definition or measurement of poverty. Indeed, poverty needs to be viewed as a contested, political concept to which are attached different meanings by a range of individuals and organizations in different situations. As such, our understanding of poverty needs to consider the complex web of inter-connections between definitions, measurements and causes of poverty within Britain (Alcock, 1993).

Several studies of poverty within (urban) Britain over the last 20 years have tended to distinguish between absolute and relative components of poverty; the former concerned with factors such as inadequate diet, poor health, lack of shelter, and so on, while the latter component involves a recognition that systems of inequality within affluent societies may act to exclude or marginalize certain groups from generally accepted standards of living.[2] Indeed, recent debates on the changing nature of poverty within Britain, particularly within political circles, have centred on the question of whether it is still possible to identify absolute poverty in the late 1980s and early 1990s. Conservative politicians, including government ministers (John Moore, 1989), and members of the Royal Family (Duke of Edinburgh, quoted in Jury, 1994) have argued that 'the end of the line' has arrived for poverty, in that, as average standards of living have risen steadily over recent years, poverty in Britain can no longer be seen in absolute terms but has become relative. However, such arguments that increased affluence benefits all sections of society, albeit at different rates, appears to be at odds with official statistics charting changing income levels in Britain over recent years. Table 5.1, for example, is taken from a recent report of *Households Below Average Income* (Department of Social Security, 1995) and highlights an *absolute* reduction in income levels (after housing costs) for the bottom 10 per cent of earners between 1979 and 1994 - a situation which contrasts with an overall rise in incomes of 38 per cent over the same period.

Table 5.1 Percentage changes in real income (after housing costs) by decile group, 1979–92/93

Income group	%
bottom 10%	–17
10–20%	+1
20–30%	+6
30–40%	+15
40–50%	+24
Total population mean	+38

Source: Department of Social Security, 1995, p. 62

Recent academic research and reports by agencies working with poverty have also pointed to increasing rates and the changing nature of poverty within (mainly urban) areas of Britain. A report by the Church of England in 1994, for example, has highlighted the worsening conditions in many of Britain's inner cities, and Oxfam announced recently that it is considering an aid programme to address issues of inequality and poverty in Britain (Meikle, 1994). Academic studies have attempted to theorize about these 'new' forms of city-based poverty and the emergence of an urban 'underclass'.[3] In both cases, academics and concerned agencies have highlighted a series of factors which are linked to and seen as evidence of the rising incidence of urban poverty within Britain - high rates of persistent unemployment, the increased visibility of the homeless on city streets, the deinstitutionalization of the mentally ill, the growth of low-paid, poor-quality employment and an increased incidence of alcohol and drug (ab)use. However, the most comprehensive studies of poverty within Britain were published in the late 1970s and mid-1980s.

Townsend (1979) constructed an index of deprivation based on key indicators of standard of living which correlated strongly with low income levels. A comparison of these deprivation scores with income levels revealed that the degree of deprivation within households increased disproportionately at a certain level of income - 140 per cent of a household's entitlement to supplementary benefit (now income support). From this analysis Townsend claimed that the welfare state is failing to raise many low-income households above the 'poverty line', and consequently benefit rates needed to be increased by around 40 per cent. The research also highlighted certain household groups which were experiencing a high incidence of poverty: single elderly households, large families, the self-employed and those in unskilled manual occupations.

A second important study of poverty in Britain was the *Breadline Britain* research undertaken by Mack and Lansley (1985) which involved a quota sample of 1174 persons in 1983. The study considered poverty in terms of an 'enforced lack of socially perceived necessities' (Mack and Lansley, 1985, p. 9), with households defined as living in poverty if they lacked at least three necessities identified by a majority of the population. According to this definition around 22 per cent of the British population (12.1 million persons) were living in or on the margins of poverty in the early 1980s. The research pointed to five important groups living in poverty: the unemployed, single parents, the sick and disabled, pensioners and the low-paid (Mack and Lansley, 1985, p. 185), although there is clearly a degree of overlap between some of these groups. Low pay was identified as a key factor behind inadequate standards of living, with one-third of impoverished households containing persons in full-time employment, although unemployed households accounted for roughly half of those living in intense poverty (lacking at least seven necessities).

Widening Notions of Poverty: Towards Experiences of Deprivation and Marginalization

These two studies by Townsend (1979) and Mack and Lansley (1985) can be viewed as attempts at simplifying the multi-faceted nature of poverty and deprivation down to key indicators linked to levels of income and other material factors (such as housing, health, diet and access to essential services). However, the notion of deprivation also encompasses a broader remit of issues and life chances - it is linked to notions of separation, non-participation and marginalization from accepted ways of life (Alcock, 1993). In this wider sense, deprivation can be seen as linked closely with notions of disempowerment and lack of citizenship (see Robbins, 1993; Scott, 1994). However, these broader conceptualizations of marginalization and exclusion may bring normative and experiential definitions of deprivation into conflict, given that:

> [need] only exists to the extent to which people perceive themselves to have needs which are not met, or are going without things which they think they ought to have. If you do not need or want something, then in what sense can you be deprived of it? (Alcock, 1993, p. 77)

Indeed, conflicts surrounding the definition of need have long been recognized by researchers of poverty in urban areas. Runciman (1966), for example, in a study of relative deprivation in the 1960s, has reported that many people living below the poverty line do not perceive themselves as relatively deprived. Households experiencing poverty (in normative terms), it is argued, due to limited social mobility, tend to compare themselves with others in their local area rather than wider society, and thus do not view themselves as experiencing any particular problems (see also Coates and Silburn, 1970). Townsend (1979) has also uncovered a reluctance on the part of households living in poverty to admit to feelings of poverty and deprivation. Moreover, he suggests that lower proportions of households defined normatively as living in poverty recognize the existence of poverty generally within society compared with those living above the poverty line.

Such discrepancies between notions of poverty and deprivation as defined externally and as experienced by households and individuals can present a series of important difficulties for researchers of these issues. Put simply, normative definitions of poverty may include groups and individuals who do not view themselves as poor, they may homogenize diverse groupings under the potentially stigmatic umbrella term of 'poverty', or fail to understand how low-incomed households and individuals draw on different strategies to cope with situations of low income; a focus on different experiences of poverty and deprivation, however, may constrain attempts at generalizing about poverty issues and deflect from efforts to raise poverty issues on to wider, political agendas. Thus, it can be suggested that within poverty research a firm grasp needs to be held of both wider processes of structuring which act to marginalize certain groups within society (in financial and other - social, cultural and political - terms) and the actual experiences of living in such circumstances. There remains a need for intervention by academics, agencies and individuals concerned with issues of poverty, deprivation and marginalization within society, given that there exists a range of factors which can act to soften, deflect and silence the voices of those experiencing poverty. Indeed, as Alcock (1993) has suggested, locating the politics of poverty solely within the politics of 'the poor' themselves neglects wider issues associated with poverty in Britain:

> it is to a shared belief in greater social justice that poverty campaigners [and researchers] must appeal if they are to secure support for policy changes to remove poverty, and this cannot be achieved if poverty is perceived and presented as a problem only for the poor. Thus the involvement of poor people in campaigning against [and research of] poverty can be a supplement to the more general activities of the academics, politicians and professionals, but it cannot be a substitute for them. (p. 213)

While it can be suggested that it is the 'academics, politicians and professionals' who need to supplement the activities of those households and individuals experiencing poverty, it is clear that researchers need to encompass a range of different methodologies and voices within their studies of and campaigns against poverty in Britain. The remaining parts of this chapter begin to consider these different viewpoints on poverty, deprivation and marginalization within one particular neglected (geographical) area of poverty research - the countryside.

Poverty and Deprivation in Rural Areas: I, Britain

A review of recent poverty research within Britain would reveal that in terms of both volume and theorization, the cutting edge of such research has remained locked generally within urban areas.[4] While such an imbalance may be linked to an urban-bias within human geography and sociology, it is also connected closely with the different scales of visibility associated with a wide range of rural and urban 'problems'. For example, households living in poverty in small and scattered rural settlements tend to remain physically hidden, in contrast to the visual concentration of poverty in the urban, and more specifically inner city arena. Indeed, in many areas of the countryside, the marked physical segregation of 'rich' and 'poor' households - suburbia and inner city - tends to be absent, with the 'rural poor' often living cheek-by-jowl with more affluent residents. Scott *et al.* (1991) have also suggested - in similar ways to Runciman (1966) and Coates and Silburn (1970) - that in many rural areas there exist restricted levels of knowledge about urban lifestyles, a more limited set of expectations and, consequently, a lower degree of awareness of poverty and deprivation within the local area. Moreover, even when problems are acknowledged within the private arena, it can be suggested that the generally reduced anonymity associated with rural lifestyles may prevent such feelings from being discussed more openly - either with concerned agencies or in household-based surveys.

A second important means by which poverty and deprivation in the British countryside may remain hidden concerns cultural constructions of rurality. Dominant discourses of 'the rural' within Britain - whether drawn from popular culture and the media, social science or policy - tend to be constructed at worst, as problem-free (sometimes people-free) environments, and at best, as arenas characterized by forms of problems which are less pronounced than in urban areas (see Cloke and Milbourne, 1992). As Bradley *et al.* (1986) have commented: 'Indeed, to admit the existence of poverty (and deprivation based on inequalities between people, rather than places) in rural areas is to challenge one of the most persuasive images of our social heritage' (p. 25). They suggest further that the rhetoric of country life in Britain is capable of interlocking certain dominant notions of contemporary rural lifestyles: the importance of a strong community, feelings of patriotism and nationalism ('England's Green and Pleasant Land'), a distaste of the dependency culture linked to the welfare state, and the reinforcement of social hierarchies. Furthermore, Cloke (1995) has suggested that new political cultures of privatized welfare provision can be viewed as symbolized by the images of voluntarism, self-help and low levels of public-sector welfare services characteristic of many rural areas.

Studies which have attempted to increase the visibility of problems in the British countryside can be traced back over four decades (see Bracey, 1952, 1959), with a number of reports having highlighted several facets of rural deprivation. However, it was not until the late 1970s that researchers started to explore the cumulative nature of problems being experienced by certain rural households. Research by Shaw (1979) and Walker (1978), for example, attempted to bring together multiple components of rural deprivation, with Shaw categorizing three facets of deprivation -

opportunity, household and mobility deprivation - which, when interconnected within certain low-income households, acted to reinforce problems of poverty and deprivation in the countryside.

In the early 1980s an important study of rural deprivation was undertaken by McLaughlin and Bradley (see Bradley, 1984; Bradley *et al.*, 1986; McLaughlin, 1985, 1986). The research, which was funded by the Department of the Environment and the Rural Development Commission and involved interviews with 876 households in five areas of the English countryside, attempted to evaluate competing (rural and urban) demands for central government resources. A key aspect of this study involved the generation of a normative indicator of rural deprivation using Townsend's (1979) analysis (described earlier within the chapter). Annual gross disposable income was expressed as a percentage of supplementary benefit entitlement plus housing costs for each household within the survey and a deprivation threshold of 140 per cent benefit entitlement was fixed. This calculation revealed that an average of one-quarter of all households in these five areas were living in or on the margins of poverty - ranging from 21.4 per cent of households in Suffolk to 27.3 per cent in Northumberland (Table 5.2). Such findings have been viewed by many rural commentators as important not only because they reveal high overall levels of poverty in rural areas but also for the relatively consistent rates of poverty associated with very different types of English countryside. Indeed, these poverty statistics have been used widely by researchers over the 1980s and early 1990s as an indication of the widespread nature of poverty and deprivation in rural areas.

Table 5.2 Poverty relative to supplementary benefit entitlement for five areas of rural England, 1980

	Percentage of households living:		
Area	on the margins of poverty (100–139% of Supplementary Benefit entitlement) %	in poverty (less than 100% of Supplementary Benefit entitlement) %	in or on the margins of poverty %
Suffolk	13.1	8.3	21.4
Essex	15.2	9.7	24.9
Shropshire	15.4	9.5	24.9
North Yorkshire	15.6	10.2	25.8
Northumberland	18.8	8.5	27.3
All areas	15.6	9.3	24.9

Source: McLaughlin (1986, p. 295)

Poverty and Deprivation in Rural Areas: II, USA

Over recent years poverty issues in rural America have been much more extensively researched than in Britain. The availability of official statistics has enabled researchers to compare the dynamics of urban and rural poverty in the USA, with such figures pointing to a growing problem of poverty within many rural areas over the 1980s (Molnar and Traxler, 1991). Indeed, Brown and Warner (1991) have calculated that, by the early 1990s, the non-metropolitan poor totalled 9.1 million persons and accounted for two-thirds of the 13.9 million poor people residing in metropolitan central cities. However, even with this visibility of rural poverty within published statistics, the image of poverty within American media, policy and academic discourses remains largely urban-focused. Dudenhefer, for example, has highlighted such a bias within poverty studies in the social sciences:

> Over the last 11 years, only 21 articles have been listed under the heading 'Rural Poor: United States'; this compares with a listing of 26 different pieces on urban poverty and the underclass in the United States in 1991–92 alone. Apparently, when urban researchers - or at least the principal sponsors of poverty research - think poverty, they think city, not town and country. (1994, p. 4)

Researchers of rural poverty in America, like those in Britain, have pointed to the physical invisibility of a range of rural problems in explaining this neglect of non-metropolitan issues - linked to both geographical isolation and the camouflage effect of picturesque landscape (see Harrington, 1981) - even though, unlike the situation in Britain, in statistical terms rural poverty appears highly visible (Brown and Warner, 1991). Attention has also focused on other factors influencing this urban-rural poverty research imbalance, including an historical acceptance of poverty among rural residents resulting from relatively weak working-class representation (particularly in the South), and a partial spatial displacement of rural poverty to the city through an out-migration of certain poor households to urban arenas (Tickamyer and Duncan, 1990; Molnar and Traxler, 1991). However, even with this predominantly urban gaze associated with poverty studies, there has been a growing interest in rural poverty among social scientists in the USA over recent years. Such interest has been linked particularly to the establishment by the Rural Sociological Society in 1990 of a Task Force on Persistent Rural Poverty, which has aimed to 'provide a conceptual classification regarding the factors and dynamics of society which perpetuate rural poverty' (Rural Sociological Society, 1993, p. 3).

Much of this recent poverty research in non-metropolitan America has highlighted important differences in the nature of rural- and urban-based poverty. Dudenhefer (1994), for example, has suggested that many of the characteristics of poverty in rural areas contradict some key discourses associated with poverty, particularly notions of an 'underclass' (see also Cloke, 1995). Rural poverty, in fact, tends to be characterized by higher proportions of households in employment, married couple families and the elderly, and a lower incidence of single parent households than in metropolitan areas. These studies have also pointed to the shifting nature of the rural economy as prime mover behind rising levels of poverty in non-metropolitan America, highlighting in particular the relative scarcity of well-paid, good quality employment and a predominance of insecure, low paid, service-based jobs. In addition to these processes of economic restructuring acting to impoverish low-income working residents, research has also focused on the experiences of the non-working poor - particularly the disabled and the elderly - who can become effectively trapped within pockets of persistent poverty. Finally, research in the USA has pointed to a series of important interlinkages between urban and rural poverty, with many of the problems associated with rural areas viewed as more deep seated than those recently identified as associated with 'new' forms of urban poverty:

> While growing numbers of working poor and a shortage of jobs offering upward mobility to low-skill workers are contributing to a new crisis in central cities, this lack of opportunity is not new to rural areas. Similarly, the deepening socio economic and cultural isolation of urban ghettos ... has been the experience of generations of the rural poor, especially in the South, where rigid social stratification has kept them out of the mainstream. (Tickamyer and Duncan, 1990, p. 70)

Poverty, Deprivation and Marginalization in the English and Welsh Countryside: Some Findings from the 1990s

The final part of this chapter returns the discussion of poverty issues back to rural Britain through a consideration of some recent research which has explored the changing nature of lifestyles and deprivation in areas of the English and Welsh countryside (Cloke *et al.*, 1994a, 1994b). The Rural Lifestyles project was funded by the Department of the Environment, the Rural Development Commission and the Economic and Social Research Council in an attempt to update the deprivation study conducted by McLaughlin and Bradley in five areas of rural England in the early 1980s.

With increased levels of funding, the research was extended to include a further seven areas in rural England and four study areas in the Welsh countryside - funded by the Welsh Office, Development Board for Rural Wales and the Welsh Development Agency (see Figures 5.1 and 5.2). In total, the Lifestyles research involved detailed interviews with around 4000 households in 1990-91 across a range of lifestyle issues - including housing, employment, income, service provision and social change. The project employed a combination of quantitative and qualitative research methodologies in an attempt to highlight both structural processes and individual experiences associated with deprivation and lifestyles in the 1990s countryside.

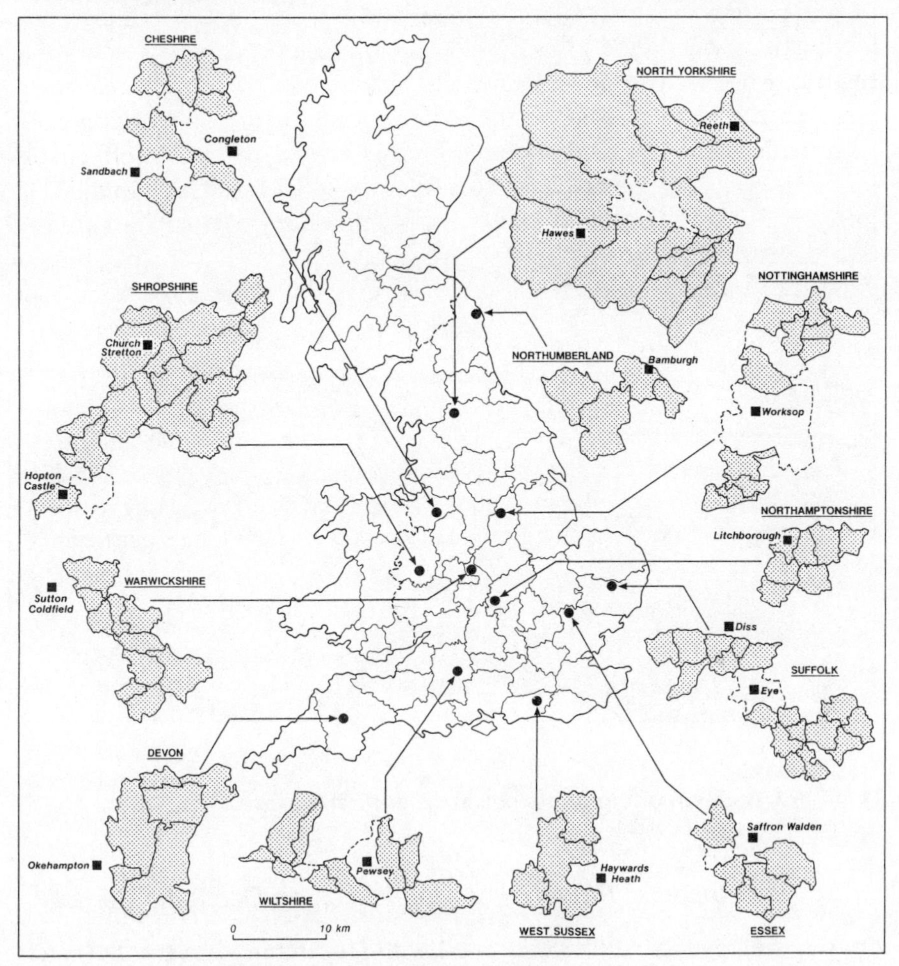

Figure 5.1 Location of the 12 study areas in rural England
Source: Cloke *et al.* (1994b)

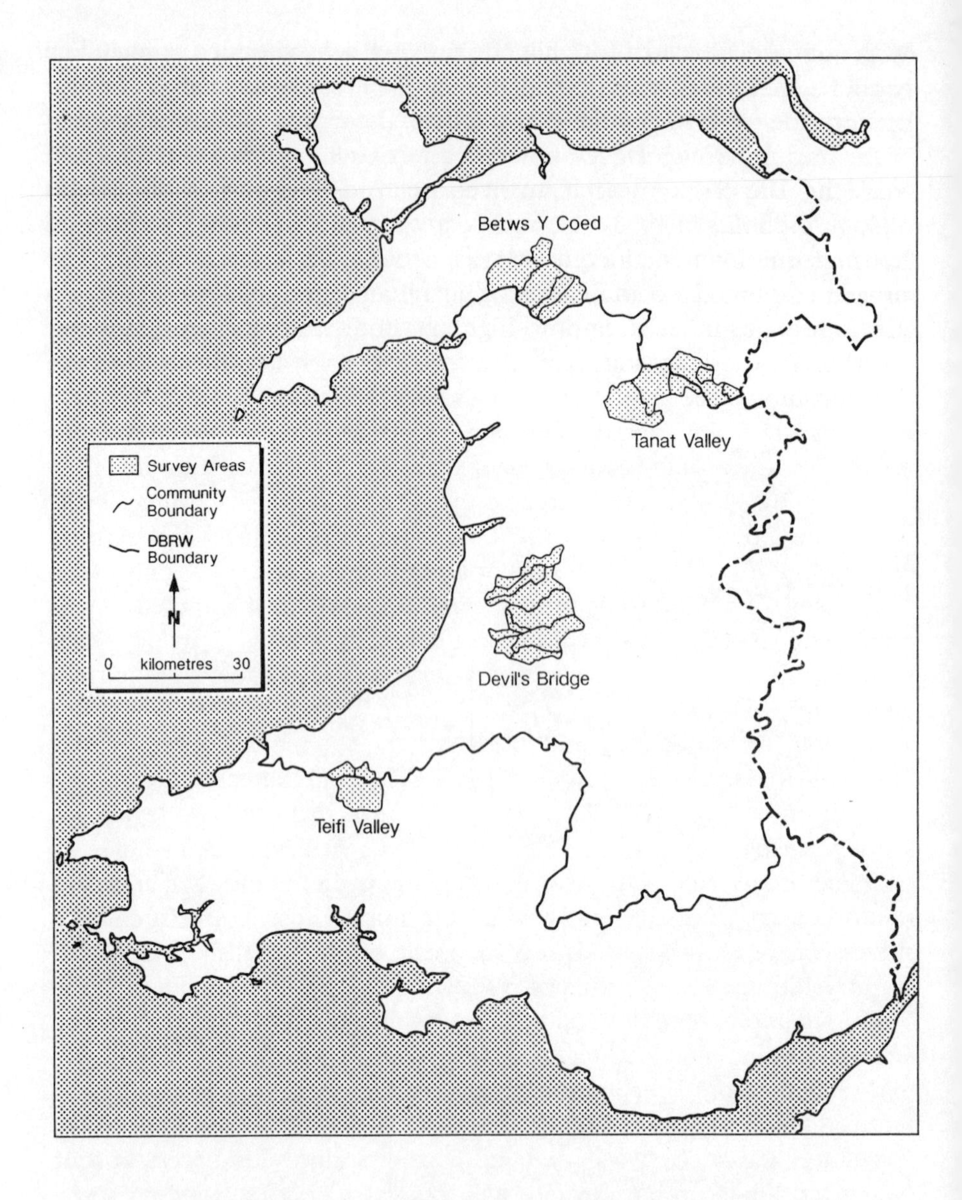

Figure 5.2 Location of the four study areas in rural Wales
Source: Cloke *et al.* (1994b)

Low Income, Poverty and Deprivation as Defined Externally

One of the key difficulties associated with researching poverty in (rural) Britain relates to the paucity of official statistics which are available at the local level. Indeed, while researchers in the USA are able to draw on a range of published data highlighting changing aspects of rural-urban poverty, their counterparts in Britain are restricted mainly to the Department of Environment's *New Earnings Survey* - an annual sample of earnings levels among full-time employees at a county level. Table 5.3 highlights the changing levels of 'rural' earnings relative to the British average income over the 1980s and early 1990s for counties containing the 16 study areas included within the Rural Lifestyles research. It is apparent from these statistics that, at an aggregate level, the earnings gap between workers in 'rural' counties and the national mean widened between 1980–94 for both male and female employees. In fact, nine out of these 16 counties witnessed a widening differential in terms of male earnings and the income gap among female workers increased in eight 'rural' counties (although income data was not available for four counties). By 1994, 12 study area counties recorded male earnings levels below the Great Britain mean income, with workers in Powys earning only around 80 per cent of this national income. Indeed, it was only in the counties of Essex, Cheshire, Wiltshire and West Sussex that income levels marginally exceeded the average for Great Britain as a whole. Such patterns of low income are also characteristic of female earnings in rural areas, with 11 'rural' counties recording below-average levels of earnings. Moreover, Table 5.3 highlights the existence of considerable gender inequalities associated with income patterns in rural areas, with women earning on average only 70 per cent of mean male income levels - a slightly greater income differential than for Great Britain as a whole.

These broad-scale patterns of low income within many rural areas are reinforced by evidence drawn from the Rural Lifestyles research. The survey of 4000 households in 16 areas of the English and Welsh countryside reveals considerable evidence of rural low incomes. Table 5.4, for example, provides an indication of the geography of what can be termed 'low-income' households - in which working adults earned less than £8000 (gross) per annum. In five of these areas, which might be referred to as the more remote rural areas - Northumberland, North Yorkshire, Devon, Betws-y-Coed and Devil's Bridge[5] - in excess of four out of ten adults in employment can be classified as low-incomed. By contrast, a much lower incidence of low-income workers is evident in several of the more accessible, commuter-type areas - Warwickshire, West Sussex, Cheshire, Northamptonshire and Essex, although even in Essex (which recorded the lowest proportion of such workers) more than one-in-five persons in employment earned less than £8000 per year. A similar geographical pattern of low income is also apparent in terms of household income (in which all sources of income within the household

Table 5.3 Average gross weekly earnings of adult full-time workers for study area counties within the Rural Lifestyles project, expressed as a percentage of the Great Britain mean income, 1980 and 1994.

County	Men 1980 %	Men 1994 %	Women 1980 %	Women 1994 %	Female earnings as percentage of male earnings 1994 %
Cheshire	104.1	103.5	97.2	95.1	66.4
Devon	86.9	87.5	94.4	90.1	63.7
Essex	101.0	102.1	99.9	101.9	72.1
Northamptonshire	92.4	93.7	89.3	90.1	69.5
Northumberland	92.2	87.9	91.2	89.7	73.7
North Yorkshire	93.0	87.2	94.8	88.8	73.7
Nottinghamshire	98.5	88.9	91.6	88.5	73.6
Shropshire	87.2	85.2	89.0	84.7	71.9
Suffolk	93.1	92.0	96.4	86.1	71.8
Warwickshire	98.5	97.1	90.5	89.8	67.5
West Sussex	98.8	103.9	98.6	104.8	66.8
Wiltshire	91.6	102.9	93.0	96.1	72.8
Clwyd	97.7	91.4	nd	91.4	67.5
Dyfed (rural)	92.6	84.0	87.8	nd	74.5
Gwynedd	91.9	87.1	nd	nd	nd
Powys	79.0	79.5	nd	nd	nd
Mean for all areas	93.7	92.1	93.4	92.1	70.1

Note: nd = no data
Source: New Earnings Survey (1980, 1994)

are considered net of deductions such as tax and National Insurance). Table 5.5 highlights the proportions of households with net incomes of less than £10,000 per annum. While an average of 27 per cent of households across the 16 areas were characterized as 'low-incomed', it is evident that in seven of these study areas - Betws-y-Coed, Devil's Bridge, Tanat Valley, Teifi Valley, Northumberland, Nottinghamshire and Devon - more than three out of ten were thus defined.

In addition to an exploration of income levels, the Rural Lifestyles research also explored some key indicators of poverty. In this chapter attention is focused solely on one of these indicators - poverty defined relative to state benefit entitlement, the indicator devised by Townsend (1979) and utilized in the study of rural deprivation undertaken by McLaughlin and Bradley in the early 1980s (see Bradley *et al.*, 1986; McLaughlin, 1986). Table 5.6 highlights the proportions of households within the Rural Lifestyles surveys with incomes of less than 140 per cent of income support entitlement plus housing costs - the same cut-off point used by Townsend (1979) and McLaughlin (1986). According to this indicator, the proportion of households normatively defined as living in or on the margins of poverty ranges from 6.4 per cent in West Sussex

Table 5.4 Percentage gross annual salaries below £8000 of adult workers in the household

Area	%
Northumberland	53.7
North Yorkshire	50.3
Devon	45.8
Betws-y-Coed	43.6
Devil's Bridge	41.1
Wiltshire	39.7
Suffolk	38.4
Tanat Valley	37.0
Teifi Valley	36.3
Nottinghamshire	35.7
Shropshire	33.4
Essex	31.9
Northamptonshire	28.7
Cheshire	27.8
West Sussex	27.1
Warwickshire	23.3
Mean for 16 areas	37.1

Source: Cloke *et al.* (1994a, 1994b)

Table 5.5 Percentage of households with net incomes below £10,000 per annum

Area	%
Betws-y-Coed	53.4
Tanat Valley	40.5
Teifi Valley	37.6
Northumberland	36.8
Nottinghamshire	36.0
Devil's Bridge	31.7
Devon	30.1
North Yorkshire	26.6
Suffolk	26.6
Shropshire	21.4
Wiltshire	18.9
Essex	18.5
Northamptonshire	16.6
Cheshire	15.0
West Sussex	14.4
Warwickshire	13.2
Mean for 16 areas	27.3

Source: Cloke *et al.* (1994a, 1994b)

to 39.2 per cent of households within Nottinghamshire, and the geography of this poverty again indicates sharp divisions between remote and accessible rural areas (although these divisions appear to be less pronounced than in the case of low incomes). In overall terms, an average of 24.5 per cent of households were defined as living in or on the margins of poverty - a similar level to that reported in the early 1980s by McLaughlin (1986) - and rates of poverty in 13 study areas accounted for more than one-fifth of all households. Such a high incidence of poverty occurring in these very different rural areas would appear to reinforce lifestyle problems associated with low incomes and poverty within many areas of the English and Welsh countryside.

Characteristics of Rural Poverty

Relatively little is known about those groups, households and individuals who are living in or on the margins of poverty in rural areas. This section of the chapter attempts to shed some light on the characteristics of impoverished households by drawing on material from the Rural Lifestyles research. It focuses on those 24.5 per cent of households with incomes of less than 140 per cent of their income support entitlements (see Table 5.6).

Table 5.6 Percentage of households in or on the margins of poverty definitions relative to income support entitlement[1]

Area	%
Nottinghamshire	39.2
Devon	34.4
Betws-y-Coed	30.0
Tanat Valley	29.7
Essex	29.5
Northumberland	26.4
Teifi Valley	26.4
Suffolk	25.5
Wiltshire	25.4
Devil's Bridge	25.1
Warwickshire	22.6
North Yorkshire	22.0
Shropshire	21.6
Northamptonshire	14.8
Cheshire	12.8
West Sussex	6.4
Mean for 16 areas	24.5

Note [1] In or on the margins of poverty: less than 140% of income supplement entitlement.
Source: Cloke *et al.* (1994a, 1994b)

Although it is recognized that the selected characteristics of households in poverty highlighted within Table 5.7 will inevitably obscure both localized differences and the considerable heterogeneity associated with the 'rural poor', it is clear that, at an aggregate level, rural poverty appears

Table 5.7 The composition of the 'rural poor'

		%
Household type	Elderly single	41.8
	Elderly couple	27.4
	Non-elderly single	10.3
	Non-elderly couple	20.5
Length of residence	Less than 5 years	24.1
	5–15 years	31.8
	More than 15 years	42.4
Close relatives nearby		60.0
Household tenure	Fully-owned	34.1
	Owned on mortgage	7.1
	Social rented	47.1
	Private rented	11.2
Occupations	Catering, cleaning, hairdressing and other personal services	33.3
	Selling	13.9
	Clerical and related	11.1
	Health, welfare, education	8.3
	Construction	5.6
	Farming, fishing and related	5.6
	Processing, making, repairing and related	5.6
	Miscellaneous/not stated	16.7
Reported housing defects		16.5
No access to private car		42.4

Source: Cloke *et al.* (1994a, 1994b)

to contradict any notion of a 'rural underclass'. For example, rural poverty is associated particularly with the elderly, accounting for around seven out of ten households living in poverty, and especially those households containing a single female elderly person. Accordingly, many households in poverty are well established in their rural area, with around six out of ten households reporting the presence of close family members living locally.

The tenure make-up of households in poverty would again appear to contradict dominant notions of poverty which are associated with the rented housing sector. In fact, our research has pointed to around four out of ten households in poverty owning their property – the vast majority of these being outright owners. However, it nevertheless remains the case that a majority of households living in poverty are residing in social rental and private rental accommodation.

Clearly, the predominance of elderly persons living in poverty means that rural poverty is generally associated with *non-working* households. However, our analysis of rural poverty also revealed a group of households in employment who were living in or on the margins of poverty – the rural *working poor*. These low-incomed workers tended to be involved generally in low quality, insecure jobs related particularly to clerical, selling and personal service employment.

Finally, for some households living in poverty, aspects of income deprivation were compounded by other aspects of deprivation linked to restricted personal mobility and poor quality housing conditions. Around four out of ten households, for example, did not have access to a private vehicle and instead were reliant on generally infrequent public transport services. In this sense, some low-incomed households, particularly in the more remote areas, were effectively trapped within their localities for a number of hours or even days. Other households living in poverty were also experiencing severe problems with the quality of their accommodation, with almost 17 per cent of respondents reporting a range of structural defects with their property.

Experiences of Poverty, Deprivation and Marginalization in Rural Areas

It is important within any consideration of poverty and deprivation issues to explore notions of poverty which are predominantly based on normatively defined aggregate statistics alongside more individualistic accounts of the experience of poverty in rural areas. This final part of the chapter provides a preliminary exploration of the varied meanings associated with residents' understandings and denials of poverty and deprivation in our 16 study areas. It begins with an examination of perceptions of poverty within the local area both generally and among those households who were defined (normatively) as living in poverty. The section then moves on to consider some commentaries provided by our respondents in rural Wales concerning the understandings of poverty and deprivation in their local areas.

The Rural Lifestyles study would appear to reinforce findings from previous research (Runciman, 1966; Townsend, 1979) that many people who are defined normatively as living in poverty are not willing to recognize the existence of poverty within either their own household or local area. Table 5.8 highlights that only 27.1 per cent of respondents living in poverty (relative to income support entitlement) considered that poverty was present within their local area, with levels of recognition ranging from 62.5 per cent of respondents in Devil's Bridge to a universal denial of poverty in the West Sussex study area. Moreover, it is clear that, in most areas, a lower proportion of respondents living below the

Table 5.8 Percentages of respondents who considered that issues of poverty and deprivation were present in their local area

Area	All respondents %	Respondents in households living in poverty %
Devil's Bridge	61.5	62.5
North Yorkshire	46.2	22.2
Devon	43.9	45.5
Teifi Valley	41.2	20.0
Betws-y-Coed	40.8	16.7
Shropshire	39.8	37.5
Northumberland	36.3	21.1
Wiltshire	35.7	41.1
Suffolk	34.7	33.3
Tanat Valley	33.2	21.4
West Sussex	33.3	0.0
Cheshire	32.1	20.0
Essex	29.3	38.5
Warwickshire	28.6	14.3
Northamptonshire	25.1	25.0
Nottinghamshire	21.0	15.0
Mean for 16 areas	36.4	27.1

Source: Cloke *et al.* (1994a, 1994b)

poverty line recognized poverty in their local area than those persons living above this line; here 36.4 per cent of all respondents admitted to the presence of poverty in their area.

The chapter now turns to explore some key reasons behind these low levels of recognition of poverty among residents within our surveys. The remaining sections draw on an initial analysis of 160 interviews with residents in rural Wales[6] (see Figure 5.2) and explore respondents' perceptions of the nature of poverty and deprivation in their local areas.

Our interviews revealed a series of factors which were acting to dilute the level of awareness of poverty and deprivation issues among residents living in the Welsh study areas. A large group of respondents pointed to the scattered nature of settlement patterns in their local area which tended to reduce the visibility of a range of problems. Indeed, while some of our respondents were convinced that poverty and deprivation existed within their locality, relatively few had actually encountered such problems on a personal basis:

> It [deprivation] probably does exist but we don't see that much.
> (Devil's Bridge, 42f, 16+ years, personal assistant, private rented)[7]

> [There is an] argument between them. She thinks those in rural areas are

better off; he thinks there is deprivation. But she mentions [the] homeless in Coventry; he comments that there are also homeless people here but they are invisible.
(Devil's Bridge, 21f, less than 1 year, not working, private rented)

No sign of it [poverty] around here - some people maybe but [they] hide it.
(Teifi Valley, 64m, 16+ years, retired post office worker, owner-occupier)

Another important issue which was seen by many residents within our interviews as downplaying local awareness of rural poverty and deprivation concerned a set of perceived differences between urban and rural lifestyles. Here, respondents considered that rural residents tended generally to hold much lower expectations of life, with a widescale acceptance of low levels of opportunities and service provision in their local areas. Consequently, although many residents recognized higher levels of opportunities and services in other, particularly urban, areas, this situation was rarely viewed as problematic. Indeed, some residents had moved to their local area precisely for reasons of isolation and a less developed service provision infrastructure:

[There is] deprivation of the things which a town can offer, but people have chosen to live here exactly for that reason.
(Tanat Valley, 44f, 3-5 years, secretary, private rented)

Poor people [in rural areas] live a simpler life; don't expect the same things [as urban people]. [They] expect a simpler life.
(Teifi Valley, 60f, less than 1 year, school teacher, social rented)

Others considered that many of the perceived 'problems' associated with rural living, particularly those related to poor quality employment opportunities and a limited range of (relatively expensive) services, were somehow compensated by a series of aesthetic, environmental and health qualities associated with their localities. These wider benefits of rural living were able to provide a kind of 'psychic income' (Cloke *et al.*, 1994a) for households living in poverty. In the two commentaries highlighted below, we begin to see these notions of a perceived 'contented rural poor':

I do not think that there is real deprivation, but where people are deprived of services they make up in other areas, such as beauty and quietness which towns are deprived of. If this is deprivation then I am content with it.
(Tanat Valley, 62m, 3-5 years, manager of caravan park, owner-occupier)

They [deprived people] are lucky they live where they do compared to children in towns.
(Teifi Valley, 64f, 16+ years, retired shop worker, social rented)

A further issue raised by our respondents which can be viewed as lowering rural residents' awareness of poverty in their area relates to some key perceived attributes of rural life. While rural problems were acknowledged, it was felt by these residents that voluntary structures of support and self-help existing within the local area were able to deal with such problems. Village people were capable of 'looking after their own', without the need for intervention from outside (national or local) agencies:

> I don't think there is deprivation – villagers look after one another.
> (Tanat Valley, 76f, 3–5 years, retired secretary, owner-occupier)

> I've not seen people go hungry – people help each other; grow food for each other.
> (Teifi Valley, 60f, less than 1 year, school teacher, social rented)

Finally, the existence of poverty and deprivation in the Welsh countryside was denied altogether by a number of, predominantly elderly, respondents. For these residents, notions of deprivation tended to be conceptualized in historical terms, making reference frequently to past periods of 'real' hardship and absolute poverty experienced by previous generations of rural people. Given the prominence of elderly persons within our classification of households living in poverty, it is perhaps not surprising that the level of awareness of poverty was particularly low among this group of rural residents:

> I don't think there is really deprivation in rural areas nowadays.
> (Betws-y-Coed, 70f, 6–15 years, never worked, owner-occupier)

> A lot of people [are] without work, but people nowadays get more on the dole than I had at work. [It's] different now than when I was at work.
> (Teifi Valley, 74m, 6–15 years, retired clerk, owner-occupier)

> There isn't any [deprivation] – I just said that. In the old days there was hunger and poverty but now even if you don't work you can still live well.
> (Devil's Bridge, 37f, 16+ years, housepartner, owner-occupier)

Among those residents who felt able to identify problems of poverty and deprivation in their local area, the most frequently cited reason behind such problems related to the failings of the individual and notions of an 'undeserving rural poor'. In the following commentaries we begin to see that many people considered welfare provision as the responsibility of the individual rural resident rather than the state; that the 'rural poor' needed to 'help themselves':

> People should get off their arses and get to work.
> (Betws-y-Coed, 74m, 6–15 years, retired clerk, owner-occupier)

> It's up to the individual to find work in this area. There are opportunities but you have to go out and ask.
> (Teifi Valley, 32f, 6–15 years, control clerk, owner-occupier)

> Those who claim to be deprived would have a lot better [life] if they spent less time in the pub and quit smoking. People [should] learn to help themselves.
> (Tanat Valley, 72m, 16+ years, retired vet, owner-occupier)

Others, however, rejected individual blame and instead highlighted a series of detrimental rural outcomes emanating from central government policies in the post-1979 period, particularly involving a switch from programmes of state intervention towards free market economics. Many residents commented that relatively little consideration had been given to the specificities of rural areas within these policies, particularly in relation to deregulation and privatization:

> [The] Government has forgotten about rural communities.
> (Tanat Valley, 78m, 6–15 years, forest warden, owner-occupier)

> The worst thing is privatization – [we] can't pay for increases with the cost of services.
> (Devil's Bridge, 34m, 3–5 years, lecturer, owner-occupier)

Residents also highlighted a series of more specific economic changes over recent years, linked partly to central government legislation, but also to wider processes of economic restructuring. Such changes were linked to a contraction of the agricultural workforce and a proliferation of low-paid, insecure, service-sector jobs, effectively trapping certain low-income groups within the working population into situations of persistent poverty:

> [There is a] shortage of local employment and low wages [and] deprivation associated with agricultural policy.
> (Tanat Valley, 61m, 3–5 years, retired engineer, owner-occupier)

> Employment [is] not available; no real jobs. [We need] higher income and better employment. [There are] too many odd jobs – not enough real jobs.
> (Tanat Valley, 36m, 3–5 years, social worker, owner-occupier)

Others pointed to a wider series of restricted opportunities affecting low-income households, linked to housing access and public transport services in their local areas. It is clear from the commentaries highlighted below that certain residents considered that the cumulative effects of a range of problems were acting to disadvantage certain groups within the rural population:

> [The area is characterized by] low incomes and a car is essential - if you can't afford to buy a house or run a car then life in rural areas can be utter hell.
> (Devil's Bridge, 34f, less than 1 year, student, private rented)

> [You] couldn't live here if you had no transport or job. You have to travel a long way to work.
> (Teifi Valley, 61f, 3–5 years, retired clerical officer, owner-occupier)

> [There is a] lack of affordable accommodation, lack of money, lack of choice of jobs.
> (Devil's Bridge, 50m, 1–2 years, TV engineer, owner-occupier)

Finally, notions of deprivation were also understood by some of our respondents in broader terms which included those aspects of social exclusion and cultural marginalization discussed in earlier parts of this chapter. Although these residents did not generally discuss these wider socio-cultural issues under the umbrella term of 'deprivation', they did nevertheless recognize such feelings of marginalization as key concerns for certain groups within their locality. Within our interviews, these notions of peripherality to the socio-cultural mainstream(s) of rural life appeared to emanate from two main sources.

A first group of respondents, characterized mainly by newcomer residents, perceived themselves as living 'outside' of the mainstream rural 'community' through reasons of non-localism, linguistic incompetence and lifestyle difference, although it can be suggested that other factors such as age, class, gender and sexuality might also be acting to maintain positions of distance from dominant community relations:

> I've been living here for twenty years but I'm still an outsider if you know what I mean.
> (Community Council Clerk, Devil's Bridge)

> It's hard ... when everybody knows your business and is watching you all the time. A lot of people ... think they have the right to judge you and discuss it endlessly. People think of kindly neighbours leaving eggs at the back door, but here they'd probably be off.
> (Devil's Bridge, 40m, 3–5 years, graphics artist, private rented)

Second, some residents, particularly those more established persons, felt marginalized by recent processes of economic restructuring and socio-cultural recomposition which had impinged on their local area. Many Welsh-speaking respondents, for example, expressed tremendous feelings of regret towards processes of cultural and linguistic change which were associated with an in-movement on non-Welsh-speaking, predominately English, groups to their local areas:

> More English coming in – they don't belong here. They would be alright if they were part of the community and spoke Welsh, but they live as if they were still in England.
> (Devil's Bridge, 37f, 16+ years, housepartner, owner-occupier)

> There's so many strangers in the village now. You can walk up the road and not know anybody.
> (Devil's Bridge, 49f, all life, housepartner, owner-occupier)

> [It] used to be more close-knit. People moving in don't seem so interested in what's happening in the village.
> (Betws-y-Coed, 83m, all life, retired forestry worker, owner-occupier)

Conclusion

In the introduction to this chapter it was suggested that within much recent research in human geography and the social sciences it is possible to identify a shift in focus from issues of 'inequality' to those of 'identity'. Furthermore, the limited amount of research which has addressed notions of inequality and poverty has predominantly been conducted within urban arenas. In many ways, the chapter has reinforced the impression of our respondent in Devil's Bridge – included in the opening quotation – that issues of poverty and deprivation remain hidden in rural areas. Various factors can be seen as acting to produce this situation of invisibility – a general urban research bias within the social sciences; dominant discourses of rurality which tend to present idyll-ized notions of rural life; and physical settlement patterns associated with many rural areas which tend to scatter those households experiencing poverty 'out of sight, out of mind'.

This chapter, however, has demonstrated a widespread occurrence of poverty and marginalization within areas of the English and Welsh countryside. In normative terms, statistical indicators of poverty drawn from the Rural Lifestyles research (and utilized within previous urban poverty studies) have pointed to a continued significance of poverty and deprivation in 1990s rural Britain. Indeed, in 13 of our 16 rural study areas in excess of one-fifth of all households were living in or on the margins of poverty (according to the income support entitlement indicator). The extent of such poverty, both in numerical and geographical terms, would appear to warrant increased attention from academic, political and media commentators, in order that the urban-dominated perspective of 'problems' in Britain may be partly redressed.

While the Lifestyles research has indicated a widespread occurrence of poverty in rural areas, it has also illustrated that the nature of this 'rural' poverty would appear, in many ways, to contradict dominant (urban-based) discourses of poverty in 1990s Britain. Relatively little evidence has been uncovered which would support any notion of an 'underclass' living within rural areas. Rather, the Lifestyles studies have suggested a poverty which is characterized more by the elderly than young people, which includes property-owners as well as households living in rented accommodation, and contains those in work alongside the economically inactive. In these respects the Lifestyles study has reiterated some recent findings from studies of rural poverty in the USA, by pointing to clear differences between urban- and rural-based poverty.

Alongside these aggregate indicators of poverty though, attention has also been given within this chapter to an exploration of individualistic understandings of poverty and deprivation within rural areas. To a large extent, the Rural Lifestyles research would appear to confirm earlier urban studies concerned with perceptions of poverty and deprivation by highlighting a general reluctance of the 'rural poor' to admit to the existence of poverty within their households and immediate environments. However, the chapter has also demonstrated a more general reluctance to recognize poverty and deprivation among residents in these 16 rural areas. Indeed, even when poverty and deprivation were acknowledged by rural residents, these issues were often conceptualized in different and conflicting ways. For some, poverty was seen as one outcome of wider forces of economic restructuring and central government policies which placed an ever increasing emphasis on the free market within rural areas. Others, however, located the responsibility of poverty clearly on the shoulders of low-incomed individuals, presenting a privatized view of welfare which would appear to concur with key elements of Conservative ideologies in the post-1979 period. In one respect then, such notions of individual politics would appear to contradict ideas of 'community' in rural areas; in another respect though, they would seem to reinforce the spirit of voluntarism and self-help, perceived by many as an essential part of country life.

Within certain commentaries provided by our respondents it has also been possible to identify a series of broader notions of poverty and deprivation concerned with feelings of social exclusion and cultural marginalization from perceived norms of rural life. Such feelings of being 'outside' the socio-cultural mainstream were characteristic of some newly arrived rural residents coming to terms with 'new' ways of living, long-established residents who felt dislocated from a rapidly changing village life and landscape, and also those residents who simply wished to 'live their lives differently'.

It is clear then that a range of factors have acted (and continue to act) to hide issues of rural poverty within dominant discourses of both rurality and poverty in Britain. Such invisibility necessitates a requirement on the part of the academic researcher to utilize a broad range of approaches to highlight issues of poverty and deprivation in the British countryside; some involving normative-based definitions, others which attempt to reveal the hidden voices of those persons experiencing poverty. There remains a need within such research to highlight issues of power - both in the academy and society - which act to marginalize parts of the rural population and rural poverty as a research area, alongside the experiences of being 'poor' or feeling 'marginalized' within areas of the British countryside.

Notes

1. A comment made by a respondent interviewed in the Devil's Bridge study area, rural Wales.
2. See, for example, Donnison (1982). Townsend (1979) has suggested that in affluent societies such as Britain, poverty needs to be considered in the context of relative deprivation:

   > Poverty can be defined objectively and applied consistently only in terms of the concept of relative deprivation.... The term is understood objectively rather than subjectively. Individuals, families and groups in the population can be said to be in poverty when they lack the resources to obtain the types of diet, participate in the activities and have the living conditions and amenities which are customary, or at least widely encouraged or approved, in the societies which they belong. Their resources are so seriously below those commanded by the average individual or family that they are in effect, excluded from ordinary living patterns, customs and activities. (1979, p. 31)

3. McCormick and Philo (1995) suggest that the rediscovery of poverty in urban Britain in the 1990s should be viewed more accurately as a revival of concern about problems rather than an increase in the problems themselves: 'It is not so much poverty that disappears and reappears as its acceptability or relevance to the agendas set by the most influential shapers of public opinion.' (p. 2)
4. Such a criticism was raised by Bradley *et al.* (1986).
5. English county names used within the chapter refer to the study areas indicated in Figure 5.1 and not the entire county.
6. I am grateful to my colleagues on the *Lifestyles in Rural Wales* project - Paul Cloke and Mark Goodwin - for allowing me to use selected findings from that research within this chapter.

7. A limited amount of background information is included alongside comments provided by respondents, although no causal relationships are being suggested. The format of this information is as follows: study area; age/gender; length of residence; current economic position; household tenure.

References

Alcock, P. (1993) *Understanding Poverty*. London: Macmillan.

Bracey, H. (1952) *Social Provision in Rural Wiltshire*. London: Edward Arnold.

Bracey H. (1959) *English Rural Life*. London: Routledge & Kegan Paul.

Bradley, T. (1984) Segmentation in local labour markets. In T. Bradley and P. Lowe (eds) *Locality and Rurality*, Norwich: Geobooks, 65-90.

Bradley, T., Lowe, P. and Wright, S. (1986) Introduction: rural deprivation and welfare. In P. Lowe, T. Bradley and S. Wright (eds) *Deprivation and Welfare in Rural Areas*, Norwich: Geobooks, 1-39.

Brown, D. and Warner, M. (1991) Persistent low-income nonmetropolitan areas in the United States: some conceptual challenges for development policy. *Policy Studies Journal*, 19 (2), 22-41.

Cloke, P. (1995) Rural poverty and the welfare state: a discursive transformation in Britain and the USA. *Environment and Planning A*, 27, 1001-16.

Cloke, P., Goodwin, M. and Milbourne, P. (1994a) *Lifestyles in Rural Wales*, Cardiff: Welsh Office.

Cloke, P. and Milbourne, P. (1992) Deprivation and lifestyles in rural Wales: rurality and the cultural dimension. *Journal of Rural Studies*, 8, 359-71.

Cloke, P., Milbourne, P. and Thomas, C. (1994b) *Lifestyles in Rural England*. London: Rural Development Commission.

Coates, K. and Silburn, R. (1970) *Poverty: The Forgotten Englishmen*. Harmondsworth: Penguin.

Department of Social Security (1995) *Households Below Average Income: A Statistical Analysis 1979-1992/93*. London: HMSO.

Donnison (1982) *The Politics of Poverty*. London: Martin Robertson.

Dudenhefer, P. (1994) Poverty in the rural United States. *Rural Sociologist*. 14 (1), 4-25.

Harrington, M. (1981) *The Other America: Poverty in the United States*. New York: Penguin Books.

Jury, L. (1994) Charities enraged as Duke says poverty is relative. *Guardian*, 10 June, 1.

Leyshon, A. (1995) Missing words: whatever happened to the geography of poverty? *Environment and Planning A*, 27, 1021-8.

Mack, J. and Lansley, S. (1985) *Poor Britain*. London: George Allen and Unwin.

McCormick, J. and Philo, C. (1995) Where is poverty? The hidden geography of poverty in the United Kingdom. In C. Philo (ed.) *Off the Map: The Social Geography of Poverty in the UK*. London: CPAG.

McLaughlin, B. (1985) *Deprivation in Rural Areas*. Research Report to the Department of the Environment.

McLaughlin, B. (1986) The rhetoric and reality of rural deprivation. *Journal of Rural Studies* 2, 291-307.

Meikle, J. (1994) Britain joins Third World as Oxfam moves to help nation's poor. *Guardian*, 2 September, 1.

Mingione, E. (1993) The new urban poverty and the underclass: introduction. *International Journal of Urban and Regional Research*, 17 (3), 324–6.
Molnar, J. and Traxler, G. (1991) People left behind: transitions of the rural poor. *Southern Journal of Agricultural Economics*, 23 (1), 75–87.
Moore, J. (1989) The end of the line for poverty, speech to Greater London Area CPC, 11 May. Quoted in P. Alcock, *Understanding Poverty*, London: Macmillan.
Murdoch, J. and Pratt, A. (1993) Rural studies: modernism, post-modernism and the 'post-rural'. *Journal of Rural Studies*, 9 (4), 411–27.
Murdoch, J. and Pratt, A. (1994) Rural studies of power and the power of rural studies: a reply to Philo, *Journal of Rural Studies*, 10 (1), 411–27.
New Earnings Survey (1980) London: Department of Employment.
New Earnings Survey (1994) London: Department of Employment.
Philo, C. (1992) Neglected rural geographies. *Journal of Rural Studies*, 8 (2), 193–207.
Philo, C. (1993) Post-modern rural geography? a reply to Murdoch and Pratt. *Journal of Rural Studies*, 9 (4), 429–36.
Robbins, D. (1993) Towards a Europe of solidarity: combating social exclusion. *Social Europe*, Supplement 4/93, Commission of the EC (DGV).
Runciman, W.G. (1966) *Relative Deprivation and Social Justice: A Study of Attitudes to Social Inequality in Twentieth-Century England*. London: Penguin.
Rural Sociological Society (1993) *Persistent Poverty in Rural America*. Rural Sociological Society Task Force on Persistent Rural Poverty, Boulder, Colorado: Westview Press.
Scott, D., Shenton, N. and Healey, B. (1991) *Hidden Deprivation in the Countryside*. Glossop: Peak Park Trust.
Scott, J. (1994) *Poverty and Wealth: Citizenship, Deprivation and Privilege*. London: Longman.
Shaw, J. M. (ed.) (1979) *Rural Deprivation and Planning*. Norwich: Geobooks.
Tickamyer, A. and Duncan, C. (1990) Poverty and opportunity structure in rural America. *Annual Review of Sociology*, 16, 67–86.
Townsend, P. (1979) *Poverty in the United Kingdom*. Harmondsworth: Penguin.
Walker, A. (ed.) (1978) *Rural Poverty*. London: Child Poverty Action Group.
Whatmore, S. (1993) On doing rural research (or breaking the boundaries). *Environment and Planning*, 25 (4), 605–7.

6

New Age Travellers in the Countryside: Incomers with Attitude

JIM DAVIS

There are few sights more likely to provoke outrage and concern in a rural community than the arrival of a group of New Age travellers. This outrage is likely to be directed at the perceived invasion of people who descend like locusts on a community to suck it dry before moving on to another location, leaving behind a state of chaos. The possibility of travellers moving into an area must now rank as one of the greatest fears expressed by farmers, parish councils and ordinary residents up and down the country. The evidence of these fears is to be found at the entrances to drove lanes, set aside fields, common land and bridle paths. The use of trenches, large boulders, padlocked gates and iron posts are common methods used to prevent access to travellers on to all kinds of spaces in the countryside. It is not unusual to see farm machinery and even straw bales blocking the entrance to fields and farmyards. The fear that at any moment a horde of travellers will push on to private land is significant. This fear is given credence by intense media reporting and the considerable policy changes and new legislation introduced by the Conservative Government. John Major made his views known at the Conservative Party conference in 1992:

> You will have seen pictures on the television or in the newspapers. If you live in the West Country you may well have seen it on your own doorstep. Farmers powerless, crops ruined and livestock killed by people who say they commune with nature, but who have no respect for it when it belongs to others. New Age travellers – not in this age. Not in any age.[1]

It is a statement that preceded the introduction of the Criminal Justice and Public Order Act, legislation aimed at tackling unauthorized trespass and giving greater powers to the police and local authorities to evict and deal with travellers wherever they might be. The Act aims to give power to those farmers and landowners with whom John Major was so concerned, powers to combat the peril of the New Age traveller. It is legislation that has been given justification and backing by the fears and concerns highlighted in the media. For example, 'KEEP THIS SCUM OUT and it is time to hound 'em Chief Constable', was the less than conciliatory headline adopted by the *Birmingham Evening Mail* in 1993.[2] The article proposed that travellers should be hounded out of the Midlands and it set up the 'Help chase this scum out of the Midlands' hotline. Other newspapers simply highlight a fear of travellers: *The Cornishman* in July 1993: 'Farmers fear hippy invasion';[3] the *Gloucestershire Citizen* in February 1995: 'Residents' fears as travellers move in';[4] the *Cheddar Valley Gazette* in November 1994: 'New caravan arrivals alarm residents'.[5] As well as regional and local newspapers raising the issues there have been accounts of travellers and their lifestyle in the national newspapers. In May 1993 the *Mail on Sunday* ran an article entitled: 'Why do we put up with the welfare state cheats?'.[6] The photograph accompanying the piece was of a group of New Age travellers collecting DSS giros. The following month the *Daily Mail* produced an article called 'Nightmare of the New Age'[7] – an account by a freelance journalist who claimed to have spent time on a site on the edge of Bath and was witness to what he called a nightmare. He described filth and squalor, drug taking and scrounging, aggression and hostility and, most of all, anti-social attitudes from the travellers. It is a clear message – New Age travellers are to be feared, avoided and repelled at all costs.

Until the end of 1994, the Save the Children Fund operated a Traveller Information Unit, and part of its remit was to collate media reporting on Gypsy and traveller issues. Each month details were produced about articles relating to Gypsies and travellers in both the regional and national press; the list of articles was always substantial. The headlines were varied but consistently the reports were of local hostility to travellers and of action by police and local authorities to either get rid of travellers or prevent them from gaining access to a site. The reports themselves reflected the general confusion about categorizing travellers. Headlines varied in the terminology but commonly the terms traveller and Gypsy were used to show a difference between groups of travellers and often to emphasize that it was New Age travellers that were covered in the report. Generally though, the term traveller is used to describe a non-Gypsy and it is this group that seems to create the greatest concern and hostility.

Politicians have contributed to the debate about travellers by vociferously calling for tougher measures to clamp down on them. According to the *Guardian*, Tony Marland, MP for Gloucester West, called for legislation to restrain New Age travellers who he says were referred to locally as 'New Age vermin'.[8] Tony Marland's comments have been echoed by John Marshall, MP for Hendon South, who has made reference in a parliamentary question to 'itinerants, didicoys and ne'er-do-wells',[9] while Lord Henderson of Brompton referred to the 'plague of so-called New Age Travellers who do not seem capable of doing anything'.[10] Perhaps many of the comments and concerns expressed by some MPs are most typified by the statement made by Sir Anthony Grant, MP for Cambridgeshire South West, who in a debate on a second reading of the Criminal Justice and Public Order Bill on 11 January 1994 commented: 'People in rural communities are fed up to the back teeth with the nuisance and annoyance caused by so-called travellers ... the provision to tighten the law on those matters is long overdue and welcome.'[11]

On this occasion the term 'so-called travellers' serves to emphasize the sense that these travellers are not perceived as genuine in their travelling and are viewed as a greater threat to rural communities than more established travelling groups.

In November 1994 the Criminal Justice and Public Order Act (1994) was given royal assent. The Act, which is extensive and covers many issues, gave new powers to the police and local authorities to evict unauthorized camps of travellers. Powers were given to the police to seize and destroy vehicles and local authorities were released from their duty to provide caravan sites for Gypsies, a duty that had existed since 1968. As stated in the Government's consultation document of 1992, the Act represents a significant shift in policy.[12] The emphasis on accommodation contained within the 1968 Caravan Sites Act has been replaced with an emphasis on eviction. The Criminal Justice Act does not refer to travellers. Rather it talks about trespassers and unauthorized campers. In doing so it focuses only on the act of trespass; it does not regard people's lifestyles but only takes account of the occasion when they trespass. The sanctions against unauthorized campers contained within the Act include evictions, fines, imprisonment and the seizure and destruction of vehicles including caravans. According to the Act the only issue to be considered is that of people camping on land which is not their own or that they do not have permission to be on.

Legislation now supports the view that travellers should be repelled from the countryside and that their presence should be resisted. The law does not now recognize people's lifestyle. Where they have come from and where they might go to is considered irrelevant; moving them on is all important. What is remarkable is that the views as expressed in the media, picked up by politicians and contained within legislation have very little basis on any analysis of who travellers are, where they come from, why they travel and what they need. In fact what has been missing almost entirely within these debates is the voice of the traveller.

A New Development?

One of the reasons given in the 1992 Government consultation document for introducing new legislation was that the rise of new forms of travellers had created the necessity for greater control, that the policy of accommodation had not succeeded and new trends in travelling had meant a different approach was needed. One concern often presented is that New Age travellers are a new, unexpected phenomenon; people who wander around the countryside, people who are different and by nature threatening. Yet nomadism has been a feature of our society for centuries, in particular the arrival of itinerant workers, Gypsies and travellers into rural communities has been a feature of rural life for generations. Aside from the movements of Gypsies, residents from major cities would make seasonal trips to the countryside to take part in harvests such as hop picking in Kent. But the need for mass labour to perform agricultural tasks has declined as farming techniques have changed. Gypsies of various categories who have traditionally moved within defined routes to do work in the countryside have found that the work has declined. In addition, traditional stopping places are no longer available because they have been blocked or developed for other uses.

The decline in the availability of seasonal and casual agricultural work combined with the loss of access to common land and greater controls on building development in the countryside is significant. Rather than this latest group of travellers representing a distinctly new phenomenon that because of its nature is to be feared, the situation is one of changing attitudes in rural life and patterns that are now seen as incompatible with a travelling lifestyle. Yet travelling is not a new phenomenon, and nor is resistance to it.

Gypsies have rarely been popular and legislation to control them followed swiftly on from their arrival in England. One of the first laws was introduced by Henry VIII in 1530 with the 'Egyptians' Act', so called because of the belief that Gypsies originated from Egypt. The Act included expulsion, imprisonment and a ban on immigration in its sanctions (Hawes and Perez, 1995). Subsequent laws have been equally determined to control and contain the presence and activities of Gypsies. There were also measures taken under the reign of Queen Elizabeth I to distinguish between real and counterfeit Gypsies as a way of determining who was deserving and who was not - a situation that resonates with current attempts to distinguish between Gypsies and New Age travellers. But since the arrival of the 'Egyptians' in the sixteenth century the pattern has always been of existing travellers being joined by emerging groups. In previous, harsher times, the need for work and shelter has forced people on to the road. The fake Egyptians of Elizabeth I's time were regarded as vagabonds, economic waifs and strays. The arrival of Irish Gypsies on to the mainland in the 1950s and 1960s in search of greater opportunities may have given concern at the time, but now Irish travellers are generally regarded as traditional whereas New Age travellers are regarded as being altogether different.

The common argument against New Age travellers is that they are dropouts from society who have no regard for authority yet are keen to exploit the welfare state and take its benefits. The perception is that New Age travellers are playing a game, that their need to party is greater than their need to have somewhere to live. In particular, there is a belief that New Age travellers are leaving houses and urban areas and are setting up home in the countryside. This view has had some support from what should be informed sources. During the passage of the Criminal Justice and Public Order Act through the House of Lords an amendment was put forward that the repeal of the Caravan Sites Act (1968) should be postponed for five years. In supporting this amendment Lord Avebury made a distinction between Gypsies and New Age travellers, reinforcing the idea that New Age travellers are urban dropouts:

> that site provision should go to 'genuine Gypsies' and not ... to New Age travellers or to persons like a correspondent of mine who took up the nomadic way of life voluntarily in his early twenties by buying a van and taking to the road ... . It is totally unreasonable for them to expect the taxpayer or local authorities to support them in what they arbitrarily decide to do. They must fend for themselves.[13]

Lord Avebury never stated whether these views were based solely on his knowledge of that one correspondent.

It seems that traditional Gypsies in the light of New Age travellers have been granted a grudging acceptance. During the passage of the Criminal Justice Act efforts were consistently made to ensure that any amendments made to lessen the effects of the Act were directed at Gypsies. Hence Lord Stanley of Alderley commented on 11 July 1994 that:

> (the amendment) delays for five years the repeal of the Caravan Sites Act 1968. As your Lordships will know, the main effect of the 1968 Act is to lay a duty on the local authority to provide sites for genuine Gypsies - genuine Gypsies being those people as defined by a recent Court of Appeal decision. I must make it clear that they are not hippies, New Age travellers or any of the like.[14]

The Court of Appeal decision referred to was the judgment made on 27 May 1994 by Lord Justice Neill responding to a case found in favour of South Hams District Council.[15] The decision sought to identify Gypsies who are not only nomadic in habit, but are nomadic for economic purposes. It is a decision that will continue to be debated and provoke legal debate for some time. Its effect is to add to the sense that there are people who travel because they have to, or who are born to it and people who travel purely out of whim.

In the context of the debate held in both Houses of Parliament as the Criminal Justice Bill went through its various stages of becoming legislation, the idea that there are credible and deserving travellers against those who are not was significant. It meant that even those who opposed the Act and sought to introduce amendments to limit its impact were not prepared to align themselves with New Age travellers and all that they were perceived to be.

The Children's Society Interest

The Children's Society is a national child care charity working in England and Wales and has not previously had a specific focus of work on Gypsies and travellers. But in 1992, prior to the publication of the government consultation document on the reform of the Caravan Sites Act (1968), one project in the West Country began to work on the issue. The Bath and Wells Neighbourhood Development Team was primarily a community development team with a focus on initiating and supporting community led initiatives for children and families within Somerset and South Avon.

The interest in travellers stems from work carried out in 1991 by the team in Bath with a group of churches concerned about the Bath 'crusties'. The term 'crusties' is somewhat derogatory and was used by the media to describe young homeless people who looked unkempt, invariably had a scruffy dog in tow and were inclined to sit in the city centre drinking cider or strong lager. There were also concerns expressed about what was described as aggressive begging; Bath, which owes much of its wealth to tourism, did not feel easy with these young people. The work the team undertook with churches in Bath was to investigate further the backgrounds, needs and aspirations of the 'crusties' (Davis, 1991). Ultimately the work led to further support for a night shelter scheme, but it raised other issues. Among the alcoholics who had been on the road for years and the bored young people looking for another way of rebelling, there were young people who were homeless and had given up on the idea of gaining conventional housing. Instead, these young people had the declared intention of buying a cheap vehicle and taking to the road as a traveller. Although they seemed to take on the appearance of travellers there seemed to be little connection between these homeless young people and anyone they knew who was a full-time traveller. The concept was simple enough; they did not have enough money to rent a flat, so the easier option was to buy a transit van for £50, put a wood burner in the back and create a 'home'. It was a home that could take them out of the restrictions of the town and into the countryside.

The appearance given was that this was simply a pragmatic solution to a pressing problem. There was no evidence that this was a whimsical decision made by university dropouts looking for a party life. Certainly there was a sense of rebellion and an awareness of how deviant this action would be seen, but the desire to become a traveller was presented as a desire to get out of sleeping rough and retain the support of friends. What was obvious to the Children's Society team even at that stage was that whereas these young people elicited a degree of sympathy from the public when sleeping rough, that sympathy evaporated when they started sleeping in vehicles and adopted a travelling lifestyle. Indeed, as a society we feel able to respond to the needs of young people when we see them as victims, but as a threat when they start to take control of their own lives.

The advantage of approaching a new issue from a community development perspective is that any new work is developed on the basis that nothing is known until it is found out, and there can be no solutions without interaction with the people who are affected by the issue. As a community development group the Bath and Wells team was well placed to conduct an investigation to see if the connection between youth homelessness and travelling was more widespread than had already been seen. This necessitated contacting travellers living in Bath and the surrounding area.

The Children's Society approved a six-month investigation into travellers in Somerset and Avon with the intention of producing an internal report on the relationship between young homeless people and travelling. In the end the work broadened and the result was a report called *Out of Site, Out of Mind* that was published by The Children's Society in March 1994 (Davis *et al.*, 1994). The investigation focused entirely on New Age travellers because of the perceived connection between homelessness and travelling, and, therefore, the key issue was why and how people became travellers, and how their situations changed as a result of their new lifestyles. The most significant difference between New Age travellers and any other group of travellers is that anyone can become a New Age traveller, whereas people have to be born into Romany or Irish travelling lifestyles. But this distinction becomes less clear when you take account of those travellers who were born in houses to parents or grandparents who previously travelled as Gypsies. One New Age traveller, Jane, represents an example of this complexity:

> How could I travel when my brother and sisters have got nice houses and jobs and 2.2 children and 2.2 dogs with a nice Fiesta? What am I doing this for when I could be in a house? But it's simple. After all, my mum did it. She was a Romany. She lived in a horse-drawn caravan and she brought up ten of us before I came along. On the tenth one they decided to go into a house so they sold the horse and the wagon, bought a 2-bedroomed house, and then I came along. So I never knew the road, I only knew the stories from my mum. (Lowe and Shaw, 1993, p. 196)

Jane's situation is not unusual. In the initial investigation the team came across numerous travellers who by appearance, lifestyle and peer contact were New Age travellers, yet whose parents or grandparents had been Irish or Romany travellers.

Although the term 'New Age traveller' is commonly used it actually has very little meaning as a descriptive term for people who happen to travel. Its use is largely a means of differentiating between traditional Gypsies and people who were originally born in houses but latterly take to the road. Even then it is hard to define those children born on the road to New Age travellers or those people born as Gypsies who live in houses and do not travel. The need to produce a label for people can become unproductive and a distraction from other issues. This was emphasized during the investigation when one staff member asked a man on site whether he considered himself to be a New Age traveller. His reply was 'what do you consider yourself to be – a loony lefty do-gooder?' After this incident, any attempts to define people were abandoned. What was found was that this New Age travelling culture is composed of people from various backgrounds and with a multitude of motivations that led them into travelling.

During 1992–93 interviews were carried out with 98 travellers on 20 unauthorized sites in Somerset and South Avon. Material gained from these interviews formed the basis of the *Out of Site, Out of Mind* report with the intention of highlighting the impact of the (then) proposed Criminal Justice and Public Order Act. Our concern was that if the common belief that travellers were acting on whim and belligerence were unfounded then the Act would result in increased hardship for such people. If travellers did not have a stable home to return to or an alternative to living in a vehicle, evictions would resolve nothing. Rather they would increase the risk of conflict and instability for children.

What was found, however, was that although one-third of the travellers interviewed said they chose to travel because they wanted to, only two had an alternative to travelling. The majority had entered into the travelling lifestyle because of 'push' factors - circumstances such as homelessness, relationship breakdown, unemployment, domestic violence or some other trauma. Such a push factor was cited by Sarah: 'I was sleeping on a friend's floor for a year waiting for a house. I was pregnant at the time. In the end I got a truck and got out' (Davis *et al.*, 1994, p. 5).

But despite such difficult experiences prior to travelling, the general feeling among those interviewed was that travelling offered a positive experience, regardless of the motivation for joining it. Initially it proved difficult for travellers to talk about why they started to travel. What was considered to be positive was the sense of community and the support given to each other on site, as well as the independence and control experienced in owning a home without the burden of a mortgage. But perhaps the key attribute of travelling was given as the ability to move on and into the countryside.

The majority of sites in the study were in rural areas or on the periphery of towns. One or two sites were quite isolated and the status of sites varied. All sites were unauthorized in that they either did not have the landowner's permission or planning permission, and most were on council owned land, common land or on land with disputed ownership. Not a single site was on productive farmland or in 'someone's back garden'. The commonly held view among travellers was that it was not only impolite but foolhardy to occupy land that was being used or had crops or livestock on it - even the children were aware of this: 'We don't like parking on farmland' (Kyle, aged 5, quoted in Davis *et al.*, 1994, p. 8). Of course even though some sites were on grass verges that did not have any productive use, farmers were still inconvenienced on occasion by extra vehicles in the road or travellers making access to fields more difficult.

At the time of interviewing, the free festival circuit was in decline with fewer events taking place and fewer travellers with children were prepared to risk travelling to such events. Although some travellers felt that free festivals, such as the event at Castlemorton in 1992, represented a distraction from travelling and contributed to people's fear of travellers, others considered that free festivals were an integral part of the travelling lifestyle. This was particularly true for people who had drifted into travelling through attendance at free festivals and for whom the festival scene gave a purpose to travelling. Indeed, Earle *et al.* (1994) have suggested that the growth of the New Age traveller movement has been closely linked to the free festival circuit:

> By 1976, the summer of the long drought, many people were realizing that vehicles provided the necessary means of travelling nationwide to the very full programme of free festivals. Combined with socio-economic factors of the time, and the belief that life on the road was better, cheaper and healthier, some individuals became full-time travellers. (Earle *et al.*, 1994, p. 10)

Undoubtedly the free festivals which attracted thousands of house-dwelling party goers and were invariably held in rural areas caused a great deal of distress and disturbance to local people. When such numbers gathered at unlicensed, uncontrolled events, crimes would occur and the site would not be left in its original state. Festivals were, for some travellers, a legitimate activity in a free society, yet one traveller's liberty can be seen as another person's nightmare. Even among travellers no consensus exists about whether festivals and the right to party are intrinsically good phenomena. At Castlemorton in 1992, for example, one traveller sub-group, the Spiral Tribe, played rave music constantly for 24 hours a day and refused to accede to other travellers' requests to turn the sound off or down. As one traveller commented: 'anarchy doesn't work unless you think about it' (Earle *et al.*, 1994, p. 49).

Travellers interviewed within our research had a clear notion of what represented a good site location. Travellers have different expectations and needs for sites depending on the season – fields that seem ideal in the summer can become mudbaths in the winter. The search for a site appeared less related to whether it would make a good festival site or had the capacity to take a large number of vehicles and more to do with the likelihood of eviction. For this reason land owned by a local authority was favoured as it was felt that other local authority responsibilities regarding site provision could be brought into effect. On at least two sites within the research, travellers had applied for a judicial review on the grounds that the local authority was attempting to evict them from their own land while they were unable to provide alternative sites.

This argument used by travellers that local authorities have a duty towards them to provide sites was often disputed by these local authorities on the ground that New Age travellers were not true Gypsies and so were not covered within the Caravan Sites Act (1968). However, such debates have become irrelevant since the repeal of the Caravan Sites Act under the Criminal Justice Act. Latterly travellers have sought to apply for judicial review on the basis that local authorities are bound to take account of their other duties under the Children Act (1989) when pursuing evictions. Thus, although not universally successful in delaying or preventing eviction, travellers tend to favour camping on local authority land because there is at least the potential for this leverage.

The fact that so few sites within our study occupied private land is not something that has been widely stated in newspaper reports. The fear persists that travellers are likely to come and park in your back garden. Of course the argument presented by private landowners of large estates is that all their land is private; whether the land is being used for anything or not is irrelevant. This issue represents the most striking disagreement between travellers and landowners: for travellers, *land-use* is the key factor which determines whether a site is suitable for occupation; for land owners, *ownership* is the dominant issue. Within the research project, one site was located on a derelict railway siding owned by British Rail. The siding had been derelict for 20 years or more due to the closure of rural railway lines and the land had no real agricultural potential. It was not used by British Rail for any purpose and to the travellers it represented an unused location that could be put to good use. From the viewpoint of British Rail, occupation of the land was unwelcome and ultimately an eviction took place and the site returned to its derelict state. The only extra work carried out on the site following eviction was the addition of a stronger gate with a better padlock.

Since the publication of *Out of Site, Out of Mind*, the research team has conducted a further study which has examined the impact of the Criminal Justice and Public Order Act (1994) on the lifestyles of travellers. This second project focused on the disruption caused by evictions to children's access to health care, schools and other essential services, as well as examining the need for stable sites and the motivations behind travelling. The results, which are as yet unpublished, confirm the findings of the earlier research. For example, over half of travellers interviewed had been homeless prior to travelling, with very few having any alternative accommodation other than travelling in a vehicle. As with the previous study, unauthorized sites were visited, although the geographical scope of the research was extended to include the counties of Cornwall, Devon, Dorset, Wiltshire and Gloucestershire as well as Somerset and Avon. Interviews were conducted between October 1994 and May 1995, and included a total of 30 sites of various sizes and in varying degrees of stability. With the exception of two cases in Bristol, all of the sites were located in rural areas.

Of the 30 sites visited, four were located on privately owned land, 17 sites were on land controlled by local authorities and the remainder consisted of land which was of unknown ownership, National Trust land or owned by travellers. Those sites that had been in existence for more than a year tended to be those owned by travellers or those on which travellers were applying for planning permission with the owner's consent. The more temporary sites were usually created after an eviction and were characterized by laybys, drove lanes or green verges. The size of sites ranged from three to 50 vehicles, with an average of around 15 vehicles per site, and appeared to depend more on the number of evictions being carried out in the area than on the types of travellers on the site or a desire to be together. For example, when travellers on a site of more than 40 vehicles were recently evicted in Wiltshire virtually all of the travellers moved on to an existing site in Somerset, simply because they were not aware of any alternative sites.

An ironic outcome of evictions monitored after the Criminal Justice Bill became law in November 1994 was that evictions on smaller sites tended to result in travellers moving to a smaller number of larger sites. Understandably anxiety among local residents tends to intensify as the size of a site increases on a daily basis. What is not seen however is the desperation felt by travellers who having been evicted from one site reluctantly move to a larger site in search of greater security from a further swift eviction.

The pattern that emerges from both research projects is that of a disparate community of travellers moving around predominantly rural areas mainly as a result of eviction. The impact of the Criminal Justice and Public Order Act 1994 would appear to have simply increased the scale and frequency of movement, with the same people moving around a decreasing number of sites. As more sites are blocked or trenched off the search for new sites becomes more desperate with the increased likelihood of more private land being occupied by travellers.

Positive Attempts to Resolve the Dilemma

Within this generally bleak picture of increasing evictions there have been some glimmers of hope and isolated examples of travellers being accommodated within rural communities. One example uncovered within the Children's Society research was a site in Gloucestershire where a group of travellers collectively purchased an area of land near the village of Tidenham, believing it already had planning permission. In reality they were mistaken and had to apply for retrospective planning permission, which was refused. Over the following months an appeal was lodged and the traveller families settled into the area. Children from the site went to local schools, travellers shopped in the local stores and a certain level of contact was made with local residents. By the time the planning appeal was heard, and lost, a degree of local support had been raised to the extent that a petition of 2000 signatures was handed in to the district council calling for the travellers to be allowed to stay.[16] Thus, with some effort on the part of travellers and local villagers the initial hostility between the two groups became weakened and the traveller site was viewed by some residents as part of the local landscape. However, other local residents opposed the site - an opinion shared by the planning inspector - and the travellers were forced to consider leaving the site or face the consequences of an enforcement action.

The capacity for New Age travellers to purchase their own land is limited. More often they have to rely on benevolent land owners. Travellers arriving at the disused Slough Green caravan site in Somerset quickly negotiated with the land owner mutually agreeable conditions for staying, which as well as paying rent included submitting a planning application. As with the Tidenham travellers the application was refused by the local planning authority, despite the fact that the site had previously been a caravan site complete with hardstanding for caravans, a toilet block and tarmac road. The most frequent planning argument against traveller sites in rural areas is that they constitute a development that contravenes Green Belt controls or other statutory restrictions such as Areas of Outstanding Natural Beauty or Sites of Special Scientific Interest. The Slough Green site did not contravene any of those statutory restrictions but was found to be contrary to the council's Special Landscape Area status. Planning law is complex and travellers face an uphill struggle to avoid all of the statutory restrictions, local policies and resistance from residents. However, at the Slough Green site the lengthy process of applying for planning permission and then appealing against the refusal meant that the site was stable for nearly two years. In that time children were able to attend the local school and playgroup, parents became volunteers in the playgroup, some travellers took local jobs and others commenced further education courses in Taunton. In this sense, travellers can be seen as attempting to integrate within the local area.

Although travellers on these sites have failed or struggled to gain permission, their relative longevity of tenure has demonstrated the potential for travellers to integrate within rural life and highlighted that feelings of invasion can diminish through localized interactions. However, such harmonious lifestyles rarely arise. The villagers of Hinton near Bath, for example, paid one group of travellers £1000 to leave their area rather than make any attempt to tolerate or perhaps welcome this new group of rural residents.[17] Travellers argue that if permission is granted for them to stay on a rural site and they are given reasonable notice, they will leave a site much as it was found. Travellers at Slough Green argued at planning meetings that if they were to leave the site having removed their belongings then the site would remain unaltered by their presence, and so they could not be viewed as a development in the same way as a house or barn. However, one effect of speedy evictions is that although a site is cleared of travellers it can remain full of other discarded belongings and rubbish.

Local authorities can risk considerable criticism from local residents if they grant planning permission for sites or invite travellers on to land they own. For example, before Christmas 1994, Somerset County Council took a political risk when it allowed a group of travellers to stay on one of its chipping stores off the A303 for 28 days. For the families on site it was a respite from the flurry of evictions they had been experiencing and it gave the children a stable site over Christmas. At the end of the agreed period the travellers moved off, back into the cycle of finding a new site, being evicted, moving on to an existing site, being evicted and so on. It is this frequent movement of travellers which serves to maintain their distance from the rural community through which they pass and maintains patterns of resistance among local residents. Such negative images of travellers become more difficult to maintain when more meaningful contact between travellers and villagers is established. Indeed, our research has highlighted that children are often the medium for this contact between local residents and travellers which can break down fears. Travelling children attending local schools and playgroups are often seen by other children and parents for what they are - children.

In the summer of 1994 Channel 4 produced a series of programmes called 'Child's Eye', a child-led collection of programmes giving children a chance to express their views about an issue that concerned them. The Bath and Wells Neighbourhood Development Team managed to link up the programme makers with Vicky, an 11-year-old girl living on the Slough Green traveller site in Somerset. Vicky was given a camcorder to produce a brief film about her life as a traveller and how she was affected by the recent refusal of planning permission for the site.[18] With all the innocent directness of a child, Vicky set about interviewing the Chair of the planning committee, the planning officer and local villagers who had opposed the application. Her questions included: 'Why don't you like travellers?'; 'why was planning permission refused?'; 'what will happen to my schooling if we are evicted?'. While most of the answers were rather weak and ineffective against the directness of a child, the most telling interview was with children from the village school where Vicky was a pupil. Vicky wanted to know what the children thought of traveller children prior to meeting her. The replies echoed the concerns and views of parents and adults in many communities: 'We thought you would be dirty, scruffy, not nice and not fit in!' However, towards the end of these interviews the children's views changed, with one commenting: 'but you're not like that'.

The Future?

Travellers should not be viewed as a 'marauding horde' to be feared, nor as romanticized figures of 'peace and love'. Instead, they need to be seen as 'normal' people living in different circumstances than the majority of the population. Vicky has every right to ask everyone she encounters: 'Why don't you like travellers?'; 'why don't you like me?'. It has become acceptable to criticize travellers, use derogatory terms and highlight specific examples of bad behaviour of a few to stereotype the many. It cannot be acceptable to label children as vermin or to present them as a malevolent force to be resisted and repelled from rural communities. But their different circumstances need to be accepted when sites are considered.

The travellers at Slough Green eventually appealed against the decision of the planning authority and their appeal was heard by a Department of the Environment inspector in June 1995. The inspector found in favour of the travellers and granted planning permission for three years. On his findings the inspector commented on the special needs of the travellers which outweighed other considerations and the fact that Somerset County Council was in favour of the site.[19] The success of the appeal shows that it is possible for travellers to legitimately gain permanent sites, but they have to struggle for them and their special circumstances have to be recognized.

There exist many examples of travellers integrating within rural communities which serve to highlight travellers' interest in the preservation and sensitive development of rural areas. The examples tend to be short lived as either sites are evicted or travellers lose the struggle to gain planning permission, but the signs are there that travellers are compatible with rural life. If travellers are enabled to become partners in developing sites rather than being restricted to the position of passive recipients of a designated site of least local resistance, then more creative solutions can be found. Travellers involved in The Children's Society research favoured a variety of options, none of which included overdeveloped local authority sites or large anarchic rave sites. One of the more prevalent views expressed by travellers was that sites should revert to old patterns of land-usage - for lanes, common land, droves and verges to be used as stopping places. This need for stopping places is based on patterns of movement of travellers and their requirement to 'pass through' various rural areas. As such, these stopping places do not need to be heavily developed; they can remain containable and unobtrusive. In addition to stopping places though our research has highlighted a need for winter sites, consisting of firm ground and water supply. Winter places allow travellers to draw breath and make use of local facilities such as schools and playgroups. However, such sites can be rotated on an annual basis so that any one site may be used, for example, once every three winters.

Finally, our interviews with travellers in the South West have revealed a perceived need for more permanent sites. Permanency can mean different things to different travellers - a site with basic facilities such as toilet, rubbish collection and hardstanding for vehicles; allowing people to secure their children's education, gain employment or further education, and convert vehicles; or just rest for a while. If a range of sites - from stopping places to permanent sites - can be developed in the British countryside in consultation with travellers then local rural residents need not fear any sudden 'invasion'. Movement could be contained within recognized but changing locations, while permanent sites could allow travellers an opportunity to attain a greater degree of stability.

During the summer of 1995 the expected rush of evictions in the West Country did not materialize. Sites became more stable and travellers could begin to see a slowing down of the eviction process. This may be in part due to a realization by local authorities that simply evicting people resolves nothing and that the needs of travellers and their children are paramount. Considering the needs of travellers and their children became a requirement of local authorities after a judge in the High Court ruled that Wealden District Council was legally in the wrong for not properly enquiring into the welfare needs of a group of travellers in Crowborough prior to trying to evict them.[20] The case heard on 31

August 1995 was heralded as a landmark case in that it could make the Criminal Justice Act unworkable as it prevents local authorities beginning eviction proceedings without first investigating the needs of each traveller. It may not prevent evictions from taking place but it will slow them down. With a slowing down of evictions and an increase in the number of stable and officially recognized sites it is possible that in the future we may see a greater level of assimilation of travellers into rural communities.

Such a vision may appear idealistic in the current climate of fear and resistance, but with fewer options open to travellers the prospect of a desperate group pushing on to a field or village green simply because it is accessible is increasingly likely. Travellers are a feature of rural life, with our research and the literature on the history of British travellers suggesting that despite punitive legislation they are likely to remain part of the countryside scene. Travellers can add a richness to rural life if they are allowed the opportunity to assimilate within it rather than being continually resisted.

Notes

1. John Major, Conservative Party Conference 1992.
2. *Birmingham Evening Mail*, 29 June 1993, author unknown. KEEP THIS SCUM OUT and it is time to hound 'em Chief Constable, p. 1.
3. *The Cornishman*, 9 July 1992, Joyce Channon. Farmers fear hippy invasion.
4. *Gloucestershire Citizen*, 18 February 1995, no author attributed. Residents fear as travellers move in, p. 9.
5. *Cheddar Valley Gazette*, 17 November 1994, no author attributed. New caravan arrivals alarm residents.
6. *Mail on Sunday*, 12 May 1993, James Bartholomew. Why do we put up with the welfare state cheats?, p. 6.
7. *Daily Mail*, 8 June 1993, author unknown. Nightmare of the new age, pp. 8–9.
8. *Guardian*, 5 May 1993.
9. House of Commons (1992) *Hansard*, volume 221, number 23, columns 916–17.
10. House of Lords (1992) *Hansard*, volume 540, number 68, columns 1320–22.
11. House of Commons (1992) *Hansard*, volume 235, number 23, columns 96–7.
12. Department of the Environment, Consultation Paper on the reform of the Caravan Sites Act 1968, 18 August 1992.
13. House of Lords (1992) *Hansard*, volume 556, number 115, column 1553.
14. House of Lords (1992) *Hansard*, volume 556, number 115, column 1562.
15. *Independent*, law report, 15 June 1994, Ying Hui Tang. Local authorities applied right definition that gypsies travel to find work as 'habit of life'.
16. *Forest of Dean and Wye Valley Review*, 17 February 1995, Karen Tregear. Let caravan kids finish school, p. 1.
17. *Western Daily Press*, 8 November 1993, author not attributed. Why we paid travellers £1000 to quit our village.

[18] *Child's Eye*, Channel Four TV, 25 September 1994.

[19] John Frears, Inspector, The Planning Inspectorate, reference APP/C/94/D3315/635640-1, page 4, paragraph 15, page 7, paragraph 29.

[20] *Guardian*, 4 September 1995, Sally Weale. Travellers win 'makes Criminal Justice Act unworkable'.

References

Davis, J. (1991) *Young, Free and Crusty*. Midsomer Norton: The Children's Society.

Davis, J., Grant, R. and Locke, A. (1994) *Out of Site, Out of Mind*. London: The Children's Society.

Earle, F., Dearling, A., Whittle, H., Glasse, R. and Gubby (1994) *A Time to Travel*. Lyme Regis: Enabler Publications.

Hawes, D. and Perez, B. (1995) *The Gypsy and the State*. Bristol: School for Advanced Urban Studies.

Lowe, R. and Shaw, W. (1993) *Travellers: Voices of the New Age Nomads*. London: Fourth Estate.

7

Diverging Voices in a Rural Welsh Community

NORAGH JONES

Introduction

Living in a locality containing groups and individuals with similar interests to yourself is relatively unproblematic; it is more difficult to share such space with 'others'. Living with a range of 'other' groups is very much part of the experience of moving to a rural 'community', particularly when the newcomer is concerned with a wider context of living than simply self-interest and amenity without social responsibility.

In 1987 I began interviewing locals and incomers, traditional women and feminists, Welsh speakers and English speakers, residents and summer visitors, New Age travellers, hill farmers and urban commuters in and around Cwmrheidol in rural west Wales, motivated by a personal need (as an incomer born and brought up in Northern Ireland) to understand the complexities of this fragmented 'community' in which I had come to live. I was intensely aware of being 'other', and I felt that I needed to make connections with the people in my new community. On completion of my community study (Jones, 1993) I had listened to many diverging voices talking about the economic, social and cultural state of the Welsh countryside, and I had tried to identify bridge building strategies which might ensure the survival of positive community values. Such strategies can be seen to be linked to a new communitarian agenda emerging in the 1990s which has sought a recommitment to moral values in an attempt to balance rights with responsibilities, where 'people can again live in communities without turning into vigilantes or becoming hostile to one another' (Etzioni, 1993, p. 1). In the communitarian perspective, active and responsible membership of communities is seen as a democratic defence against faceless bureaucracies, against distant and legalistic government, rather than a retrograde clinging to the repressive values of close-knit communities which stifle the modernist individual, or to unfounded folk dreams of romantic solidarity. Indeed, community studies in rural Wales carried out in the 1950s and 1960s (see Rees, 1950; Frankenberg, 1957; Rees and Davies, 1960; Emmett, 1964) were criticized for 'treating communities as homogeneous holistic and harmonious entities unarticulated to the wider society' and for a tendency 'to portray a "Welsh way of life" as a single homogenized entity under threat from external forces' (Williams, 1986, p. 178). By the late 1980s, however, it was scarcely possible to fall into either of those traps, since many rural communities in Ceredigion are now clearly fragmented and their *cymreictod* (Welsh-speaking culture) has been culturally and economically penetrated by external forces.

The following extracts from my Cwmrheidol study, *Living in Rural Wales* (1993), explore these processes of change from the diverging viewpoints of individual experiences of living within fragmented rural communities.

Ways of Seeing the Countryside

Ieuan: The Welsh-speaking Hill Farmer

Ieuan is an unmarried hill farmer in his forties who has worked the same land as his ancestors with 'dog and stick' for many years. Following the death of his mother seven years ago he lives alone in his hillside farmhouse. In many ways Ieuan typifies the traditional hill farmers working in the area with his resentment of official bodies such as the Forestry Commission and the Countryside Council for Wales. Such organizations are perceived to have dramatically transformed local landscapes, particularly through the imposition of blanket coniferous plantations on hill sides. Moreover, many local farmers are angry with agricultural policies initiated by the European Union, which are seen as forcing them into different ways of work and life. Here is the voice of Ieuan, one such resentful hill farmer:

> Since the educated men got hold of farming it has gone from bad to worse. First they persuaded us to build up our dairy cows and gave us subsidies for that. Then they announced there was too much success in that and they were going to stop it. So many a family that had held the same farm for

> generations were forced to sell out to pay their debt to the banks. They were out of a living, but you never see those educated boys out of a living, do you? Now it's happening again with the sheep subsidies. The educated men think there are too many sheep in Wales, so they're trying to stop us doing what we have done for hundreds of years. And what else can you do on land like this? Oh yes, they talk about set aside money, but do you really believe they're going to give us money now for doing nothing at all, and watching the fields we've drained and cleared of bracken go back to a wilderness? Or grants to cover the land with trees, that we've broken our backs turning into good pasture? Trees! Look at what the Forestry Commission have done to the Welsh hills with their blankets of conifers. They've killed whole areas. Now the plan is for us to join in the killing. I'll tell you when the Forestry Commission came here in the 1950s they made compulsory purchase orders on family farms and they drove the people out. Now they're selling it off to private companies and pop stars, and what do they care about those families that were driven out? It's always profits for the big boys who've already got the money. There's no help for the small people ...

Resentment about the effects of agricultural policies on the familiar landscape is partly based on a sense of powerlessness in the face of officialdom. It also stems from the perceived impotence of agricultural planners at matching supply and demand on global markets:

> The worst thing of all is that they say we're overproducing food and that we have to cut back and let the land lie idle. But half the world is starving. How can you have it both ways? Is there nothing the educated boys in their offices can do to get the food we can grow to where it's needed in the world? That would be good work they could be getting on with instead of tormenting the life out of the farmers with their chopping and changing the rules and regulations every few years.

Diversification into tourism is considered impracticable by this hill farmer. He is critical too of the thoughtlessness of tourists in the way they use the countryside:

> We're supposed to be diversifying into tourism next, no matter if you have a remote place like this, and the weather coming over it in waves that would keep the townees shivering in their beds at night and longing to get back to their pubs and their discos ... I often see the summer visitors walking past here and I wonder what it is they get out of walking, for they don't seem to see the country they're walking through, the most of them. They just keep going, a big line of them, often, like it was an endurance test. A few of them come for the red kites, it's true. But the bird watching brigade see as little of the real country as the rest of them. Their eyes are glued to their binoculars the whole time and they fail to see what is going on – unless it's to find a

fence in their way and go over it without a thought for the work that's gone into keeping it stock proof.

Crow's Farewell Poem: A New Age Traveller's View of the Land

Crow lived for a winter in a bender in the Forestry Commission woods nearby that hill farmer's sheep pasture. He explored the locality thoroughly on foot, seeking out plants to make alternative medicines (according to the Bach flower remedy formulas, to which he was devoted). He also carved wood and wrote poems and stories. Crow can be seen as a healer and story teller, travelling lightly across the land, leaving behind him recipes for healing ointment, a squirrel totem and a peace symbol of white quartz stones. However, officialdom views Crow as a trespasser in the forest, against whom court action is necessary. The court injunction repossessing the land and giving him ten days to leave is pinned to a tree adjacent to the tree containing Crow's poem:

Are we the last stand of the oppressed of this land?

Are we the incarnate Celt who was called for aid
When the initial invasion of this nation was made?

What do you see?
Think about it if you dare.

They don't want us
They don't want you
Except to do as you've been told to do.

You pull down our homes
And make us move on
But you'll be the target when

We have gone.

Can you not understand that they
Are the spoilers of your beautiful land?

What will you do
When they've killed the soil
Wasted your valleys and ancestors' toil?

When they move you on –
As you once did us
What will you do?
Live in a bus?

Ros: The Dropout in Quest of Community

Ros rented a derelict cottage from an old bachelor farmer in order to live the simple life away from the urban ratrace. She arrived with her partner Alex but he disappeared after a couple of years when their relationship broke up under the strain of heavy drinking and shouting matches loud enough to alarm their neighbours some distance away. Her future tenancy of the cottage is uncertain because after six years the old farmer Dewi is trying to get her out and sell the cottage for renovation, as he has very profitably done with a couple of other ruins on his hundred acre land holding since the property boom at the end of the 1980s. The relationship between Ros and Dewi was close for the first year or two, involving dropping in and having a glass together. But since he decided to sell the cottage and she cannot afford the high price it will undoubtedly fetch on the open market, they are no longer on speaking terms.

> When we first came we were ostracized – literally. Taboo. They wanted us out, full stop. They didn't tell us to our face. That's not their way. But Dewi told us, 'They want you out', again and again in the first six months. Even now they've accepted us, well, they haven't really ... they've just stopped positively trying to get rid of us.
>
> We're not going to change the valley. I don't want change. I want it to stay the way it is. It's Dewi who's always on about conversions and modern bungalows. When you talk about who's changing rural Wales it's the bloody Welsh themselves. If you go up Cwmystwyth there's a load of travellers living there, but those kids don't want to change the place either. They're there because they like it the way it is. Same with us. We've come here because we like the peace and quiet, so I'd be the biggest anti-change person there is. Like when Dewi talks about building housing estates in the valley, I'd go mad. If the new owner of that ruin up the road tries to knock it down and build a new bungalow, I'll do a Prince Charles, I'll go and sit down there and say, 'You can't do it' ...
>
> In the end, after the first round of disappointments, what we found was that the old locals talked to us, because we were in with Dewi, and he told them we were helping a bit round the farm. He was in hospital for a while last winter and we fed the cattle, because it seemed the natural thing to do. I mean if you live in any sort of community, you do that sort of thing by instinct when anybody needs help. But the old locals, they're a community on their own, aren't they? Whereas, like, the rest of the people in the valley are foreigners like us, only they've been here a bit longer. The people who don't acknowledge you, or the ones you don't know, are probably foreigners anyway. They might wave from the car occasionally, but you won't catch them stopping to offer you a lift. They don't want to know you.

'Alison' and 'Phil': Green Incomers from England

Alison and Phil were formerly university students at Aberystwyth who fell in love with the area. Although they were unable to secure 'professional' jobs which matched their qualifications, they now own a small business which they run from home. They do not want to return to their previous English city lifestyles, having experienced a distinct form of 'community' in this area of rural Wales. Both Phil and Alison have attempted to protect the local landscape of their new found rural life through participation in a range of campaign groups which have been formed to oppose increased housing development and the siting of a rubbish tip in the local area:

> I suppose you could call us Greens (though not too fanatical veggieburger). It's good here if you're green minded. We grow a lot of our own stuff, but you can also get organic vegetables just for ordinary in the market in Aber[ystwyth], not costing the earth like they would in your urban Sainsburys. We've planted a lot of trees around the place, made our own birdboxes to nail up .... The kids love it now, but I suppose when they're older they'll make a beeline for the nearest English city, just to be healthy rebels against us. I hope they don't, especially as they're completely bilingual and into Welsh pop groups like Sobin a'r Smaeliaid.... But it's rural Wales' tragicomedy that so many brought up here want to get out and so many not brought up here want to come in. They say young people have to go to find work, but I'd say it's much more complicated than that, because look at all the incomers around here who have set up their own businesses and made a go of it - including us, I suppose (keeping my fingers crossed against the recession). Well you don't know you're in Paradise till you've been outside - and for some people even Paradise is not enough.

These few extracts from *Living in Rural Wales* (Jones, 1993) indicate something of the current diversity of ways of seeing the Welsh countryside, but also hint at unusual alliances cutting across the cultural polarities normally drawn, for example, between locals and incomers, alternative and straight lifestyles. Green incomers have children who are now fluent in the Welsh language, even if they themselves fail to become Welsh speakers. An old Welsh-speaking farmer living on his own enjoys the company of alternative young people. A New Age traveller sees himself as a guardian of the old simple folk ways, while some of today's *gwerin* (folk) are market driven and take advantage of rising property prices to sell off derelict cottages to incomers - effectively, if not consciously, diluting the *cymreictod* (Welsh-speaking culture).

The voices of the Cwmrheidol study suggest that building bridges among these diverse elements in rural Wales begins with reviving hospitable and friendly everyday contacts between 'them' and 'us', as neighbours, as dwellers in a shared and loved place, as consumers and contributors within the local economy, society and culture. It requires too some inspiring ethos within a community, and this often comes from a few key individuals who take their community responsibilities seriously and live out in their own lives, consciously or unconsciously, the communitarian agenda proposed by Etzioni (1993, pp. 253-67). Underlying the cultural tensions over the survival of the Welsh language culture are economic problems common to both locals and incomers. These include the problems of earning a living, providing for a family on low local wages, and finding a house at an affordable price. The following voices of significant bridgebuilders in the community suggest positive ways ahead.

Ian Jones: The Property Developer

Ian Jones is a strong advocate of diversification in rural employment. The major problem he identifies is the conservative mentality which resists any kind of change. The answer he proposes is a shift in education and training to encourage the spirit of individual enterprise:

> Here in west Wales we need a fairly major diversification out of farming but that will require a change of psyche into the enterprise frame of mind.... The young people who leave the area have great pressure on them to get their A levels and a nice professional job - doctor or accountant or solicitor. But there's a very limited demand for those jobs in an area of small population like this. What nobody says to them is, 'Why not start your own business? Develop a service or a process and get out there and sell it.'

He emphasizes the need for personal models of the entrepreneurial spirit, drawing on his own family experiences:

> I remember when we were little and looked after the chickens or other bits of work for my father, it was on a joint venture basis, not payment by the hour. We got a percentage of the profit on the eggs or whatever it was. There is an idea around that you're a victim of your own circumstances - that's very prevalent .... The Bateman Report says that because farming is going down the jobs are going down too. But you can in fact put more work into farming and increase the labour side, by cutting the heavy input costs (of fertilizers, chemical sprays and expensive machinery). You can also go direct to the market with your products, as Rachel's Dairy does. What our farming leaders are telling us is that we're victims of the CAP, so all we can do is wring our hands and wait for someone to rescue you. Instead of asking, 'What are *they* going to do about it?' people should be asking, 'What are *we* going to do about it?'.... So I think what we should be aiming for in

> our schools and in our communities is the enterprise way of thinking . . . . To get an omelette you have to break eggs. We're back to the problem of people being against any kind of change even though the present situation isn't helping rural Wales to keep its young people or create work.

While Ian Jones emphasizes the need to develop the enterprise mentality, the *cymry cymraeg* (Welsh-speaking Welsh) give priority to preserving the culture, but have initiated *Menter a Busnes* (Enterprise and Business) to encourage more entrepreneurial spirit through the schools and community organizations like young farmers' clubs and the Welsh women's movement *Merched y Wawr*.

Patrick Thomas: Vicar

A role for the churches in community bridge building is outlined by the Vicar of Brechfa, Patrick Thomas, who lives out in his own community his proposed role for rural clergy – as mediators in fragmented communities. He holds bilingual services, provides free language classes for incomers, and brings together, through his church activities, old and young, Welsh speakers and English speakers, locals and incomers. He urges individual responsibility for maintaining (or restoring) traditional values of belongingness, of mutual and personal interchange between neighbours, rather than labelling people as 'them' or 'us'. Patrick argues that these community values are often what incomers have moved to rural areas to regain. These values are also those of the values of the early Celtic Christianity which can be seen as part of the heritage of churches today. Individuals in a rural community can help to restore these values by building bridges and refraining from labelling people as 'other', which acts to fragment community to the extent that:

> the members of one subculture or group become effectively invisible to the members of another group (except where conflict breaks out between them). When a local councillor in one parish remarked that '*dim ond tri theulu sydd ar ol ar y mynydd erbyn hyn*' (there are only three families left living on the mountain now), he meant only three Welsh-speaking families – the dozen or so English families didn't count. A similar attitude is apparent among the hippy subculture who talk about 'people' (meaning people like themselves) – those who are not 'people' are of no importance.

Voices of Women

A further source of conflict lies in tensions between traditional roles for women in rural Welsh communities and emerging feminist perspectives, which are often regarded by Welsh-speaking women as an alien Anglo-American import. But there is an increasing number of both Welsh- and English-speaking women who are starting to enter into a dialogue in which feminist ideas may be accepted provided they can be rooted in existing cultures. One Welsh-speaking woman with whom I talked sets out her own future scenario in the following terms:

> For me my Welshness is so much a part of my identity that I probably wouldn't even think of it as an issue were it not for the changes I see going on around me in the rural communities. We have small children and we always speak Welsh at home. But they go to the village school and there is a big shift happening as more English-speaking children enrol there. They may all be taught to speak Welsh as well as English, but you notice how hard it is for Welsh-speaking children like ours to spend their whole day in their own language .... What do I want to happen? Well, I certainly don't want to draw up the drawbridge and keep the stranger out, because that is no answer in the long run. What I would like to see is the newcomers being ready to meet us halfway, so that we could all be part of a community that keeps what is valuable in the old traditions, but is also part of the modern world I want for my children. What kind of modern world? Well, I went to Greenham Common, and I'm one of the many Welsh-speaking women working for peace. I'm all for women moving outside their traditional domestic interests, though I wouldn't want to throw those out or undermine their importance, for it's very important for me and other Welsh-speaking women to have a strong home base for venturing out into the 'political' world, in our own communities or further afield. What worries some Welsh women about feminism is that it sometimes seems to be throwing the baby out with the bathwater, or getting rid of a very important reason for changing the world - that you want it to be a better place for your children, and that means keeping your own culture alive for them ....

How can incomer women and local Welsh-speaking women work together to achieve a cross-cultural dialogue in their communities? This open-minded Welsh-speaking woman suggests that:

> If we could join with incoming women to work for a fairer place for women in every department of Welsh life, that is something I would be happy to be part of. But both sides have to feel easy with each other and you only reach that position if you're prepared to really get to know each others' valued things ... you can't just turn up and want to work for peace or equal opportunities, without understanding about the community and the culture which these causes have to be rooted in, if they are to have any meaning for Welsh-speaking people .... It's better to be sincere than to be fluent, but a lot of Welshwomen are scared stiff to argue with confident fluent English incomers, even if they're women too ... who might be glad to have their

> views broadened. After all they have chosen to come and live here and have sometimes an angry sense, I think, that it is a different country that they can't understand ... I think Welshwomen have a part to play in explaining our communities and our culture to incomer women, and getting them to be part of this culture of ours. Because women are better than men at connecting, aren't they?

Conclusion

In collecting my 'Voices of the Future' for the final chapter of *Living in Rural Wales* I came to realize the intricacy of fitting together the diverse pieces of the Welsh rural community jigsaw. It became clear that the traditional Welsh-speaking culture cannot build a future on its own without economic and cultural support from outside. It is in any case not the monolithic culture that many outsiders take it to be, but contains its own 'others' - Welsh-speaking media professionals, for example, in relation to the *gwerin* or rural folk. It needs further injections of enterprise culture to keep its young people in work at home. The enterprise culture in turn cannot build a future on its own without a greener face and a concern for local sustainable development, for otherwise profits are exported and the skills imported with little advantage to the locals. However, the Green culture cannot build a future on its own, but has to translate its generalized ideals into practical strategies that are seen to be concerned with local livelihood and local cultures. Building bridges between Welsh-speaking, enterprise and green incomer cultures can be assisted by public bodies and by supportive policies but cannot succeed without the active work of bridgebuilding individuals (whatever their origins) working towards a sustainable future in their own communities. This requires an attitude towards the 'other' which embodies the old Celtic symbol of the Fifth Province. The first woman President of Ireland, Mary Robinson, in her inaugural speech in 1989, described this bridgebuilding symbol in these terms:

> The fifth province is not anywhere here or there, north or south, east or west. It is a place within each of us - that place which is open to the other, that swinging door which allows us to venture out and others to venture in ... tradition has it that the fifth province acted as a second centre, a necessary balance. (quoted in Jones, 1993, p. 355)

References

Emmett, I. (1964) *A North Wales Village*. London: Routledge.
Etzioni, A. (1993) *The Spirit of Community*. New York: Crown Publishers.
Frankenberg, R. (1957) *Village on the Border*. London: Cohen and West.
Jones, N. (1993) *Living in Rural Wales*. Llandysul: Gomer.
Rees, A. (1950) *Life in a Welsh Countryside: A Social Study of Llanfihangel yng Ngwynfa*. Cardiff: University of Wales Press.
Rees, A.D. and Davies, E. (1960) *Welsh Rural Communities*. Llandysul: University of Wales Press.
Williams, G. (1986) Recent Trends in Sociology. In I. Hume and W.T.R. Pryce (eds) *The Welsh and their Country*. Llandysul: Gomer, 179.

8

From Cream-making to Coq au Vin: Finding Images in Rural Devon

JACQUELINE SARSBY

Devon is an agricultural county with literally thousands of dispersed farms (11,946 holdings at 1 June 1994). Small dairy and rearing farms of cattle and sheep give the landscape a continuity with the past - the remembered past of mixed farming - which is gone from the arable areas of England, divided into the huge ploughed fields of agribusiness. The small farms have a certain independence, the authority of their own ways. Devon farmhouses are often secluded in the curve of a valley to protect them from the winter gales, but they are the centres of what has been until now the dominant culture of the inland villages: farming, described by farmers as 'a way of life'.

Farming, however, is a way of life that has had to contend with a constantly changing context of national and international markets, advice, subsidy, premium and quota, a bewildering succession of carrots and sticks from the Ministry, and more recently, daunting quantities of CAP paperwork - all for a community that prided itself on its independence from the need for school learning: it used to be said, 'Jack was a fool, so we sent him to school'. This has not been the only intrusion. Since the 1970s, the middle class rural exodus has brought with it a clash of cultures, in which the townspeople's quiche and coq au vin has been asserting itself over roast beef and Yorkshire pudding, fromage frais over jelly and trifle, the cosmopolitan values of the supermarket over the post-war traditions of the farmhouse. I was interested in the meeting of these two worlds, and in getting to know and understand better the 'farming way of life' in which rural Devonians felt at home.

Initially, I did two periods of fieldwork, in the South Hams in 1986–87 and on a farm on the edge of Dartmoor in 1989–90. I collected taped life histories, mainly of farm women, and worked on a reconstruction of life in a moorland parish in the early part of the century - and I also took photographs. My first exhibition[1] had an undeniable sense of the past in the present. Captions underlined and dutifully emphasized changes in farming, but the camera delighted in what remained - the Devon longhouse with its winter wood-pile, the little Fergie tractor which was still doing good service after nearly 40 years, the old harrow knitted into the living hedge and above all, the relationship between men and their animals. Established documentary photographers, like Chris Chapman and James Ravilious working in Devon, had already trodden this path well. But my emphasis was different: I was interested in the social organization of households and their relationship to the size and viability of farms, and I wanted photographs which reinforced research and were reinforced and given further meaning by research and captions.

The first exhibition, 'Indoors and Out, a Portrait of the Small Farm', concentrated on the life-cycle on the farm, from the farm-child's apprenticeship to the problems of splitting or increasing the size of a farm for a new generation, the difficulties of the couple who had no adult child or paid help on a small farm, and the options for retirement or old age - often a bungalow on the farm, or a widow's move to a house in the village. It also showed a facet of farm life which was less familiar: farms where brothers had remained, living and working together into maturity and old age. I showed farms where they lived with a parent or a sister, depending on the age of the brothers. Very often, one or both of the brothers had not married, and sometimes the sister who looked after them (and before them, looked after her parents) was unmarried too. This was another example of the past in the present, a form of household which W.M. Williams had described and theorized in Devon (Williams, 1963, pp. 263-5). It was also reminiscent of rural society in pre-industrial England, where late marriage and celibacy were more common than in the modern population (Wrigley and Schofield, 1981). It was no less a feature of the present-day farming community in Devon, for all that.

It is not difficult to see why brothers and sometimes a sister, remain unmarried on their home stock farm. Single sons who marry late or who remain bachelors, do so for some of the same reasons. A farm of 100-200 acres can be run conveniently by two men doing the outdoor work together and one woman indoors. Many jobs with cattle or sheep are done more easily if there are two people to catch an animal and control it - a father and son or two brothers. Where the wife helps outdoors with the stock, she must also do the work indoors and has a double burden of work.[2] When sons grow up, they introduce the most comfortable moment in the developmental cycle of the farm, being strong enough to do a man's work, but without the expense of a wife and family. In the past, often a farmworker would be sacked, when the farmer's son was old enough to do the man's paid work. It was tempting for parents to want to prolong the presence of unmarried sons. Some parents made it well nigh impossible for their children to go out and meet other young people, keeping them short of free time and pocket-money. They rarely had any wages and there was always work to do.

Other factors were and are specific to brothers rather than single bachelors. Brothers may like and be used to working together. Marriages would split the farm and make it less viable, or introduce unwelcome change into a set-up they were all used to. Isolation can still be a problem. On the one hand there is the comfort and familiarity of home, on the other, the difficulties of getting to know other people: the isolation of the farm in the midst of its fields - or in the midst of an alien culture - can lead to shyness and insularity. This is true today, no less than yesterday, for farming is a less convivial, less gregarious activity than it was 50 years ago, and what used to be called 'foreigners' are on all sides.

In the past, as Williams theorized, farms without heirs provided a pool of farms into which non-inheriting farmers' sons might dip. Nowadays, when such farms become vacant, they are likely to be split up. Neighbouring farms can get bigger, and the executors profit from the sale of a farmhouse and a few acres to an incoming professional buyer from the South East. This is part of the transformation of the countryside: other factors are the reluctance of sons on small farms to follow in their fathers' footsteps - or their realization that a small farm may no longer be viable. Barn conversions and the rise in village house-prices in the 1980s are other indications of change, fuelled by the middle class retreat from city life. This, in turn, has been facilitated by road building - the new A30 and the M4, M5, A38 links, which have brought all the middle and south of rural Devon within commuting distance of cities and of the railway to London. On the edge of the moor, in particular, the pressure of the market for fine old granite farmhouses seems to have almost killed the local farming community, producing a few larger farms and a great many hobby farms with horses and decorative poultry. In the National Park, it is more difficult for farmers to sell off a house and build a bungalow and barns for themselves, because of planning restrictions. The exhibition 'Changing Rural Devon' tried to address this subject in the autumn of 1993.

Before this, the exhibition 'The Family Farm in Devon' at Dartington enabled me to think about the different world-views which visitors, farmers, picture-editors and curators brought to images of Devon farming, and what they required of them. The exhibition was tailored in some sense for the farming audience. No longer arranged according to themes dealing with the character of the farm, its isolation and self-containment or with the life-cycle, the 49 photographs were now organized geographically – the South Hams, Dartmoor and Mid-Devon – focusing on particular farms and aspects of life on them.

I knew that publicity was terribly important, if one was going to bother to exhibit, so photographs appeared, first in the *Farmer's Weekly*, then *Country Living*, the *Lady*, the *Dartmoor Magazine*, *Devon Life* and on the local television news. This enabled me to see media preferences. Picture-editors regularly picked out a photograph of cows in the sunlight and shadow of a green lane, 'Robin White with his Cows in Coombe Lane' (see Figure 8.1). It may have been chosen because it evoked a kind of farming which was not rushed or industrialized, a 'way of life' which had nothing to do with traffic or city life. It was not an unusual picture: cows were regularly driven along the lanes on the farm where I stayed, but it showed something which is undoubtedly different from photographs one could take in most other parts of the country, where cows themselves, especially small groups of them, are now a rarity.

The second most popular photograph also evoked – quite mistakenly – an image of country life more redolent of the past. This was 'Birthday Party at Aysh Farm' (see Figure 8.2), which showed two women and 12 children at a birthday tea-party. Looking at it, people frequently said: 'Oh, look at all those children!' as if it were a photograph of a large family. The child on this farm was an only child, but this other quite unintended interpretation was regularly placed on the photograph in spite of its caption. Both these photographs appeared in magazines, were chosen by curators for brochures at various times, and were the first to be bought as prints. Two people also asked whether they could copy the photograph of the green lane, one as an embroidery, the other as a watercolour. Thatched cottages used to be the subject of postcards with captions like 'Dear Old Devon', but now people were being drawn to images of quiet animals, tall hedges and (apparently) large families.[3] This nostalgia, if it was such, related very specifically to concerns of the present – in this case, contented-looking farm animals, landscape conservation and family life – although it offered nothing but an image, an ideal and not a solution. In fastening on such images, the viewer is keeping alive something which he or she wants; it is not a political statement, but cumulatively, it helps to maintain an ideal – the question is, as American Indian writers have pointed out, when rejecting images of 'the proud primitive', whose ideal?

The farmers themselves had already seen and been given at least some of the pictures. Their reactions to being photographed had varied according to their previous involvement in photography: the Helmer twins of Chillington had been photographed all their lives, knew exactly what was expected of them, and always courteously gave it, posing happily for joint portraits. In the South Hams, where no one else seemed to be doing documentary photography on farms, the exhibition was very helpful in showing my subjects what I was trying to do. On the north side of Dartmoor, everyone knew Chris Chapman, a highly successful documentary photographer who had been working there for decades, so the idea of photographing people in their everyday surroundings was not novel, even among people whom he had not photographed. But for me, not a well-known photographer, just a woman with a camera, photography required a little negotiation.

Most people were more interested in photographs of their children or their animals rather than themselves: some farmers wanted photographs of their pets, while some younger farmers wanted photographs of their stock. The kind of photographs which I wanted to take - in black and white, with people going about their business, in everyday clothes - were different from the photographs which they normally treasured at home. Most obviously, family snaps, wedding photographs and group family portraits were invariably in colour. Older people were nearly always pictured at favoured moments, wearing their best clothes at a party or family gathering, in a village hall or hotel. The coloured, school portraits of children, lively but formal with unifyingly anonymous backgrounds, were in almost every family home and highly valued on mantlepieces and ornamental shelves. There were also press photographs taken at agricultural shows - formal poses of beautifully coiffeured and rosetted bullocks beside proud owners in white coats. There were hardly any photographs taken at home except a few snaps of children, but even family snaps tended to be framed, often in oval Victorian vignettes. The photograph had a formal, celebratory function, and even the snaps defined, through the photographer almost as much as the subject-matter, who belonged to the crucial episodes of family formation and success. All of them were highly valued. Patricia Holland has described how images in family albums reassure us of family solidity and cohesion (Holland, 1991).

My photographs tended not to be added to these family shrines unless they conformed to one of these portrait styles - for instance, a person pictured with a prize or favourite animal. The fact that I was working in black and white revealed (to me) that I was more interested in the photographs within a social documentary tradition - for others - than as fieldwork tools - for my subjects - in the sense that they were probably not what people really wanted. The photographs were, of course, fieldwork tools in other senses, as John Collier has described them, when they were the means of gathering complicated visual information - in the layout and furnishing of rooms, for instance, or in watching the performance of a skill, like helping a cow with a difficult calving, or making butter, but here again, colour might have been more informative (Collier, 1986).

In Autumn 1993, South West Arts gave me a grant for a small-scale rural touring exhibition called 'Changing Rural Devon', which was intended to visualize some important aspects of change in the countryside, especially the difference between life on the farms and the new culture of the villages. One half of it was called 'Farming on the Edge of the Moor': I had been working on the early twentieth century history of a farming parish on the edge of Dartmoor, and had been interviewing people there since 1986. I had also studied nineteenth century censuses and deeds, agricultural censuses, school registers and log books, electoral registers, Farmers' Union Minutes, farmers' accounts and letters all relating to the farming community in that parish, since discovering a sequence of diaries by a farmer and his daughter. I now knew much more about the past, and it helped me to contrast the present: there were, now, fewer farms, hardly a farming community at all in the village, but still the relentless work with animals continued in all seasons and in all weathers.

The second part of the exhibition was about a village in the South Hams in South Devon, which had had to cope in the last 20 years with a large influx of newcomers. Between 1971 and 1991 the population of the South Hams had increased by 15 per cent, the largest increase in the South West and one of the largest in the whole country, and this particular village had increased from 492 persons in 1971 to 643 in 1991, of whom 459 were under 50 years old. For comparison, at County Hall, I was quoted a study sample of Dartmoor parishes in which in 1991, 38 per cent of the people who had moved house in the last five years were in the 25-44 age group, and often from the South East. My periods of fieldwork had left me with the same impression of an influx of relatively well-off young families in both areas, on Dartmoor and in the South Hams, and, because of their very numbers and spending power, some inevitable strain had resulted in their relations with native Devonians. A point was being reached where the newcomer was becoming the norm and the Devonian was beginning to feel the 'other'.

I had visited the South Hams village continually since 1967 and I had carried out fieldwork, renting a cottage there in 1986–7. I photographed the modernized cottages and bungalows, the council houses, shops, pubs, the school and the church which had made the village attractive to people with a wide range of incomes and backgrounds, and I photographed some of the exuberant flowering of activities – morris dancing, Bonfire Night, a village school concert, church decorating (subsequently, I photographed Worm-charming, VE-day and the village pantomime) – by which people got to know one another, and became absorbed in village life. I also showed the outlying farms with their very individual mix of the old-fashioned and the modern. On both sides of the moor were farming families with their strong sense of family solidarity, their belief in progress and thrift. A whole culture lies uneasily alongside the nucleated villages – the youthful villages still with primary schools – with their fitted kitchens, their marital breakdowns and their bottles of wine in the fridge.

'Changing Rural Devon' went to seven venues in rural Devon. I was now ready to bring together photography and some of my original oral history research on farming women in an exhibition called 'Farm Women'. I had tape-recorded over 70 farming people (about two-thirds of them being women) and had interviewed some of them many times. Women's situations, their histories, activities and responsibilities were, for the public, some of the least known facets of farm life. Visually, the interior of the farm was even less known. Interior design magazines constantly referred to 'farmhouse kitchens', but these celebrations of consumerism bore absolutely no relation to the kitchens of many of the farmers' wives I knew, simply because most male farmers felt that money spent on the house was money wasted. I was very drawn to rooms which had not undergone a restyling – the imprint of magazine articles and superstores of the last 20 years – but of course farmers' wives did not always feel the same, especially if they felt their environment showed a lack of consideration for their sphere of influence: didn't their husbands want to be up to date with their huge barns and round-balers? Over time, some of the rooms would change, since women form the bridges between the farming world and the world outside. Many make compromises and alliances with this world for the sake of their children, their holiday cottages and their summer visitors, and also their contact, discussions and feelings of kinship with other women make them more open to change. Very often, coming into their husband's farm, they have long borne the weight of their mother-in-law's ideas about cooking and furnishing.

The exhibition did not just indulge the voyeurism of views indoors.

Nine photographs under the title 'One Woman's Day' showed different aspects of a particular woman's life, working indoors and out, and with a school-age child to look after. A tape of a woman's voice accompanied the photographs, and on the tape, she described very simply some of her work. Another young woman, shown hosing down her cattle-lorry, talked about the resistance she had experienced in her schooldays to the idea of her becoming a farmer. An older farmer's wife, photographed with her husband, talked about marrying as an outsider into the farming community just after the Second World War. Another woman, seen in her kitchen, pouring tea, described changes in the village - the disappearance of farms, houses sold off and the feeling of not knowing anybody any more. A small woman shown lugging a bale of hay commented: 'In the old days, the women belonged to the men ... then in my generation we were equal partners, and nowadays, the new generation, they're women in their own right, they've got their own lives to lead...'

The exhibition helped me to resolve some problems in my photography, in particular the relationship between the past and the present. At Dartington, some visitors had commented with evident pleasure that the pictures brought back memories of their childhood on the farm; one person, more critically, wrote, 'Where are all the young people?'. There had been, in fact, photographs of children and young people, but the focus was more on the households of farmers over the age of 50; those people who had made the transition from the small farms of their childhood, with maybe no more than a dozen cows, to the herds of upwards of 80 cows in the intensive farming of the 1980s. But the criticism was valid. I had been filtering out, or more literally, editing out, younger farmers, whose presence in their slim, sky-blue boiler-suits was less appealing than the older farmers in their seasoned old woollies and their coats tied with binder-twine. As I spent more and more time on a farm, and the first excitement of childhood revisited began to fade, I started to photograph and really to begin to be able to see the changing culture of the farms, their resistance or attraction to the consumer culture of the 'new' villages, and the generational differences which meant that young farm women had careers, while older women cooked and 'helped' whenever and wherever needed. I started to show the past and the present drawn apart more clearly: in 'Farm Women', portraits of elderly women were shown beside photographs of them in their youth, and they talked about the past with a full awareness of how it was different from farming today.[4]

'Farm Women' was a success, and after an article in the *Farmer's*

Weekly, a number of Devon people travelled to Glastonbury to see it, having missed it in Exeter. Taped sound and images worked well together. Still photographs allowed one to contemplate, but the addition of voices gave them an immediacy; the realization that they did not just refer to people 'out there', but people with their own world-views, their own problems and projects. In the photographs, however, or in the very best of them, something was expressed about their situation, which would not have fitted easily into a paragraph or a page. One can understand different things visually – in the bend of a neck, the sharpness of a gaze, the space between people (or between them and the photographer), and in the furnishings of a room or the darkness of a cow-shed. One needs time to contemplate images singly, then in relation to each other, and always in relation to those other images which one carries about in some inner album, checking them for family resemblances to one's own ideas and sentiments and one's own experience. Well constructed images have a path into the catalogue of one's experience, leaping effortlessly from memory to memory and often asserting themselves more powerfully than the ordinary tread of words – like poems, they are alive with metaphor and association. For a social anthropologist who wants to communicate, it is a path and a set of skills worth learning.

Notes

1. The first exhibition was 'Indoors and Out, a Portrait of the Small Farm' at the Museum of English Rural Life (September–December 1992). The second, with 19 new pictures and 30 from the first exhibition, was 'The Family Farm in Devon', shown at Exeter University (February 1993), Dartington Hall Gallery (April 1993) and the Guildhall, Dulverton (June–July 1993). After an exhibition called 'Pottery Workers' at Keele Gallery for the BAAS Conference in September 1993, South West Arts gave me a grant for 'Changing Rural Devon', a small-scale rural touring exhibition of about 40 photographs, which went to seven venues in Devon. In April 1994, I combined photographs and the voices of women on Devon Farms in an exhibition called 'Farm Women', which was first shown at Exeter and Devon Arts Centre, went on to Somerset Museum of Rural Life and the Museum of English Rural Life, and then to Newport College of Art as part of the Signals Festival of Women Photographers. In 1995 it went to the Hereford Photographic Festival. It continues to tour.
2. Cooking is considered women's business by both farmers and their wives. Men appreciate meals that are ready for them, when they come in after working in all weathers, but a woman must do it, whether she works outdoors or not. It is worth remembering that in winter, while women are doing housework, men are out in the barns cleaning out slurry and feeding cattle, while in the summer, they are doing the tractor-work, seeing to the corn, hay, or silage. This division

of labour has a certain symmetry, as long as women have no desire to do tractor-work. The problem is that although women may be called upon to work outdoors on particular farms, men are more resistant to feeding and looking after people. This is not seen as farm-work. I call it a problem because the fact that the farm is identified with outdoor work marginalizes women; daughters do not inherit unless there are no sons, and in reality this means 'unless they do outdoor work instead of sons'. Divorce laws which apportion the value of the whole farm between husband and wife are thought to give a woman more than her due.

3. I had produced four postcards from my photographs; the image of the cows in a green lane was invariably the favourite. I have no doubt that the birthday party, if made into a postcard, would sell equally well.
4. I was particularly impressed by *Images de Campagne* (1992) produced by the Centre des Sciences et Techniques Agricoles agro-alimentaires et Rurals/ Conseil General du Pas-de-Calais, who had brought together very contrasting old photographs and contemporary images in the two halves of a book.

References

Collier, J. (1986) *Visual Anthropology: Photography as a Research Method.* Albuquerque: University of New Mexico Press.

Holland, P. (1991) History, memory and the family album. In J. Spence and P. Holland (eds) *Family Snaps: The Meanings of Domestic Photography*, London: Virago Press, 1–14.

Williams, W.M. (1963) *A West Country Village: Ashworthy*. London: Routledge & Kegan Paul.

Wrigley, E.A. and Schofield, R.S. (1981) *The Population History of England and Wales 1541–1871*. London: Edward Arnold.

Figure 8.1 'Robin White with his Cows in Coombe Lane' (1990) from 'The Family Farm in Devon'. This photograph appeared in the *Farmer's Weekly*, the *Lady*, and the *Dartmoor Magazine*.

Figure 8.2 'Birthday Party at Aysh Farm' (1992). This picture was included in all the exhibitions and it appeared in the *Farmer's Weekly*, *Devon Life* and the brochure of the Hereford Photographic Festival.

Figure 8.3 'Moorland Farmer with his Dog' (1992) from 'The Family Farm in Devon'.

Figure 8.4 'John and Wilfred Rowdon with Bets' (1992), from 'The Family Farm in Devon' and 'Changing Rural Devon'. This photograph appeared in the *Farmer's Weekly* in 1992 and *Country Living* in 1993.

Figure 8.5 'Mrs Rowdon and Phyllis' (1992). This has been used in all the Devon exhibitions and appeared in *Country Living* in 1994.

Figure 8.6 'Morris Dancing at Blackawton' from 'Changing Rural Devon'. The morris dancers were mainly professional incomers to the village and they danced on most village occasions.

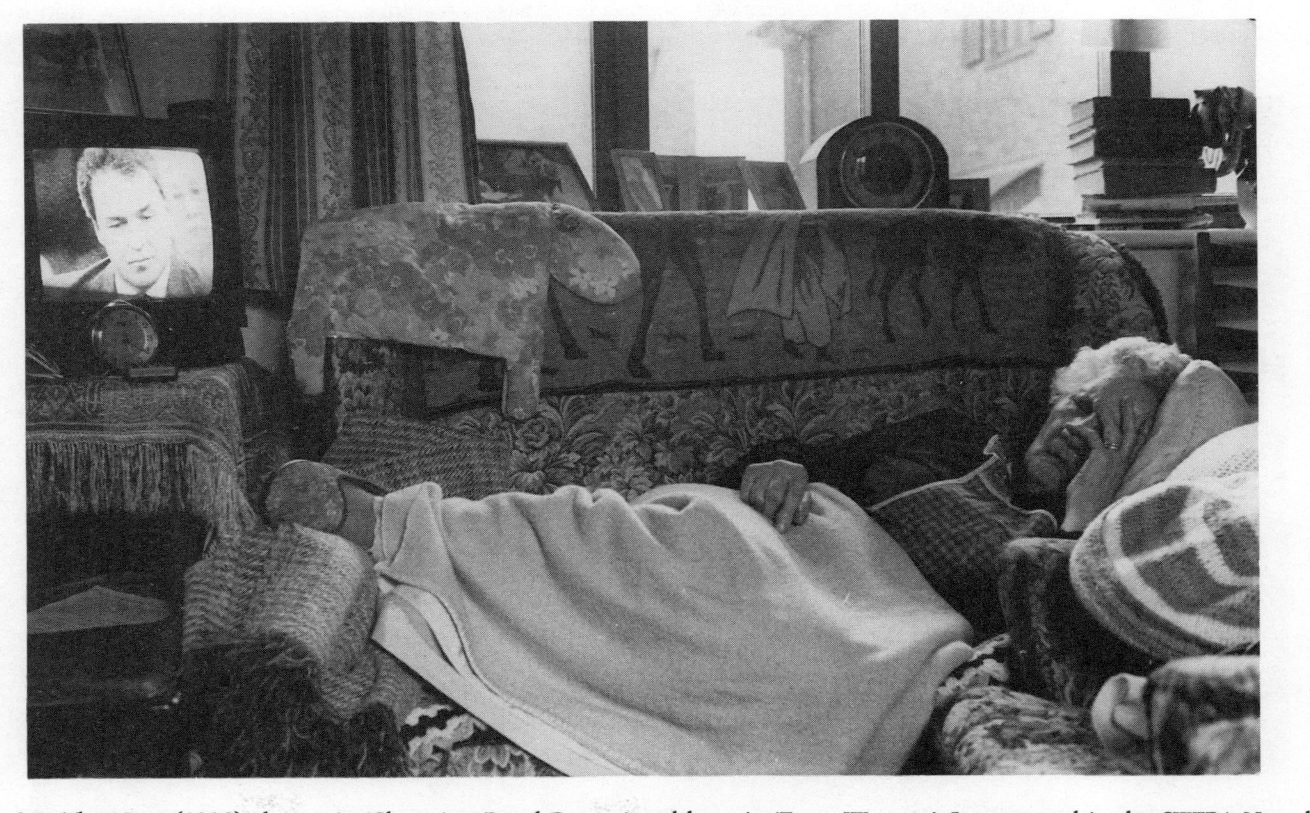

Figure 8.7 'The Nap' (1993) shown in 'Changing Rural Devon' and later in 'Farm Women'. It appeared in the SWIPA Newsletter, *Light Reading*, also the *Photographic Journal* and *Art Monthly*.

Figure 8.8 'Hazel Pearse of Barramoor Farm' (1993). Hazel and her husband, Colin, work as a team outdoors on this Dartmoor farm, rearing South Devon cows and mostly white-faced Dartmoor sheep. This appeared in 'Farm Women'.

Figure 8.9 'Phyllis Rinsing out her Butter Tub' (1994) from the butter-making sequence for 'Farm Women'. This appeared in the *Farmer's Weekly*, the Signals Catalogue, the *Photographic Journal*, and later, *Country Origins*.

9

Women and Rurality: Gendered Experiences of 'Community' in Village Life

ANNIE HUGHES

Introduction

The main aim of this chapter is to begin to uncover the 'hidden' geographies of rural women and their experiences of rural life. It is argued that dominant paradigms in rural geography have consistently obscured women's experiences of rural life by failing to recognize gender as a meaningful and legitimate cleavage in the organization of rural society (Little, 1987). With an increasing awareness of the 'sociology of knowledge' in human geography a critical epistemological and theoretical reflection is called for which acknowledges, and subsequently engages with, these 'neglected rural geographies' (Philo, 1992). The chapter is, therefore, intended to redress some of the criticisms set out by Philo (1992) who suggests that rural geography as a sub-discipline has made little attempt to step beyond the bounds of its traditional paradigms to incorporate studies of 'other' peoples and their geographies. By adopting a feminist epistemology which legitimates women's subjective experience as a valid way of understanding the dynamics of rural life, the chapter begins to assess the importance of gender as constitutive in the experience of rural lifestyles.

In the main body of this chapter the experiences of women and their rural geographies are examined. Conceptualizing rurality as a social construction, it is suggested that popular discourses of the rural are in fact highly gendered and incorporate specific ideas about the correct and proper roles of men and women.[1] In other words, it is argued that particular gender identities are bound up with how 'the rural' has been, and is being, imagined and represented. Furthermore, it is suggested that the everyday experiences of women living in the countryside are informed by these 'imagined geographies', with their lives influenced, at least in part, by what they perceive to be a 'woman's role' in a village community. Additionally, the chapter highlights how women's lives are shaped by other people's perceptions of their correct and proper role and more particularly by a pressure to conform to what is expected of them. Although gender is taken as the key focus, this chapter also investigates how women's community experiences are influenced by the interweaving influences of class, age, marital status and personal background.

The focus of this chapter is women's experiences of 'community' in one village, Ditton. The term 'community' refers to an idea or a lived experience rather than a geographical entity (such as the village), and should be seen as much as an imagined concept as a real one, with different people drawing on different, sometimes diverging, 'imagined geographies' of rural communities to make sense of their everyday lives. Therefore, 'community' is conceptualized as a 'lived experience' unlike the early rural community studies (see for example Rees, 1950; Littlejohn, 1963; Arensberg and Kimball, 1968) which defined the term as 'a place with a structure of institutions capable of objective definition and description, and through which everyone is supposed to be integrated into consensual ways of thinking and behaving' (Wright, 1992, p. 214). In this way, the differences between people's images and realities of rural community life can be conceptualized and subsequently examined. It has been suggested that within dominant discourses of rurality (academic, policy and also popular) women have been viewed as the linchpins of rural communities. This chapter is concerned with the interrelation between how women's community role is perceived (by them and others) and how this influences the real community experiences of women. The aim, then, is to investigate how women's experiences of 'community' in the contemporary countryside are (re)shaped by their 'real and imagined geographies' of rural life and more specifically how they adhere to, and contest (both consciously and unconsciously) these dominant representations of gender identity in rural discourses. However, before I go on to discuss how women's community experiences are shaped by the 'gendered geographies of rurality' it is important to question the reasons for the dearth of any sustained theoretical analysis of gender relations in rural research. To do this, the relationship between power and knowledge in rural research needs to be briefly addressed.

Power and Knowledge in Rural Research

Recent literatures in human geography have begun to question, rethink and subsequently redefine academics' claims to knowledge (McDowell, 1992). The impetus for such epistemological reflection has arisen out of post-structuralist, post-colonial and feminist critiques concerned with the 'sociology of knowledge'. These critiques recognize that knowledge *per se* is a social construction and they have begun to question who intellectuals have defined as 'knowers' and what kinds of knowledge have been elevated to positions of importance. This literature emphasises how dominant paradigms in the academy have influenced the construction of knowledge and how academics' positionality has affected what they have deemed worthy of study. However, rural geographers have rarely stepped beyond the bounds of their traditional paradigms to question their geographic imagination.[2] It is only in the last three years that rural researchers have begun to question their own claims to knowledge (see Philo, 1992, 1993; Murdoch and Pratt, 1993, 1994).[3] This may reflect what Buttel *et al.* (1990) describe as the 'theoretical lag-effect' manifest in rural studies. The research documented in this chapter draws on a feminist epistemology, which highlights the subjective nature of knowledge,[4] to argue for the legitimation of women's subjective experience as a valid 'way of knowing' and understanding the rural.[5] In the past, academic agendas in rural geography have consistently concealed women's experiences, hiding behind claims of objectivity and science. Therefore, not only has rural geography neglected gender as constitutive in the organization and experience of rural society (Little, 1987), it has normalized masculinist research strategies as the correct and unbiased way to study rural issues (Whatmore *et al.*, 1994). Although this chapter is not intended to document the achievements of feminist rural geographers over the last ten years (see Whatmore *et al.*, 1994), it is important to note that there has been an increasing awareness of the gender divisions particularly within farming households (see for example Sachs, 1983; Gasson, 1989; Whatmore, 1991). As this literature has developed it has become more theoretically informed and moved on from merely 'adding women' to a more substantial critique of the dominant paradigms in rural research.[6] However, although this heightened awareness of the uneven experiences within the household has been studied in relation to farming households, far less attention has been given to the broader rural community (Little, 1986, 1987; Redclift and Whatmore, 1990).

The aim of this chapter is to add to the growing literature within feminist rural geography concerned with the gendered nature of rurality and rural research. However, the intention is not to merely 'add women and stir', a tendency that Sandra Harding (1987) has termed feminist empiricism.[7] This critique of rural geography goes beyond the suggestion that the exclusion of women has been a result of an empirical oversight (McDowell, 1992). Rather, it is due to the fact that dominant agendas in rural geography have focused on non-gendered experiences and academic discourses of rurality, neglecting both the importance of gender as constitutive in the experience of the rural and secondly neglecting the more sensitive 'lay discourses' of rurality (Jones, 1995). It is, therefore, based around a more fundamental questioning of the epistemological and theoretical basis adopted in rural research. By adopting a feminist epistemology that legitimates women as 'knowers', it is intended to highlight the voices of 'ordinary' rural women, rather than measuring their experiences against a masculine norm.

(De)constructing Rurality: Gendered Assumptions Underlying Constructions of the Rural Community

In the last ten years geographers have become more interested in the ways that people construct spaces, places and landscapes and how society has imbued meaning on to certain places. The impetus for such a re-evaluation of the meanings of place has followed the so-called cultural turn in the social sciences (Whatmore, 1993). As urban geographers have begun to address questions of city life, how people experience it and identify with it, rural geographers have begun to embrace these debates and their implications for understanding rurality. Indeed, some contemporary rural research has begun to acknowledge the need to recast and reinterpret the meanings of rurality (see for example Mormont, 1990; Cloke and Milbourne, 1992; Halfacree, 1993). This work has begun to investigate the links, and 'break the boundaries' between, on the one hand, the rural as physical space and on the other, the symbolic significance of rurality. Although this chapter is not intended to provide a detailed review of this literature it is important to rehearse some of the main points. Put simply, it is argued that the rural cannot be defined by trying to objectify it but needs to be understood through the social and cultural meanings that have become bound up within it; as rural space 'becomes imbued with the characteristics of these representations, not only at an imaginative level but also physically, through the use of representations in action' (Halfacree, 1993, p. 34). Therefore, rural geographers are moving to a new vision of rurality centred around its importance as an idea, as a lived experience, rather than merely a territorial definition.

It has been argued that rural areas in Britain have been accorded 'mythical geographies'. Constructions of rurality have emphasized ideas of harmony and happiness, through notions of organic community and 'natural' ways of living. Cloke (1992, p. 269) suggests that rural areas have been used as a 'repository of ideological virtue'. He continues:

> the rural landscape has been characterized as offering natural beauty, health, fulfilment of life and freedom from problems. Equally rural communities have been viewed as friendly, desirable and secure living environments where traditional values are upheld.

It has been suggested that as Western society has become more industrial and urbanized such idealized conceptions of rurality have become more prominent in contemporary society (Bunce, 1994). These powerful images which represent the rural as a good place to live have become incorporated into popular culture (see James, 1991) and seem to be as strong now as in the past. Davidoff *et al.* (1976) highlight the endurance of this ideology by suggesting that:

> to many of us the adjective 'rural' has pleasant, reassuring connotations – beauty, order, simplicity, rest, grass-roots democracy, peacefulness, Geimeinschaft. Urban spells the opposite – ugliness, disorder, confusion, fatigue, compulsion, strife, Gesellschaft. (p. 149)

In other words, the rural must be conceptualized as more than a physical space, but as a symbolic construction which incorporates specific ideas about the worth of the organic community, kinship networks and 'natural' lifestyles. This symbolism embodied in rural areas has been acted upon, reproduced and integrated into contemporary rural discourses. Furthermore, it can be argued that only when we understand the multifaceted meanings underlying representations of rurality will we begin to make sense of the relationship between rural discourses and contemporary rural experience. As Laing (1992, p. 133) suggests:

> experience is ... not a matter of direct and unmediated encounters between individuals and the material world, but rather of the construction of meanings through language and symbol, through the available stories and images circulating within their culture.

Put simply, rural people's everyday lives are shaped by their experiences and understandings of and in place.[8] Although a number of authors have uncovered the class-based relations involved in the development of what could be termed the 'pastoral myth'[9] and the ways that it has been bought and controlled (see for example Howkins, 1986; Short, 1991; Cloke and Milbourne, 1992; Bunce, 1994), relatively little work has addressed the importance of gender relations and the construction of gender identities within these rural discourses. Representations of rural life must be understood not only in terms of class and property relations but also through gender relations given that dominant discourses of rurality encapsulate specific ideas concerning masculine and feminine identities. In particular, it can be suggested that a specific construction of femininity has been strongly represented within such discourses linking womanhood, domesticity and the family with notions of the organic community. Women have been constructed as being central to both the family and also the community. Moreover, just as authors such as Bunce (1994) and Howkins (1986) have suggested that the 'pastoral myth' developed as a result of crises in Victorian urban society, Davidoff and Hall (1987) see the construction of the 'domestic ideology' as centrally placed within the development of the capitalist economy. They highlight how its development was a material and ideological response to these changes, with womanhood being re-coded and linked to domesticity, morality and the family.[10] However, what is important here is that the ideal location for the 'domestic woman' was viewed as the family house in the country. Women were centrally placed within the home and community and in fact were seen as the linchpins, holding both ideal locations together (Davidoff *et al.*, 1976). Rose, following Nead (1988), highlights the centrality of gender difference to the construction of rural discourses. As she suggests:

> The rural idyll was envisioned as a village community. Everyone knew their place, and the harmony of such a community was centrally represented through 'natural' gender differences. Ideas about the natural order were epitomized in the 'natural' difference between men and women, with women naturally natural mothers. (Rose, 1993, p. 95)

Such historical gender images are being reproduced within a range of contemporary writings about the rural. Two recent reports have highlighted the continuing presence of a stereotypical ideal of a 'rural woman' (NCVO, 1991; Braithwaite, 1994). Indeed, Braithwaite (1994) states that the stereotype of a rural woman is that of 'a family woman, traditional and conservative, absorbed in the care of the home and the farm or garden' (p. 12). It is interesting to note that many contemporary books concerned with village life still reflect and reinforce these traditional gender identities. For example, in Joanna Trollope's popular novel *A Village Affair* the main character, Alice, sees village life as the perfect place to live out her utopia of domestic and community life giving her the chance to play her part in the community, to get involved with the church fete, the flower rota and driving old people in to town for their shopping. Recent academic research has also highlighted the prevalence of these images of the 'domestic rural woman'. For example, Stebbing (1984) argues that women in rural areas seem to have very strong ideas about what it is to be a 'countrywoman'. Although many women found the concept of the countrywoman difficult to define, most, she suggests, believed it to be related to a 'rural background' and traditional ideas about gender difference which:

> encapsulate the very essence of the rural and domestic idylls – the calm, well-ordered home as a refuge from the whirl of meaningless urban activity, presided over by a woman in touch with nature and with life's real values. (p. 202)

Little (1987, p. 340) suggests that 'the majority of voluntary activities rely to a large extent on women's unpaid labour, time and caring skills. Local fund raising ... is seen predominantly as "women's work", particularly where it involves the extension of so-called "female" domestic skills'. Moreover, she highlights how women's status in the rural community is by and large dependant on their willingness to get involved in community events and 'do their bit' to help out irrespective of their other commitments. In fact, for many women, living in a rural community was viewed as a 'full-time job' in itself (Little, 1994b). Such a viewpoint has been highlighted in a recent policy document, produced by the NCVO (1991) which suggests that:

> women are the backbone of the rural community – they hold the fabric of rural life together ... most rural volunteers are women, especially in 'caring' activities. They undertake a huge variety of tasks from 'just helping out' to organizing large events. (p. 2)

While this research seems to be suggesting that women play a central role within the rural community, it fails to consider the ways in which (different) women are influenced, and their own lives subsequently shaped, by their and others' (dominant) constructions of rural life. Interestingly, Little (1994a) has begun to investigate the links between the images and realities of rural life and how such images influence gender relations at the household level. As she suggests:

> popular perceptions about rural living appear to create a greater acceptance or tolerance of the lack of employment opportunities for women while the importance of the family, the community and the role of women as mothers ensure that their careers generally assume second place. (p. 26)

In the remainder of this chapter these issues are explored using case-study material of women's experiences of community in village life. In particular, attention is given to women's roles within the community in an attempt to highlight the ways in which gender is constitutive in the experience of rural lifestyles.

Women's Experiences of Rurality: Femininity, Community and Rurality

The research drawn upon in this chapter is part of my doctoral research. This work was based around intensive interviews and group discussions with women living in the contemporary countryside over a seven-month period. This chapter includes research findings from one of three villages studied, Ditton[11] (where 16 in-depth interviews were carried out), situated in mid-Wales in close proximity to the English border. A qualitative method of enquiry was adopted as these techniques provided the best tools to investigate and understand women's subjective experiences of living in the countryside.

To put the village in context, Ditton is a small hamlet of just over 100 residents located in a parish of around 500 people (the parish also included a second village slightly larger than Ditton and many outlying farms). Although originally dominated by farming, some villagers now commute to work in nearby towns and the village has experienced in-migration over recent years, predominantly involving English households retiring into the area.

A Sense of Community?: Women's Perceptions of 'Community' in Ditton

The women interviewed in Ditton were adamant that a community feeling existed in their village. However, when asked to elaborate on this many had difficulty in defining what they actually meant by a sense of community as if it represented some kind of 'taken for granted set of social and cultural norms' (Cloke *et al.*, 1994, p. 114).[12] Initially, they suggested that it was simply the friendliness of everyday meetings, the concern for neighbours, knowing and caring for people living around you and a 'pulling together'. Many said that it was just a feeling that they experienced when they moved in but could not pin-point any one thing. Elaine, a middle-class mother of two who had moved into the village 15 years previously after her husband changed jobs, argues: 'it is lovely being part of the community and walking around and talking to people'. These feelings were very real to the people in Ditton and as such were important to their feelings of belonging. These comments flowed from the incoming population as well as from the more established residents. Mary, a woman in her early fifties, who had moved into the village with her husband to start a business 18 months prior to our conversation, summed up these feelings of community by saying:

> Um, I walk along up, up the lanes ... they'll all speak to you, they're very friendly and that's what I have never had before. I could walk in the middle of Berkshire and nobody would speak a word to you ... I've never met anything so friendly as here. You can drop into it just like that.

Mary suggests that it is a feeling that she had 'never had before'. She had moved from an urban area and she continued by stating 'it's being part of a rural community, isn't it'. She seemed to be suggesting that being part of a community was a taken for granted aspect of a rural lifestyle. This is an important point as Mary seems to be arguing that community feeling was inevitably stronger in rural places than in other areas and this was taken for granted by herself and others. Women constantly compared life in the village to that experienced in the towns positing the 'community spirit' as much stronger than in other places that they had lived. Judith, an incomer in her late fifties who had semi-retired to the village, argues that: 'the sense of community is very strong. I think it is stronger here than in the town. My mother is lonelier [in the town] than I am here, yes, there's a great sense of community'.

Comparison with urban living was one of the main ways by which the interviewees felt they could describe the community spirit. Therefore, although it was a difficult concept to pin down, community in Ditton appeared different from anything which they had experienced in the towns. Locals as well as incomers adopted this comparison using anecdotal evidence from family and friends who had experienced living in urban areas. Jean, who had moved to the village five years ago after a holiday in the area, highlights how she hated the anonymity of living in an urban area:

> Although I was born and bred a townie I hated every minute of it .... In towns particularly in the winter you are going out to work and coming home in the dark, you are too busy in your little wrapped up world, you are very insular in towns ... you are not really in a community .... You can be as alone in a city as you can be on the top of a moor somewhere.

The feeling of being able to help one another was seen to enhance the community spirit. However, women who had lived in the village all their lives felt that the community spirit was declining. Phyllis, a farmer's wife in her sixties who had lived in the village all her life, highlights this feeling. She argues that people are now less reliant on their neighbours; that helping each other created a bond in the village community which is now being broken:

> It is not like it used to be in neighbours ... when our new neighbours moved in I went down and told them that we were up here if there was ever something that we could do. But we don't. I wouldn't say that we have nothing to do with them but it is practically nil. Whereas the people that were there when we came, we would give them lifts to town every week and we would stop and have a chat.

Clearly, the sense of community was perceived to be strong in Ditton although there was a feeling that the community spirit was declining. This was particularly the case among women that had lived in Ditton all their lives (both young and old, well off and not so well off). They were also more sceptical of the community spirit surviving intact with the recent social change in the village. Incoming women were much more acutely aware of the sense of community. Indeed, as Mary suggested above, some assumed that a sense of community was inevitable in a rural village.

Inside and Outside the 'Village Community': Joining in

Initial accounts suggested that everyone was involved in the community life of Ditton. Initially, then, it seemed that the shared geographical location provided the 'sense of community' and everyone was party to it. Being part of a 'community' was a part of village life that was quintessentially rural. However, it became progressively clear that 'belonging' and being part of the community meant joining in with the activities in the village. It was, therefore, not fostered through a shared residency alone. This was much more apparent for women who had moved into the area. You did not belong to, or fit into, the community unless you got involved with what was happening and co-operated with other people. Joining in seemed to be a precursor for being part of the community and more importantly being accepted. The community, therefore, was not just there, something abstract, a shared value system. Rather, it was something that had to be participated in, and created by, those that chose to become involved in it (or were accepted into it). In Ditton, community life was fostered by the locals with incomers joining in activities already 'up and running'. This is reflected by Judith, who states: 'it is the people that have been here, they are the ones that organize things, and if you want to join them you can, they welcome you with open arms'.

The attitude of having to join in to be part of the community was shared by incomers and locals alike. Jean, a recent incomer to Ditton, pointed to the importance of getting involved with activities in Ditton, arguing that although she made the effort and 'thrust' herself into the community life some people chose not to:

> I mean I am a townie born and bred and I have thrust myself into the community life and I want to get involved with everything that's going on and you get ... new people move in and you don't see them ... they don't get involved with the community .... They can be involved as they want to be .... There are just a couple that want to keep themselves to themselves.

Jean is suggesting that everyone can get involved in the community if they want to. In her opinion, it is by choice that people do not enter into the community spirit.

The women in Ditton argued that a few incomers did not join in and this caused some friction in the community. This was a result of their attitude that everyone should 'do their bit'. In this village helping in the community was perceived more as a duty and it was expected of the residents, especially of women. The most common complaint in Ditton concerning tensions in the village was the fact that some incomers moved in and did not participate and help out at community events. Such a point was highlighted by Emma, a young mother who had lived in the village all her life: 'People move in and they don't tend to mix as much as the locals will ... it is the people that come into the village that don't take part.'

It became clear as the research progressed that incoming women were not accepted into the Ditton community if they did not conform to what was expected of them and this entailed getting involved with village events and 'doing their bit'. If they did not participate they were excluded from being part of the community. This is not to say that they were actively excluded from village events but that they were noticed and condemned for their lack of participation. The women in Ditton seemed to be annoyed that some incoming women were not taking their turn to help with the smooth running of the community. Such feelings were probably due to Ditton being a small village and thus, as Elaine (an incoming mother of two children) points out, the 'responsibility falls on so few'.

Women and the Village Community: A Central Role?

Joining in was a precursor for being accepted in the village. However, with further investigation, involving interviews with both men and women, it became clear that women played a pivotal role in village life.

Women were instrumental in getting fun days, bonfire parties and dances organized to raise money for the village. It is important to note that men did 'help out' but women were the primary organizers. Pat, who had retired into the village with her husband twelve months previous to my research, noticed this as soon as she moved in:

> they're trying to build a new community hall and ... I think that if it was left to the men nothing would ever have been raised for it, it's the women in the community who have a fun-day, the men do help with the heavy things, the side shows and things ... it's the women in the community that do it all.

Similarly Rose, who had also retired to the village with her husband, pointed to the central role of women in the community:

> Funnily enough, very often it is the women that do all the organizing. In fact yes I have noticed that it is more often than not the women in the village. The men do help out but the majority of the real work, you know, is done by the women in the village.

Jean, an incomer of five years, noticed this tendency and picked up on the role of the Women's Institute (WI) in organizing community events and activities: 'The WI is very much the hubbub of the community ... very much so. If they want something done, you know, they usually ask the WI to get involved.'

Women moving into the village noticed the gender division of labour in organizing community events more acutely than more established female residents. Local women were much more likely to stress men's involvement, as Catherine, a farmer's wife who had lived in the village thirty-five years, suggests:

> Well I think that the women have to persuade their husbands that they must join in. Men are very good, there are some men that are very good and are quite happy to do it anyway but a lot of men won't unless they are pushed to do it. Things like that don't come easily to men don't you think? They are not good at community things like women are.

Such differences may be due to the fact that local women have always undertaken the organizing and accepted this as their duty. Indeed, Catherine is suggesting that women are somehow naturally better at 'community things' and that although men should help out, in her opinion it is not really their place. This is reiterated by Elaine, also an incomer, who argues that women are expected to help out – it is seen as part of living, and being involved, in a village community: 'Women are very powerful in this community. They organize everything .... Women are very instrumental and I think that it is accepted that they do it.'

Conforming to 'the Norm': Women in the Community

Women's involvement in the community, then, is perceived as a duty in Ditton. Local women exert pressure on incoming women to take part in community activities. This pressure is far stronger because it is a smaller community and those who don't 'come up to scratch' are more visible. Indeed, women in Ditton actually pin-pointed and talked about other women who did not participate. Phyllis, a farmer's wife who had lived in the village all her life, stated:

> one particular couple, I don't think do anything in the village ... not everyone just one particular couple and they have their lace curtains up and she doesn't go to WI and she doesn't go to church or anything in the community. At a community event you don't see them.

It is this woman's lack of participation that is noted even though neither of the couple is seen at community events. It is the fact that she is not involved in organizing the events rather than just attending them that is the key point. A lack of participation among certain women was also noted by Rose, who had moved to the village a couple of months prior to our conversation: 'there is a couple in the house behind, they were here before us but she goes out to work ... she hasn't integrated as much as I have .... This is a great pity'.

While these two interviewees may have been talking about the same couple, it is clear that women are being pin-pointed and judged on their lack of community involvement. Elaine summed up the situation perfectly:

> I think there is a lot of pressure in the countryside to conform to what society wants of you. If you don't try to fit in with the village and what is organized you are not accepted .... You have to work at it to prove yourself to feel as though you belong, there is a lot of pressure, while in the city you don't have to make any effort really. You've got to conform to expectations ... I think that it is accepted that women go out to work but you have to do your bit, to get involved I think .... You can't just hide yourself behind closed doors or people think that you are odd.

In suggesting that women are expected to take part in community activities Elaine recounts her own experiences moving to the village:

> The week that I moved here the old lady next door said, church is 9.30 and 3.30 on alternative Sundays and WI is the first Wednesday in the month ... I'll pick you up. There wasn't any question about it (laugh) ... because when I first moved in there was only one other woman that had moved in and she was very active in the community ... I was just accepted nicely and in a

> friendly sort of way ... I don't know if I would have been if I didn't try and be helpful .... It was presumed that that's what women did.

The view that women are instrumental in community life was particularly apparent when discussing the decline of community feeling. It became very clear in the village that people linked such decline with an increasing number of women partaking in paid employment. Although it was accepted that women need to go out to work they were still expected to 'do their bit' in the community. Rose, for example, discussing the woman living next door, points out that women who have paid employment are less likely to get involved with the community: 'She (the woman next door) goes out to work ... she hasn't integrated as much as I have, because she's working you see ...'

Catherine, a farmer's wife, points out that getting involved with the village community is far less important to women who go out to work:

> It (the community) is not so important for young women I suppose now. They have got their own lives and they are so busy that the community work comes second place, doesn't it? You see that is what is happening here.

Not only were these working women seen to have less time for the community but getting involved with the community was seen as less important to them. When women were at home all day the village provided much needed support and encouragement. With women developing other support networks, however, particularly through their work, the importance of getting involved with the community tended to decline. As Catherine continues:

> For women I think that the community was more important but things change and a lot of younger women go out to work and they do not need the community as much as before. I have noticed that anyway. Do you think?

Imagining Rurality: Incoming Women's Attitudes to Community

Clearly women are the linchpins of this particular rural community. Moreover, it is argued that it is a role expected of village women. Women who did not conform to this community role were not accepted as being part of the community life. Indeed, women are still expected to 'do their bit to help' even if they possess a full-time job. Women who helped out were held in very high regard and were well respected. On the other hand, women who did not participate were labelled as 'letting the side down' and were talked about and commented on. Incoming women were more acutely aware of the gender divisions of labour in the community, while women who had lived in Ditton all their lives were less likely to question the situation. This reflects an attitudinal difference between village women, with incoming women seeming to fall into one of two groups: those who were central in the village community, and women who did not integrate at all. Elaine argues that this reflects different perceptions of rural lifestyles, suggesting that people had moved into the village for two reasons: to 'get away from the pressures of city life and try to opt out' of society; and secondly to get more involved in the community. Elaine continues:

> Some come to adopt a rural lifestyle, some come for the social aspect and some people are only interested in getting away and shutting themselves off ... and a lot of people bring their city lifestyle with them.

Elaine is suggesting that there is a perceived 'rural way of life' which some incomers reject by 'bringing their city life' into the countryside. Interestingly, she herself moved into the area to become more active in a community, something she felt would be more difficult in an urban area:

> I have always lived in the country and I am into community things ... I think it is very much more friendly and I wanted to get to know people and play an important part in society. In a bigger place it is much easier to be incongruous ...

Elaine is, therefore, suggesting that women's roles, particularly those of incoming women, are, in part, influenced by their perceptions of rural life. For Elaine, living in a rural area meant getting involved in the community, reflecting her 'imagined geography of rurality'. Although she felt that there was a pressure to conform she states that it was a desire to be part of the community that spurred her and her husband to move into the village. However, the situation for Pauline, a mother who had moved into the village two and a half years ago, was almost the reverse:

> we moved here to get away from the pressure and commitments. We wanted to spend more time with each other and the children. I didn't want to be out every night at this committee or that committee. Before we moved I had a high pressure job and I felt I wasn't spending enough time with the family ... we thought this area could offer us a change, to get away from all that ...

Pauline perceived moving to a rural area as a way of escaping from people and the pressures of modern living and not as the 'community utopia' so prevalent in popular discourses of rurality. In her interview she said that the last thing on her mind when they decided to move was to be 'hounded' into taking part in community activities. She talked of the pressure to conform to what was expected. This pressure, she suggests, was not overt but became apparent in subtle comments by other women in the village. This introduces a key issue, that rural experience is not the same for all women; that there is no one rural experience. Nor does everyone share the same notions of rurality and what it can offer.

Conclusion

It has been argued in this chapter that being part of the 'community' in Ditton required an involvement with the social life in the village. This was particularly the case for women, highlighting popular perceptions of a woman's role in rural communities. The gender division of labour in the organization of village activities is clear. Women were the backbone of the village community and, moreover, they were expected to carry out community work. Community participation was perceived to be their duty, their natural role. Women who were instrumental in organizing community events were highly respected for their commitment to the village. It could be suggested that this created a hierarchy among the village women and, as a result, caused tensions and arguments. Importantly, this antagonism was not between the sexes but between women themselves. This hierarchy was visible when I attended my first local WI meeting. I asked every woman if she would agree to be interviewed. The classic response was 'oh I wouldn't be any use to you, you should go and talk to so and so'. 'So and so' was invariably a woman who was deeply involved with community activities and not, as I had expected, a local woman who had lived in the village all her life (although there was a relationship between local women and community participation but this was not exclusively so). Although local women accepted their community responsibilities, some incoming women were reluctant to adopt this role. This, it is suggested, was partly influenced by their own imagined geographies of rurality. For example, Elaine moved into Ditton to fulfil a community role while Pauline, on the other hand, had different ideas about rural living. Rurality can, therefore, be viewed in terms of partial and unstable representations of place, reflecting multiple lived experiences. Indeed, if a different village in a different part of the country was studied, take for example a Welsh-speaking village, antagonisms may have been more likely to be based around notions of Welshness and Englishness. Rose, an incomer of 18 months who had retired to the area, stated that in the last village in which she had lived 'there was resistance to the English'.

It is important to note that although gender is constitutive in the experiences of rurality, a non-essentialized view of gender identity is advocated. In other words, as gender influences how we understand and experience rurality so do issues of class, race, age, sexuality and background. Clearly women's rural experiences are shaped not only by their gender but also by these other cleavages.[13] For example, all the women, except one, that had moved into the village had moved in with their husbands. Having a partner to share household responsibilities with and who is available to look after the children facilitates community involvement. Single parents or women who had less supportive partners would find community involvement much more problematic. Women who spent most time in the community tended to be those who were married with children (or grown-up children). Although many of these women did have full- or part-time jobs, it begs interesting questions about the social status of, for example, single parents in villages who may be unable to partake fully in community activities. Similarly, the majority of women who had moved into Ditton possessed comfortable lifestyles. Sufficient money was available to partake in community events, fun-days, carol services and children's parties. Although not being expensive individually, the cost of these events, as Rose suggests, 'adds up'. Indeed, Elaine states that she had spent a considerable amount of money on baby-sitters just so she could get involved in community meetings and events. Women who were less well-off would not be able to afford this childcare option. These are very interesting issues and additional research is required concerning the situation of these 'other' groups in rural society.

This chapter, then, has endeavoured to highlight how the adoption of 'other' methodological and epistemological devices can enhance our knowledge and understanding of the dynamics of rural life. In particular, by drawing on a feminist epistemology which legitimates women's subjective experience as a way of understanding rurality (both real and imagined), the importance of gender as constitutive to the experience of rural lifestyles has been highlighted. The research drawn upon here adds new ways of understanding women's lives as they are influenced by, and negotiated through, not only material space but also their understandings of the symbolic meanings underlying rural places. In other words, 'place matters'; women's gender identities are influenced, at least in part, by what they perceive to be a rural woman's role within the rural community and secondly shaped by what others in the community perceive as their role. Furthermore, my research while assessing the ways in which women draw identity from these imagined geographies of rurality, also addresses the ways in which women contest dominant representations. As a result of this multiplicity of experience they will, at different times in their lives, engage with, contest and rework dominant conceptualizations of rurality and particularly the feminine identities bound up within these constructions. More and more rural women are going out to work, and although the employment available is usually part-time and often low paid, it is providing rural women with different social outlets leaving less time for community involvement. These women are beginning to contest the dominant view of the 'domestic rural woman'. However, it is clear in Ditton that a woman's social standing is very much related to her willingness to partake in community activities and women are expected to do this as well as engage in paid employment. This adds an extra burden on to their already busy lives. Clearly much more research needs to be undertaken on the importance of gender relations and the experience of gender identities in the rural context. What is required is a rural geography which takes account of the gender divisions in rural society (and also rural research) and is also sensitive to the diversity of female (and male) experiences in contemporary rural society.

Notes

1. By the term 'rural discourse', I am referring to 'the rural' not only as a physical space but as a symbolic and imagined place imbued with a whole set of meanings bound up with ideas of community and natural ways of living. Rural discourses, therefore, encapsulate not only the physical reality of 'the rural' but also how it is imagined, represented and made sense of in everyday life.
2. Additionally there has been little attempt by rural geographers to locate themselves as subjective beings within the research process, acknowledging the bias and values they bring to their research – although see Cloke (1994) for a notable exception.
3. For example Murdoch and Pratt (1993) argue that the imposition of a set of definitions of rurality is itself a practice of power. They argue that rural geographers should be exploring the ways in which the rural is constructed in a 'variety of contexts' rather than trying to pin down a definitive definition of rurality. Therefore, they are suggesting that rural specialists should be investigating the multiple rural experiences of place and the multiple experiences of people within those places. There is no one rural Britain (Cloke, 1992), neither is there one rural experience.
4. Such epistemologies critique the principles of enlightenment scholarship which attempted to lay bare universalized truths revealing the basic features of social reality. Feminists challenge this notion arguing that 'what had most frequently been presented as objective because supposedly devoid of the influence of values, such as those related to gender, actually reflected such values ...' (Nicholson, 1990, p. 3).
5. One of the distinctive features of feminist enquiry is that it generates research

questions from women's own experiences. Indeed, feminists argue that traditional research paradigms have normalized male activities and experiences, leaving women's lives untheorized (Stanley and Wise, 1993). Feminists, therefore, adopt women's experiences as a 'significant indicator' against which hypotheses can be tested (Harding, 1987).

6. For example Whatmore (1991) argues that women's rural experiences were obscured by inadequate conceptualizations of work and the family.
7. Stanley and Wise (1983) highlight the danger of just 'adding women' into academia as a separate discipline. They argue that if women are separated off, feminist work has little implication for mainstream research and, therefore, does little to challenge traditional orthodoxies.
8. For example, in a recent paper analysing the reasons for the re-population of many British rural areas, Halfacree (1994) highlights the importance of the 'rural ideal' to migrants moving to the countryside. He suggests that the literature on counter urbanization 'has failed to appreciate adequately the extent to which a desire to live in a more rural residential environment is a crucial constitutive element of this migration phenomenon' (p. 185).
9. These authors argue that the construction of the so-called 'rural idyll' was a result of the social and political power relations prevailing during its development in the late Victorian era. Village life was represented as the epitome of stability and order as a method of social control in an increasingly unstable world. In other words, the development of the rural idyll was primarily linked to the onset of capitalism which had led to the undermining of previous hegemonic power structures.
10. Feminist anthropology has highlighted how womanhood is not culturally stable and is, therefore, not reducible to biological determinism (Moore, 1988). Similarly feminist historians have also suggested that gender identities and ideas of gender difference are also specific to particular times in history (Hall, 1992).
11. The name of the village and the names of all the interviewees have been changed for the purposes of anonymity.
12. This reflects academic concerns with the ambiguous nature of the term 'community' (see for example Bell and Newby, 1971; Day and Murdoch, 1993).
13. It is telling that there were no coloured women living in Ditton, highlighting the exclusively white nature of much of rural Britain. A black woman's experiences of village life, for example, may be quite different from that of a white woman's even though they share the same gender and possibly class position and background.

References

Arensberg, C. and Kimball, S. (1968) (2nd edn) *Family and Community in Ireland.* Cambridge MA: Harvard University Press.

Bell, C. and Newby, H. (1971) *Community Studies.* London: Allen and Unwin.

Braithwaite, M. (1994) *The Economic Role and Situation of Women in Rural Areas.* Luxembourg: Office for Official Publications of the European Communities.

Bunce, M. (1994) *The Countryside Idyll: Anglo-American Images of Landscape.* London: Routledge.

Buttel, F., Larson, O. and Gillespie, G. (1990) *The Sociology of Agriculture*. Westport CT: Greenwood Press.

Cloke, P. (1992) The Countryside: development, conservation and an increasingly marketable commodity. In P. Cloke (ed.) *Policy and Change in Thatcher's Britain*. Oxford: Pergamon Press, 269-98.

Cloke, P. (1994) (En)culturing political economy: a life in the day of a rural geographer. In P. Cloke, M. Doel, M. Philips and N. Thrift *Writing the Rural: Five Cultural Geographies*. London: Paul Chapman Publishing, 149-90.

Cloke, P. and Milbourne, P. (1992) Deprivation and lifestyles in rural Wales - II, rurality and the cultural dimension. *Journal of Rural Studies*, 8 (4), 359-71.

Cloke, P., Goodwin, M. and Milbourne, P. (1994) *Lifestyles in Rural Wales*. Cardiff: Welsh Office.

Davidoff, L., L'Esperance, J. and Newby, H. (1976) Landscapes with Figures: home and community in English society. In J. Mitchell and A. Oakley (eds) *The Rights and Wrongs of Women*. Harmondsworth: Penguin, 139-75.

Davidoff, L. and Hall, C. (1987) *Family Fortunes: Men and Women in the English Middle Class 1780-1850*. London: Hutchinson.

Day, G. and Murdoch, J. (1993) Locality and community: coming to terms with place. *Sociological Review*, 41 (1), 82-111.

Gasson, R. (1989) *Farm Work by Farmers' Wives*. Farm Business Unit Occasional Paper No. 15, Wye College.

Halfacree, K. (1993) Locality and representation: space, discourse and alternative definitions of the rural. *Journal of Rural Studies*, 9 (1), 23-37.

Halfacree, K. (1994) The importance of 'the rural' in the constitution of counter-urbanisation: evidence from England in the 1980s. *Sociologia Ruralis*, 34 (2/3), 164-89.

Hall, C. (1992) *White, Male and Middle Class: Explorations in Feminism and History*. Cambridge: Polity Press.

Harding, S. (1987) (ed.) *Feminism and Methodology*. Milton Keynes: Open University Press.

Howkins, A. (1986) The discovery of rural England. In R. Colls and P. Dodd (eds) *Englishness: Politics and Culture 1880-1920*, London: Croom Helm, 62-88.

James, S. (1991) *The Urban - Rural Myth - or Reality*. Geographical papers, No. 107, Department of Geography, University of Reading.

Jones, O. (1995) Lay discourses of the rural: developments and implications for rural studies. *Journal of Rural Studies*, 11 (1), 35-49.

Laing, J. (1992) Images of the rural in popular culture 1750-1990. In B. Short (ed.) *The English Rural Community: Image and Analysis*. Cambridge: Cambridge University Press, 133-51.

Little, J. (1986) Feminist perspectives in rural geography. *Journal of Rural Studies*, 2 (1), 1-8.

Little, J. (1987) Gender relations in rural areas: the importance of women's domestic role. *Journal of Rural Studies*, 3 (4), 335-42.

Little, J. (1994a) Gender relations and the rural labour process. In S. Whatmore, T. Marsden and P. Lowe (eds) *Gender and Rurality*, London: David Fulton, 11-29.

Little, J. (1994b) The village as a full-time job. Paper presented to a conference of the Rural Economy and Society Study Group, University of Manchester, March 1994.

Littlejohn, J. (1963) *Westrigg: The Sociology of a Cheviot Parish*. London:

Routledge and Kegan Paul.
McDowell, L. (1992) Doing gender: feminism, feminists and research methods in human geography. *Transactions of the Institute of British Geographers*, 17 (4), 399–417.
Mitchell, J. and Oakley, A. (1976) *The Rights and Wrongs of Women*. Harmondsworth: Penguin.
Moore, H. (1988) *Feminism and Anthropology*. Cambridge: Polity Press.
Mormont, M. (1990) Who is rural? How to be rural: towards a sociology of the rural. In S. Whatmore, T. Marsden and P. Lowe (eds) *Rural Restructuring: Global Processes and their Responses*. London: David Fulton, 21–44.
Murdoch, J. and Pratt, A. (1993) Rural studies: modernism, post-modernism and the 'post-rural'. *Journal of Rural Studies*, 9 (4), 411–27.
Murdoch, J. and Pratt, A. (1994) Rural studies of power and the power of rural studies: a reply to Philo. *Journal of Rural Studies*, 10 (1), 83–7.
National Council for Voluntary Services/National Alliance of Women's Organisations (1991) *Women in Rural Areas: Challenges and Choices*. London: NCVO Press.
Nead, L. (1988) *Myths of Sexuality: Representations of Women in Victorian Britain*. Oxford: Blackwell.
Nicholson, L. (1990) (ed.) *Feminism/Postmodernism*. New York: Routledge.
Philo, C. (1992) Neglected rural geographies: a review. *Journal of Rural Studies*, 8 (2), 193–207.
Philo, C. (1993) Post-modern rural geography? a reply to Murdoch and Pratt. *Journal of Rural Studies*, 9 (4), 429–36.
Redclift, N. and Whatmore, S. (1990) Household, consumption and livelihood: ideologies and issues in rural research. In S. Whatmore, T. Marsden and P. Lowe (eds) *Rural Restructuring: Global Processes and their Responses*. London: David Fulton, 182–97.
Rees, A. (1950) *Life in the Welsh Countryside*. Cardiff: University of Wales Press.
Rose, G. (1993) *Feminism and Geography: The Limits of Geographical Knowledge*. Oxford: Blackwell.
Sachs, C. (1983) *Invisible Farmers: Women's Work in Agricultural Production*. New Jersey: Rhinehart Allenheld.
Short, J.R. (1991) *Imagined Country: Society, Culture and Environment*. London: Routledge.
Shurmer-Smith, P. and Hannam, K. (1994) *Worlds of Desire, Realms of Power: A Cultural Geography*. London: Edward Arnold.
Stanley, L. and Wise, S. (1983) *Breaking out: Feminist Consciousness and Feminist Research*. London: Routledge and Kegan Paul.
Stanley, L. and Wise, S. (1993) *Breaking out Again: Feminist Ontology and Epistemology*. London: Routledge.
Stebbing, S. (1984) Women's roles and rural society. In T. Bradley and P. Lowe (eds) *Locality and Rurality*. Norwich: Geobooks.
Trollope, J. (1989) *A Village Affair*. London: Black Swan.
Whatmore, S. (1991) *Farming Women: Gender, Work and Family Enterprise*. London: Macmillan.
Whatmore, S. (1993) On doing research (or breaking the boundaries). *Environment and Planning A*, 25 (5), 605–7.
Whatmore, S., Marsden, T. and Lowe, P. (1994) (eds) *Gender and Rurality*.

London: David Fulton.
Wright, S. (1992) Image and analysis: new directions in community studies. In B. Short (ed.) *The English Rural Community: Image and Analysis*. Cambridge: Cambridge University Press, 195–217.

10

'Others' in the Rural: Leisure Practices and Geographical Knowledge

DAVID CROUCH

Introduction

Leisure is often 'othered' in the cultural debate about the countryside. It is imagined as outside, even 'inappropriate', as contesting the proper use of place. Types of leisure can be appropriated from the possibility of power in rural areas, evidenced in the debates over the interpretation of leisure as 'peace and quiet' in the earlier legislation on National Parks and Areas of Outstanding Natural Beauty. This is despite the evidence that landed estates were seen, significantly, as sites of 'leisure' among the gentry. This is a story of contested country; landscape claims, unstable identity but more than this, an exercise in power in contemporary culture and in the academy. Leisure is an important component in the process of geographical knowledge of the rural. However, leisure itself has often been regarded as 'other', even though sites of leisure are a crucial part of this knowledge.

Leisure considered in this chapter is not principally structured through formal production. Therefore, these practices, as we identify them, happen in places outside the boundaries of those formally labelled for leisure, including theme parks and heritage sites, although in our example of caravanning, large numbers of people participate in them (House of Commons Environment Committee, 1995).

Philo (1992), and then Murdoch and Pratt (1993), have been astute in unearthing the prevalent yet unnamed others in the countryside: unwrapping groups, who may or may not welcome that unwrapping; groups who have been overlooked, or found inappropriate in rural geography, rural sociology and, I would add more recently, absent in cultural studies. It is no accident that these same groups have been similarly disenfranchised, or never offered the franchise, of identity among what is called the rural in contemporary culture. 'Othering' may be part of imposing order, confounded by the intractably complex world (Shurmer-Smith and Hannam, 1994). For Bourdieu, making distinction is part of a social process of cultural capital, whereby we both identify ourselves and locate our position in the world around us, and discover our position in terms of hierarchy (Bourdieu, 1984). Gramsci referred the making of 'others' to the exercise of hegemony, power and knowledge, where the dominant culture not only asserts itself but its assertion is interpreted by people at large as 'natural', even welcome as part of necessary social order and social life (Gramsci, 1971). Imaginatively, Deleuze (1990) envisages the making of 'others' more playfully, as enabling the realization of places not engaged in an everyday life and allowing them to enter our own being. These perspectives in their different ways inform this chapter.

Elsewhere I have suggested an instability and diversity associated with the ways in which we make sense of the rural in popular culture, if we take that popular culture not only as what we consume through media and market, but through the everyday practices of our own lives that are also shared socially (Crouch, 1992). Those lives happen alongside signs of value and rejection; they happen in particular and contested knowledges; they happen in particular places. Some of those signs include versions of the rural; some of the practices happen in bits of space we call rural. The diversity and multitextuality of this defies formalistic boundaries, but ideas of the rural, and links between these and where we happen to be, do make connections between the metaphorical and the concrete - the physicality of everyday cultural events - and free our imaginative possibilities. Taking cultural studies a moment further, place is informative, sometimes distinctive, in making geographical knowledge and cultural identity, in an unstable weft of sign, place and life (Crouch, 1994).

One of those arenas of cultural practice is leisure. It also happens in particular places, as well as with a 'baggage' of signification. The rural itself is seen as 'other' in contemporary cultural forms and the representation of culture, used both imaginatively and in the manipulation of power; this has been typical of proscribed interpretation of modernity and has now slipped into a post-modern interpretation that similarly finds the rural and countryside culturally difficult. It is rejected, marginalized, reified and incorporated into a predominantly metropolitan culture. In prevailing academic writing, leisure is marginalized within notions of the rural, as being outside the life of people who make life in the countryside. Ironically, tourism seeks otherness. Yet leisure practices themselves diversely pick up these signs and possibilities. It is argued that understanding leisure practices, in the city or the countryside, is a valuable means to unpack the way signs interact with the consumption of particular places in making geographical knowledge, an unstable, intermittent and challenging process.

There are several important questions that this chapter addresses. How does this process, seen through particular examples, become 'othered', engage its 'otherness', and why is it 'othered'? What does this inform us, in the academy, of geographical knowledge and what we have come to call the 'othering' process? Focusing leisure practices in places makes possible a number of connections: the geographical knowledge in leisure and its semi-detachment from dwelling (is leisure part of dwelling anyway, and vice versa?); notions and signs of community as using temporary or permanent places; leisure geographies and power.

The next section of this chapter outlines the ways in which this 'othering' of 'rural' and of 'leisure' happens. This is developed within three key sections: 'Rural "Othered"?'; 'Leisure Practices and Rural Places', 'Leisure and Geographical Knowledge'. The chapter then turns to a consideration of two distinctive arenas of leisure practices; caravanning in Britain, and leisure in the lives of people in Weardale, on the eastern side of the Pennines in north-east England. Although in this second case we consider places constructed around productive cultivation, these same places are also consumed in leisure; they are crossed en route to leisure elsewhere and remembered.

Rural, Leisure and Geographical Knowledge

Rural 'Othered'?

Considering the ways in which the rural is 'othered' opens up interesting concerns of power and ownership, the availability of 'othering', and of signs of the rural. The rural was always an 'other' in modernity. A problem in the investigation of the rural has been a presumption of a unified geographical/cultural knowledge of the rural (Crouch, 1992; Murdoch and Pratt, 1993). 'Rural' studies have traditionally investigated diverse groups, frequently around notions of coherent 'communities', and this has given room for culturally/economically marginalized groups, linked with notions of poverty and policy response (Harper, 1989). In general, these studies have lacked sophistication in the identification of diversity, and have tended towards bipolarity, community and its decline, poverty, and an uncomplicated relation of power and identity, where distinctive versions of the rural have been either marginalized or romanticized. Furthermore, this itself has been complicated by the rural being compared as a whole with what is called 'urban', the 'rural' has been made the 'other' to so-called urban and metropolitan. In classical mid-century writing, in literature and in policy, the countryside was 'othered' as requiring special conservation and identified with 'nature'. The 'country' and the 'city' were mutual outsiders and 'others', enshrined in planning legislation after the Second World War, and sustained by bodies such as the Council for the Protection of Rural England (popularly celebrated in George Orwell's *Coming up for Air*, 1949; Williams, 1976; CPRE, 1994). This is a distinctly modernist construction (Short, 1992). In terms of power, this required urban interests to assert control (Hardy and Ward, 1984).

In very recent writing this classically modernist position is replayed. Popular culture is presented as essentially metropolitan (Chambers, 1986). This is celebrated typically in a metropolitan swirl of totalizing de-differentiation, but still looks into the urban:

> the migrant landscapes of contemporary metropolitan [*sic*] cultures, deterritorialized and de-colonized, re-situating, re-citing and re-presenting common signs in the circus between speech, image and oblivion, a constant struggling into sense and history is pieced together .... It is perhaps something that we can hear when Youssou N'Dour, from Dakar, sings in Wolof, a Senegalese dialect, in a tent pitched in the suburbs of Naples. (Chambers, 1994, pp. 14–15)

The present author listened to, met and talked with a pipe player from a Peruvian village in another village of Casteljaloux, near the hamlet of Bouglon, in France in the summer of 1994. But unlike Chambers we do not need to see this as postmodern. It is a continuity of travelling people over a very long sweep of history; not an exaggerated contemporary cultural shift, but an existing cultural complexity and as likely to be observed in the country as in the city (Hannerz, 1992).

In modernist discourse, this 'othering' was connected with the presentation of capital as urban, although that much simplifies the relation (Williams, 1973). In postmodernity, the rural has not been associated with the metropolitan dimensions of cultural complexity. Instead, the rural is the object of 'new' leisure practices (CPRE, 1994; Lash and Urry, 1994; Urry, 1995). In both that modernist sense and in the post-modern version, this relation concerns notions of power and control which produce signs that influence both the making of geographical knowledge and the contesting of the rural. This chapter is concerned with the position of leisure practices in these processes of geographical knowledge. These practices are understood to be situated in the meanings and norms of the actors, but also in the imagination and materiality of the practices themselves, and rooted in social practices, intersubjectivities and mutual action (Taylor, 1979; Hemingway, 1995), where meanings are communicated through the practice itself (Ricouer, 1981). Collective memory is acknowledged in contemporary writing as palimpsest but also as refuge from modernity and other modernizing cultural processes (Urry, 1995), and power is contested through these very practices themselves and sometimes as a search for reconstructing identity, remaking or challenging power relations (Smith, 1993).

Leisure Practices and Rural Places

Rural is 'real' in people's lives – acknowledged, spoken of, referred to and used as an imagined frame of reference in people's lives, however much this may be at a metaphorical level. That notion, sign or metaphor influences decisions, cultural practices and the way in which place is taken and worked, perhaps playfully, into geographical knowledge and cultural identity (Thrift, 1987; Crouch, 1992). As well as playing with 'signs' of the rural, people may also participate in the actual materiality and physicality of rural places – the countryside.

It is argued that the modern, and post-modern countryside is imagined as the abstracted sweep view or gaze (Cosgrove and Daniels, 1989; Countryside Commission, 1992; McNaghten, 1993; Urry, 1995), but leisure happens in 'bits of countryside'. Although we enjoy a broad sweep of countryside, as a gaze, people visit individual sites in leisure activities, and may be deeply aware of intimate places around us – enclaves – and their immediately adjacent geography rather than the distant encompassing view. How then, is deeper imagination mobilized through the practice, often in small corners of the rural? Leisure practices may provide an everyday means of making sense of the rural, whether over a sustained dwelling or through fleeting, intermittent visits. There are important gaps in our knowledge of how this everyday geography is understood. It is contended that this everyday use of countryside (re)positions the rural in our identity.

Contemporary writing about the rural has privileged the market in awarding it a prolific involvement in remaking the rural – especially in tourism, new leisure forms of heritage, theming, and delivering a consumer version of the rural. This arguably takes 'the rural' into Chambers' metropolitan palimpsest as simply further contextualized by a metropolitan market, 'people are free to appropriate meanings in their lives from just about everywhere they see it' (Tyrrel, 1990). Does this adequately explain countryside consumption in leisure? Has this open possibility removed 'othering', as everything is an 'other', and as such is engaged fleetingly and without reference point into our lives? John Urry's writing suggests three possibilities: a post-modern version of making sense of the countryside as commercially contextualized consumption (Sack, 1988); the Countryside Commission as exemplar of a 'modernist' approach to diversity in the rural; and a third version, of 'new sociations' of people, often sharing leisure practices and identities through leisure alone, alert to a 'critical' version of the rural in rejection of the consumerist image – where environmentalism and collectively generated leisure 'enthusiasms' predominate as resistant, or rather alternative models (CPRE, 1994; Urry, 1995). These are presented as polarities. However, what do people involved in the 'new sociations' make of the rural? How and in what ways are these forms actually new? Is, and if so how is, this three-way leisure practising interpenetrated with 'othering', or is 'othering' diminished in this process?

Particular components of place consumption are of central importance in taking this explanation further. First, the process of geographical knowledge is unstable, it has multiple reference points, and is a cultural process. Following Fiske (1990) and Miller (1987), the production of cultural objects (here we may read 'the rural') in both sign and materiality, is met by consumption that can be passive and active, critical, subversive. In this more active phase, there is a recontextualization of the signs that convey the product, and sometimes of the product's materiality; Fiske uses the example of a pair of jeans, ripped, shrunk and embroidered away from the Levi 501 advertisement. We may see the countryside similarly – commercial leisure contextualized and packaged, often ironically with the wrappings of pre-modern and modern versions of heritage (Crouch, 1992). What influence does this production and complex consumption have on 'othering' particular groups, both among leisure practices, and among people who spend most of their lives in what they would call 'the rural'? Does leisure practice become a means of 'othering' across margins between distinctive leisure identities? How much do signs conveyed in the delivery of commercial leisure, or in the positioning of particular cultural groups, 'other' either kinds of leisure practices or places where those leisure practices happen? Place is crucially important in leisure practices.

Leisure and Geographical Knowledge

The way we come to know place, however fleetingly, is engaged in a wider, fragmented and uneven, but none the less existing world, and thus also a set of other places to which it may be related. We may visit a theme park or a heritage site, but we return to other places which we engage in everyday practice - the pub, golf club, park, bingo hall, work, home - and life continues in particular places. Both the leisure practice in the rural, and the practice in the village or in the city are likely to happen in forms of sociality (Hetherington, 1992; Shields, 1992), and possibly in familiar forms of family and friendship. 'Exposure' to heavily coded leisure sites mingles with other activities as itself part of everyday cultural intercourse (Warren, 1992). It may be that the identity we discover from both sides is slightly changed. This is surely unexceptional, and hardly provides anything new, however heavily laden 'new' sites of leisure may be. Moreover, the engagement with these 'new' sites does not happen on a 'tabla rasa' (Hannerz, 1992), but rather within collective memory. Many of these often uncertain, fragmented engagements with place mean that we make leisure in particular bits of countryside, fragments of the rural. These fragments of the rural may have, however, very clearly positioned meaning in the leisure practices we may pursue. Commercial contexts for leisure frequently appeal to the abstract 'rural', but not always. How does 'othering' happen with regard to the promotion of particular leisure practices and the promotion and positioning of the rural in those practices?

Geographical knowledge is continuously transforming and being transformed; signs are brought into the situated materiality of practice; that practice is anticipated and realized through the conveyance of signs (Lash, 1993; Crouch, 1994). Exactly how this works requires attention to particular sites in the practice of leisure. Whitt and Slack (1994) draw attention to the need to position notions of environment in this way. They acknowledge the reappraisal, in much more flexible versions, of 'community' and 'mutuality', and argue for investigating notions of 'environment' with close reference to specific, local environments. We may translate that case for attention to distinctive (to risk Bourdieu's term) leisure practices. Are particular leisure practices 'othered'; in what ways does that 'othering' use a contextualized picture of the rural; in what ways is that 'othering' contextualized by cultural capital, versions of the rural, and do geographical knowledges become thereby 'othered'? The present chapter investigates the geographical knowledge of distinctive leisure practices, and the ways in which knowing particular places engages with other knowledges.

Distinctive leisure practices may include heritage tours, paintballing, historic enactments, a theme park outing or fell running. This chapter posits that distinctive identities are being played, challenged and reformulated in these practices. Place is likely to be informative in the way this happens, as distinctive places are used in each case. Notions of rural inform both the selection of practice - where it happens - and how it is reworked in place knowledge. Some of these leisure practices are more evidently contextualized by the commercial market; consumption as a response to a specific moment of delivery. In other cases, this is more obscure, and in some, leisure is effectively self-generated. By this I mean produced, contextualized and participated in by a group of people themselves. Purchased products promoted with an image of 'rural' may feature in this practice, such as walking boots, and may peripherally inform the imagination of the practice. Of course, there are wider signs through which a practice is made sense. In turn, each practice may utilize distinct places through which those signs and cultural identities may be realized (Crouch and Tomlinson, 1994). Taking our contentions from the beginning of this section a step further, how far did modern interpretations of the rural 'other' particular leisure practices, and through what ideological and hegemonic system? Has that been transferred into contemporary (late modern? - see Giddens, 1990) leisure imagery and leisure practices, and how do those processes of 'othering' influence geographical knowledge of the rural?

Situated Mobility and Shifting Collective Memory: Caravanning

Nearly a million households own caravans which they take with them on holidays and weekend trips; a further half of that number rent a caravan from a site. Caravans are richly represented in literature in particular ways - they are candidates for the archetypal leisure of a mobile and unattached age, of romancing the road (Cresswell, 1993; Eyerman and Lofgren, 1995), enabling the enjoyment of flickering images *en route* and a short sojourn with the knowledge of its temporality (Thrift, 1994). However, they are also the object of substantial criticism in terms of certain ways in which sense is made of the rural. This emerges in particular relation to both modernist versions and post-modernist remakes of those versions. To understand the process of 'othering' requires a reading of how geographical knowledge is made in a particular leisure practice, and how this may be observed in contrast with other constructions and contexts of geographical knowledge.

Caravanning combines important threads in the making of rural knowledge. It is a freewheeling phenomenon and consumes those flickering images of the figural as rural, as people shift aimlessly and privately in the celebration of mobility and individuality itself. It becomes everybody's desired place and nobody's 'other'. The wider iconography is more complex. Caravanning in the UK is shaped around two main clubs that most travelling caravanners belong to, either because of the friendship or the fact that the clubs own particularly good sites that can be visited only as a member. With thousands of families who are members of local neighbourhood, company or other leisure-linked clubs (there is a four-wheel-drive Land Rover Club) this absorbs nearly one million households. Many of these people go on weekend rallies, which are described below. Another quarter of a million are estimated not to belong in this way, but caravan alone, or informally with friends, at weekends and on holidays.

The main club - the Caravan Club - was inspired in the first years of this century by the late nineteenth-century story, *The Voyage of the Land Yacht Wanderer* (Stables, 1886), a story of the travels of a Victorian Gentleman who took his two children and valet (not his partner/wife) to explore the wider reaches of rural Britain. For women this experience was considered inappropriate, a transgression of domesticity among the middle class. They stopped in 'waysides' and commons all over an England only selectively conscious of this transgressive act. More widely, the caravan and 'doing caravanning' are contextualized in a collective imagination that combines class identities. There is the romantic gypsy, hobo, freedom and power in one's life. This is epitomized in different, but generally middle-class ways, in Kenneth Grahame's *Wind in the Willows* children's story, whose rider of the 'canary coloured cart', Toad, is of course the re-lived and disappearing figure of the rural, the English Gentleman; in Enid Blyton, where good middle-class children can share the limits of freedom on leave from public school in *Five go off in a Caravan*. For Grahame, this proves to be a celebration of modernity; the caravan over the horse; the caravan giving way to the 'motorcar'. It is again a very gendered image of 'progressive' [sic] masculinity. Modernity is celebrated in the design of the caravan - a mobile machine, full of gadgets and adjusted for a mobile 'lifestyle'; a marvel of modernist design that has been adapted throughout the century (Gutmen and Kaufman, 1979).

However, there is also a powerful strand of working-class culture and the shared freedom of a displaced cultural space in the rural outdoors. These roots are formed in the impossibility of other holidaymaking; the enjoyment of beer, translated from the pub - long an important leisure place among the working class (Smith, 1983), and the chance to earn money while holidaymaking, on hop picking holidays (Ward and Hardy, 1986). Of course, the caravan can be cheap, and today they can be bought second hand for £200. The more expensive sector of the market reaches over £20,000, and there is a flourishing market among Caravan Club members that embraces the whole range. However, the paintings of Harry Allen, a working-class painter whose work charted a changing life of the rural in Yorkshire in the middle of this century, are alert to the powerful 'othering' of gypsy culture in Britain, which has been deeply investigated by Judith Okeley and David Sibley (Okeley, 1980; Sibley, 1980), while Van Morrison celebrates a more international dimension of the hobo in 'Caravan, 1986'. These various signs are replayed in contemporary advertising, alongside images of up-market cars - Volvo and Range Rover appear in Caravan Club magazines, identifying the continuity of caravanning with the Land Yacht Wanderer, appealing to a middle-class acceptability. That acceptability is important, because the caravan is interpreted with much 'othering' in other reaches of popular culture. However, these are informative 'signs'. I will turn in the next section to the way place is positioned in a process of leisure. Before that, I highlight how the caravan and the practice of caravanning can become 'othered'.

For decades since the Second World War, the caravan has been 'othered' because it has been interpreted as a 'blot on the landscape'; seen to transgress the image of the rural that has been dominant in British cultural traditions (Wright, 1985; Howkins, 1989). Thus, in the 1980s there has been criticism of Fay Godwin's non-romantic rendering of caravans on the Sussex coast (Godwin, 1990), while her photography of the expected romantic places - in the Scilly Isles and around Howarth in the Pennines - has been applauded. The caravan is positioned in branches of contemporary visual culture and conservationist literature as 'other'; discordant with the visual imagery of countryside and landscape and the icons used to support these. The evaluation of 'leisure landscapes' by Lancaster University's Centre for the Study of Environmental Change, albeit for the Council for the Protection of Rural England, continues this reading (CPRE, 1994). Local councils and government agencies have similarly labelled these sites; 'many sites [are] environmental eyesores with little privacy and charm; operators of the 1950s and 1960s spent little time on landscaping' (East Anglia Tourist Board, 1984). The caravan was seen as a technological, modernist-industrial intrusion into the country-side. Thus, in the middle of this century, while other technologies were roundly praised (Putnam, 1993), the caravan was rejected because it was used in the countryside. Countryside, then as now, was predominantly imagined as pre-industrial, pre-technological, pre-modern and picturesque (Shoard, 1982; Short, 1992).

'Solutions' to this 'other' are sought unsurprisingly among those 'enriched' by post-modernism, in theming: 'Wildwest', 'Seascape', 'Spacescape' and 'Eastern city', and most ironical, self-referential 'gypsy' decorations and film-set 'landscapes' [*sic*] are proposed to contextualize and hide the caravans. This would be 'amplifying imagery of the site by giving theme to parts of the caravan park' (East Anglia Tourist Board, 1984). Caravanning becomes a means to be themed (East Anglia Tourist Board, 1990). In the Policy and Consultants' documents that describe these ideas and designs, the sites are presented in views from the air, where hardly anyone can see them, and completely miss the way these places are experienced 'on the ground' - how these places are engaged through the practice of leisure and in the process of geographical knowledge by those who do caravan is not understood.

This 'othering' is applied especially to large caravan sites. These sites provide a valued means of access to 'beautiful places' for millions of people each year in the UK. Unsurprisingly, because the people using these sites go there because they want to enjoy beautiful places, these sites are most effectively located near them. The many thousands of households who caravan at weekends, especially at 'rallies' as well as those who take their caravan with them on the road, often to join static caravans at the large sites, are also 'othered'. In 1992, an action group called the Anti-Caravan Club was formed. Its members are opposed to the presence of 'unstable vehicles on the road' and would like to see 'a dawn to dusk curfew restricting caravan movements to night hours' (Clouston, 1992).

What had been a remarkable modernist design becomes rejected, because of its intrusion on a classical version of the rural. The 'othering' of the moving caravan is linked with its 'othering' in groups, in mass sites, in association with a mobility that is not seen to 'fit' in the late twentieth century version of either the rural or mobility. Although caravans are often sited temporarily, their presence is familiarly associated with fixed sites, and more widely with images that contradict the rural as 'unpeopled views', wide expanses. People in the countryside are often 'othered', especially if they are creating their own leisure, which can be seen as wilful:

> the hoards of hikers cackling insanely in the woods, or singing raucous songs as they walk arm in arm down the quiet village street .... There are

> tents in meadows and girls in pyjamas dancing beside them to the strains of the gramophone ... (CEM Joad, quoted in Hardy and Ward, 1984, p. 40)

Those sites become acceptable as 'themed', organized, situated and placed within an imposed version of the rural. Behind this lies an attitude that 'others' caravanners in a way that reflects attitudes to gypsies; outsiders, 'others' in a rural image; mobile, uncertain, bringers of buildings, however humble, into a place reserved for something, or someone, else. Just like the allotment, regarded as neither urban nor rural, yet actually both, the caravan is 'home' and 'escape' (Crouch and Ward, 1994, Chapter 10). However, this difference in view is a confrontation between applying a 'picturesque' view of countryside, of regarding it as an object for contemplation at a distance, and being actually involved in its spaces, through everyday social practices. Caravanning is one such social practice that, as we observe, is also significantly cultural, where the practice is rich in metaphor too, engaged in a complex process of geographical knowledge and cultural identity. This emerges through an investigation of people who use their caravan for rallies, and for those who spend a holiday based on a large caravan site.

Culture in a Field

> It is a question of contingencies overlapping. The events which take place in this field – two birds chasing one another, a cloud crossing the sun and changing the colour of the green – acquire a special significance because they occur during the minute or two which I am obliged to wait. It is as though these minutes fill a certain area of time which exactly fits the spatial area of the field. Time and space conjoin .... The field that you are standing before appears to have the same proportions as your own life ... (Berger, 1984)

'The main reason we go caravanning is to make freedom and to make friends.'[1] 'Freedom from the phone' is the most frequent expression of this feeling, and many caravanners use the expression which is published in club literature, 'you can go where you like when you like'. For these caravanners, many of whom spend most weekends of the year going to rallies, the telephone is a real intrusion, but is also a metaphor of the 'trappings' of everyday working life; it is a tie to commitments, the office (and many caravanners we talked to work from home, or are 'on call' at awkward hours). This is also an effort towards freedom to make socialization, to seek empowerment through a distinctive cultural identity and practices 'over which you have your own control'. People who caravan comprise a fair spectrum of socio-economic groups: the Caravan Club itself has 71 per cent of its members in socio-economic groups A, B and C1 (Caravan Club, 1994). Our interviews focused on lower-middle income households. Those who had caravans in the upper price range tended to be older, who had slowly moved up market as they became 'empty nesters', as their children had left home. Others spent more money on their caravan as they had received redundancy payment and decided that the caravan provided an important social lifeline. Some caravan clubs are organized around the workplace; others among neighbourhoods. The Caravan Club and the second largest national club – the Camping and Caravanning Club (called the Friendly Club because it accommodates people with tents as well as caravans and has fewer 'rules' about using sites) – are organized on a regional and local basis. People join with friends, others join to meet and make friends. To almost every caravanner, the social dimension of the rally is the most important facet of the practice, more so than simply being in the countryside, or having free time, or being able to visit places: 'there is a bond among caravanners that doesn't exist anywhere else; here you are among friends'. For other members, this can be too close: 'we were active members, but now we only keep going so that we can use the sites'. Friendship like this is not universal.

'Caravanning is a great leveller; you can let your hair down.' These people construct a different world. There are different non-exclusive sets of social relations (although some find it claustrophobic). 'Nobody mentions work; work is kept out of rallies.' Momentary imagination is possible in this new place, this new social situation: 'It is like being a rich person and inviting your friends down for a weekend in the country'; this is also an expression of sociality and control. Each one in the group is a host; and the things that happen are part organized, part spontaneous, or familiar by ritual. Some people spend the whole of the weekend in a deckchair, talking and sunbathing, and, when there is a chance, enjoying beer.

Women can discover the experience of rallying to be a transfer of 'duties' from one kitchen sink to another, and there may be limits to the possibility of constructing new realities in a weekend. Others do discover a new possibility: 'Even when you are cooking on a rally, you're not stuck in the kitchen like at home. You're amongst friends, amongst the talking.' Confined space has its benefits. It is frequently felt among our respondents that men are more likely to share childcare within a place where they can both be free, and where space is shared with people with whom they can spend time talking.

Rallying can be a transferred or created community. Among people who live near to each other or who share workplace, there is often a strong income solidarity and shared preference of cultural capital for the way they use their weekend leisure time, which resembles Savage's evidence that similar class fractions share preferences for countryside recreation (Savage, 1992). For those who share 'neighbourhood' or workplace, this is more easily achieved, but many caravanners meet only when on rallies, or originally met through rallies. Some keep these friendships over generations; some transfer their friendships on rallies to meeting when they are at home; others keep their friendships for rallies only, as a distinctive component of their lives, where social identity is reserved for practice in a distinctive kind of place. The social relationships are sustained through a series of rituals; the culture is a series of shared activities, and a shared value and ideology about how to spend time, and how to enjoy mobility, making place, visiting. Ritual plays an important role in this leisure activity in a way that denotes its conscious making of community (McNaghten, 1993) and also efforts towards making identity. Typically the rally includes a flagpole, and a ceremony that happens around it; people gather at the end of the rally for prizes won at games played over the weekend; rally 'officials' – club members who take turns at the job – receive badges of thanks from other members; children get their own prizes for their own competitions, achievements and games. These events inevitably happen with a lot of laughter and little seriousness.

Many different venues are chosen for these events; members develop their favourites, but there is always felt to be room for trying new sites; holding the idea of touring, exploration and coming across a place unawares, although the rally convenor always checks the site before making a booking. Both national organizations have a regional structure, and although sites chosen for rallies may be located in many places, they favour sites within the local district, although visits to more distant sites, sometimes involving larger meetings with members of other districts, are important in the calendar. Sometimes the site may be only a quarter of a mile from where a member lives. Even that is felt to satisfy the sense of sociality and freedom, and the place where they meet is important in the way they value the event. Most groups that go rallying require ease of access for caravans to be parked, relatively flat ground to make parking and manoeuvre easy, and there are certain characteristics that are favoured that make significant geographical knowledge.

The site where the caravans are parked is the focus for social activities; it can also provide a centre from which to explore footpaths, events in a nearby village that often feature on the calendar for the weekend or an adjacent historical centre. Some of these rallies happen at sites owned by the clubs; most are rented for a small fee from local landowners. Commercially owned sites are frequently avoided because 'they don't have the freedom the club sites have', the freedom to arrange caravans, organize events and activities, to use the site as the members prefer, rather than have commercially provided events that they cannot control and make themselves; again, a sense of power. There is never merchandise for sale on a club site.

Many of these rallies include games, barbecues and dances. Weekends can be organized around events known to be happening in villages near the site. Caravans can be arranged on the site as an expression of making community, and to show how the surrounding materiality of the site is valued. Many clubs arrange the caravans in a corral, others group them more irregularly and some make lines to make an apparently neat arrangement: 'we are very conscious of our public image, so we make sure the site looks neat when we are here, and when we have left you can't tell we've been here'. Caravanners are conscious of the importance of the site in other ways. The flagpole ceremony provides the physical and social focus of the rally. 'The site' provides an important symbolic identity for the caravanner which makes everything possible; it brings people together. Sites are well researched by rally organizers; people who go alone, or informally with friends, gather a knowledge of sites that 'feel right'. This usually means a combination of straightforward accessibility, and the selection of small intimate places with interesting features - good views, footpaths, trees, not enclosed and without buildings close by. Buildings are expressed as metaphors of 'having people around who bother you'; trees are a metaphor for a sense of nature, which is also referred to in terms of effortlessness, remote from pressures, freedom, accessibility to 'get away' and a lack of controls. Commercial sites are found to fail in these crucial qualities.

A Kind of Geographical Knowledge

This is a mixture of classical rural and a rural that combines strong sociability; that is culturally situated in social relations, individual and usually collective freedom; shared responsibility without those responsibilities felt to be oppressive. There is an imagery of 'traditional' post-war farming countryside in this which is unconstrained. Caravanning enables people to get close to 'bits of the countryside', and this is unexpectedly acknowledged in the official literature; the caravanner can 'reach areas with many natural assets, areas of unspoilt countryside allow caravanners and campers to get closer to the natural world than other holiday accommodation could provide' (South Lakeland District Council, 1979). Memory of the countryside in childhood is frequently invoked among caravanners of all ages which includes the influence of childhood literature. There is a collective memory of previous visits to the same site and to others where sites begin to merge into a distinctive cultural practice, shaped by the requirements and possibilities of having a caravan with which to travel, creating a longer identity in an abstracted place where you can 'be yourself'. This would seem to be very different from the totally detached 'freewheeler' of the 'road' movie and literature, where there is overriding individuality (Cresswell, 1993; Eyerman and Lofgren, 1995). Instead, the caravanning experience, embedded in sociality, place and mobility, is relevant to particular sites in which situated practice occurs. However, while 'counter-culture' may over express this leisure practice, among caravanners there is a pervasive sense of freedom from conformity in the way of using the countryside (not by implication 'irresponsibility'), and a strongly held and felt identity.

Commercial promotion is unobtrusive or absent, and consumption generally is collective and not delivered through the market. The experience of the rural is produced and consumed essentially through shared, self-generated leisure. The place makes possible the sense of freedom, togetherness, the possibility of self-generated leisure and a shared identity. Place is important in the imagination of that shared identity; the site is its metaphor. These people come to share many values together – the need for each other (although they frequently say that they do not need to be 'in each others pockets'), a sense of conscious valued individuality and self-respect; an attitude to the countryside, and towards commercial countryside that is often as disliked as their home telephone. Caravanners do visit theme parks, but these are noticeably referred to as marginal to what they are doing: 'we might go to Sega World while we are here, but we don't like to drag the kids away too early; they prefer to spend the morning around the site'. There is a sense of land, of owning land, albeit for a fleeting time, linked with a sense of return – the site left clean and its ownership extended to next time. Ownership of land is not a matter of legal and financial ownership, but identity; cultural identity in a geographical knowledge that is owned, held, carried, and shared.

Contextuality and the Making of Geographical Knowledge: Weardale[2]

Weardale is not a typical part of the contemporary British 'rural', which in any case is essentially confined to certain more prosperous parts of southern England or particular versions of the Lake District (Howkins, 1989; Crouch, 1992; Urry, 1995). For generations Weardale has been both a mixed economy and community, with residents participating in several occupations - most notably farming, forestry and mining. This has meant that the 'farming landscape' has continued interrupted by other activities, and has resembled more a changing unstable space than a framed picture revered in classical depictions and icons of the rural (Short, 1992).

The economy, culture, and materiality of Upper Weardale are in flux. Mining in the valley is marginalized, and many mines have ceased operation; industrial plants have developed in the lower reaches of the valley and increasing numbers of people commute from up-valley to these commercial sites. The area has also witnessed shifts in its population which include new households using second and holiday homes, and increased numbers of commuters. Parallel with such changes, new leisure facilities have been developed by both the public and private sectors.

The smallholding population is unstable, with some households inheriting land, farming and cultural practices from their parents, including attitudes to land, landlord and change. Other smallholders are newly arrived - pioneers after a version of the rural, and making hard work on the land. Both recent and continuing generations of smallholders find it necessary to combine time and labour on the land with part- or full-time jobs elsewhere, usually in the towns down the valley, but sometimes in those public sector jobs associated with leisure delivery. The men's lives are made up of fragments; of lorry driving, factory work and stockrearing; the women are now usually the holders, who are concerned with the land, the home, the family, and who may hold paid employment outside the holding themselves and share the stockwork.

These people are marginal because their land is small in size, their influence small, and they do not participate in the closer identity among larger farmers, even in the Dale. They participate in a farming community 'on the edge', but their identity leans towards a wider population whose lives lie beyond the land, and so their identity shifts and becomes more complex. Leisure practices offer one means of making identity in this wider shifting, unstable and sometimes uncertain 'community', unmistakably different from farming and other imagined and earlier measured 'occupational communities' in rural Britain (Harper, 1989; Crowe and Allan, 1994). The valley becomes contextualized by the wider population within the context of work and leisure (Cohen, 1982), by the wider farming political economy and becomes recontextualized by tourism promotion. For the holders, the Dale is still embedded in ritual and the collective, through negotiated and shifting memory, which increasingly partakes a new set of relations and new cultural practices. Their pieces of land become re-envisaged in this new cultural identity. This contextualizes contemporary leisure practices, along wider signs of the rural that typically contain notions of nature, beauty and landscape (Cosgrove and Daniels, 1989; Katz and Kirby, 1991; Crouch, 1992). These notions resonate with other sources of signification.

Smallholders are marginalized by the contemporary farming political economy, of ownership, farm pricing and profitability. Smallholders are 'othered' because they are not in the mainstream of commercially 'profitable' agriculture. As we saw with the metropolitan version of popular culture and popular places, these are 'other'. They are seen to use materials in transgressive, regressive ways, for example, corrugated iron rather than 'modern' ready-made components. The lives of the smallholders, distinctive among other groups of people living in the valley, are doubly 'othered'; their lives are imagined as out of touch with contemporary cultural practices; and they are positioned in the romantic 'rural'.

Leisure Practices and Rural Places

Smallholders in Weardale know that their land becomes less important in their everyday lives as that identity becomes shared with other workplaces, but balancing income has long been part of the unstable economy, and rather than depart, the land shifts in their identity. This time change includes other dimensions; more individual places become part of their identity and people become familiar with those who come from a wider geographical area; more places are visited and passed through in everyday life, and in many of these, friendships are made. Leisure is especially important in this process.

Aline lives in the middle of the long Dale, halfway to the height of the Pennines. She has only five acres of what was a larger holding in her early life. She is in charge of the land, with her husband working down the valley at Beamish in a heritage theme park. She retains a close relationship with families among the immediate smallholding lives, who have for years shared values in land, shared a similar home, church, struggles with land, money and work. They are conscious of the distinction of the physicality of their 'place' and of its position in their habitus. The holder next door has 33 acres, which provides her with hay for her horses, and visits Aline each day for dinner. Aline has three children and several grandchildren - one is unemployed, one works at the leisure centre in the small town five miles away - and she participates in all the shows in the Dale, with whatever produce she has available at the time. This practice survives as a ritual, and most of the smallholders do this. She enjoys these shows as an opportunity to talk with the other smallholders, but distinctively she does not identify with 'farmers' - their life is the land only, only a commercial practice.

Leisure practices are frequently shared, self-generated and important in cultural identity. Another smallholding household, the Nelsons, came to the upper Weardale from Kent less than a decade ago. The Nelsons have discovered the significance of leisure in shaping their identity, and geographical knowledge informs and is informed by this practice. Their move from the South was linked with achieving an idea of 'rural', a more conscious attempt at engaging in the land than people like Aline and her family. However, their 'rural' is more than simply cultural capital (Thrift, 1987): 'We have certainly made loads of friends since we came up here. Right from the first, everybody was helpful; jumble sales, events, shows, babysitting. We are part of the church, and our children are in the choir.' This 'involvement' may be part of making the 'rural', realizing an image, but also partaking of a materiality of everyday cultural practice.

Consuming Places: Leisure and the Rural in Geographical Knowledge

The land has an important symbolic meaning in Aline's identity that is partly childhood and partly collective memory shared with other household members along the Dale: 'I used to climb over there, when I was a child. I don't think there's anywhere as pretty as this. I love the Dale but particularly here. I would never leave this place, and don't want the pasture that remains flattened.' The pasture, now a small field, is visible from her kitchen window. It is in that kitchen that all of her children visit, married and single parents, with their children, and where the neighbour who pays to take the hay, visits each day for dinner. This kind of metaphorical significance is not really nostalgic - the pasture is not detached from contemporary life. The land, and the pasture in particular, are symbolic of memory, and of being in the Dale; of a remembered and still tangible way of life. But this is disrupted, and Aline and her large family consciously negotiate this change.

The wider valley is seen from the kitchen window and is crossed on the way to take children, now grandchildren, to the school leisure centre and swimming pool. Leisure activities again become important in the way the valley is known and felt as part of cultural identity: 'I can't say where our land stops and the valley begins; the boundaries merge.' In this sense, the private and the 'wide countryside' overlap. This is a physical and a cultural merging. Physically, it is difficult to identify a hard boundary of protected territory, as territory is not felt in that way. Instead, the edges are held very loosely. Culturally, the 'community' is widening, consistently permeable, merging different spheres of social contact and financial uncertainty, resembling communities in the city rather than the romanticized, commodified 'rural' (Reville, 1993). The wider rural is grasped with the wider culture: 'the other night I stood outside at twelve o'clock. Planes flew over from Newcastle airport and it was lovely and peaceful and calm'. She shows a tapestry of a tractor that she wove that hangs in the room where the family gets together every day, along with the neighbour and a wide circle of friends from school and her son's work at the leisure centre: 'I like anything that depicts the countryside on the wall, anywhere in the house.' Because they have long used the land, this does not preclude their engaging with it at a level of gentle spectacle, but this is contained within a longer perspective about land, life and labour.

The more newly arrived Nelsons intertwine their participation in local leisure with an identification of the Dale as both site of leisure practice and familiarity, and sensuous imagination in its materiality: 'I just love the hillside ... that view ... I could sit and look at it all day. It changes so much you can sit and look at it for an hour, and it changes in that hour, even in bad weather it is spectacular. It is just so open up here.' It is a mixture of realized vision and an everyday coping along with other people on whom they mutually rely in making the struggles of a living: 'It is much more lateral up here (at the top of the farmed Dale); this house used to be on the edge of the valley, hanging, looking over into the long Dale.' Like Raymond Williams' view from the Black Mountains (Williams, 1990), Mrs Nelson can look at these contours and identify a cultural and social as well as material identity.

'Othering' People; 'Othering' Geographical Knowledge

This chapter has used two different examples. Caravanning is an example of contemporary leisure of an essentially city-located population. It foregrounds mobility and uses spaces in the countryside intermittently. Smallholders living in Weardale make their leisure both across their daily lives in that rural place, and also elsewhere. They constitute a changing community but are mobilized in popular culture as archetypal rural although, paradoxically, they are part of a landscape under stress. The people, not the place, are 'othered'. Leisure is important in the lives of both. Together, these two examples bring complex evidence of how the rural is understood through leisure practices and how predominant versions of the rural are flexible and contested. The ways in which these two groups engage in leisure practices provide insights into their empowerment and distinctive geographical knowledges, and in turn, the ways these work between hegemonic versions and othering processes. This provides important insights for understanding othering, power and the consumption of rural places.

Both examples are 'othered' in contemporary discourses. However, in both of these, others are components of the same. Caravanners do not subscribe to what may be labelled overtly 'deviant' ideologies or lifestyles; smallholders in Weardale are engaged in what might be termed fairly 'straightforward' and 'non threatening' lives. They are 'othered' by their practices in using the rural. The significance of this is that 'othering' is more in the exercise of power than in terms of transgression. To each group, the rural is an 'other'; making possible imagining 'being'; liberated from constraining influences in everyday life; but these also are themselves part, if an imaginative part, of that everyday life. Both cases offer examples of 'othering' as creative process, and as an exercise of hegemony.

This 'othering' as hegemony is both political and cultural. That hegemony imposes a taken-for-granted iconography of practice upon each group; each is 'othered' as transgressive, as either consumer or producer. Their signs are read alongside the promoted norms of 'othering' within the tourist and conservation imaging, for example the promotion of the Lake District (Urry, 1995). The Lake District is taken out of any other cultural context and social life; everyone and anywhere that does not 'fit' with this imagined rural is excluded. Diversity in the rural is increasingly acceptable but only within the limits that are prescribed as useful in terms of profitability by the market place in uneasy collaboration with the State. Caravanning is less easily controlled and organized, culturally and physically, than, for example, theme parks, which can be designed along particular versions of the rural – a rationalization of leisure (Heywood, 1994). In their leisure practices, both groups are 'othered' since their experience opts out of 'consumer citizenship' (Urry,

1995), where people are citizens by virtue of their (market place) consumption rather than their political rights and duties (although this remaking of citizenship may itself be challenged and be changing rapidly in the new political culture of the late 1990s). The two examples investigated within this chapter make their own versions of the rural through distinctive processes of geographical knowledge. In each case, knowledge is semi-detached from these dominant forms.

In both these cases, the leisure practices involve negotiating self and social identity through actual practices that mobilize metaphor in relation to values and ideologies and in making empowerment. Identity is not rooted in leisure, but leisure mobilizes elements of collective memory and identity, through ritual and practices that are both celebrated and reworked, reaffirmed and contested. Land and place, like music, is important in this process, where the empowerment and the mobilization of identity can be both enabled and frustrated.

Place is a site of sociality and of cultural practice. In the cases highlighted in this chapter, we observe a reworking and negotiation of social relationships, although class remains important, and caravanning continues to offer opportunities to a large number of people with lower income - which can be a cheap means of knowing countryside. The identification of caravanning with 'low' culture, and smallholders with economic and political marginality, helps to keep both 'othered', but the reality is of course much more complex. People who caravan and those who have smallholdings are making community, sometimes in a very conscious way, to realize aspirations and to hold on to their lives. Community may be temporary or intermittent but it is no less important in becoming an imagining individual tapping into collective identity. For the caravanning household its practice offers an ever accessible possibility of making community and making cultural identity; smallholders can exert their own lives through the way they make leisure, and imagine another possibility of being.

Place is very important in these examples. Space is traversed, occupied, and provides the situation for shared rituals, for meeting people and knowing them. These ordinary places, that may be called, purposefully, 'bits of countryside', to distinguish from the picturesque 'grand view', and now ubiquitous 'gaze', are used in making culture, and places are made cultural, just as in the example of the 'street' in Jackson's carnival (Jackson, 1988). Making places like this may be temporary, as we observed in caravanning, but acts as an important and familiar part of the way the rural is consumed. Smallholders know places through situated labour; through crossing land in order to get children to school, through other work and leisure; this includes meeting people as well as traversing space linked with collective memory. Space is signified as people move across it, and views are important as places are crossed in the meeting of people, in a process of making community. Space spreads out towards and contains identity; space within which cultural practices happen. Visiting a local show, smallholders cross land in a way that culminates at the event, mirroring what Nielsen (1993) has argued in terms of the power appropriated to space as scattered participants in a football crowd arrive for the game, excitement heightening as they approach the ground as it emerges into view; increasingly intermingling across space with others in the crowd, who may be recognized or completely unknown; a version of making collective memory.

Land is imagined as ownership in complex ways; as legal title and 'private'; as a site of shared cultural practice; as evoking collective memory, empowerment and resistance, a transgression of imposed and other codes. These values and meanings can become invested in other people, in particular sites and particular pieces of the rural, and can be shifted from site to site in the repetition of intermittent practice. Weardale holders envisage the valley as theirs, as well as the fragments to which they have legal title. These fragments are negotiated and constantly changing; the valley is felt to be contested as it becomes reimagined and reimaged through the process of geographical commodification.

Land is powerful in metaphor and materiality; as site to use and to hold on to; and as iconographic of cultural practice, where its geographical knowledge is held, contested and remade. Thus everyday practice produces its own signs, and informs others; its own signs semi-detached from those of dominant culture and commodified representations, which may be engaged and positioned within this everyday context. At the same time, both the smallholders and caravanners, through their leisure practices, mobilize myths and signs of mobility, nature and home; of rural community, freedom, and land. Through their practice they situate and contextualize, affirm and contest these signs. These leisure practices happen in particular situated pieces of the rural. The materiality of the situated encounter of people with each other, and with place, becomes translated through and into metaphor that informs events and practices, and is thereby challenged and reworked.

This positions a relationship between signs, places and lives. Collective memory is invoked and mobilized in leisure practices that are situated in distinctive places, social relations and intersubjectivities. Everyday leisure practice re-situates expectations and remembered meanings of places socially. These meanings are reworked through relationships and engagements that happen in these places, each a piece of the rural semi-detached from the iconography of the wider countryside, and of commodification. The rural in both cases highlighted earlier is also about a wider iconography contextualized through an active process of everyday geographical knowledge that is objective and subjective.

Both modern and post-modern interpretations have emptied the rural of situated practices and local knowledges - a vacuum which becomes filled with abstracted and global signification, more recently argued and conveyed in terms of the figural (Lash and Urry, 1994; Urry, 1995). However, when we investigate how people make and remake geographical knowledge we discover knowledge culturally constituted of both, and hence semi-detatched, unstable, and involved in contestation between local and global signification. It is however convenient and necessary for dominant influences - and perhaps, too often, dominant theoretical interpretations - to reduce this complexity; perhaps to 'other' this complexity.

People who rally caravans, and smallholders in the Dales know that the rural is powerfully sensuous, and engages with emotions and ironies. Commodified imaging is also consumed by both, and the fragments of commodified infrastructure are composed in this way, not seen as necessarily antagonistic (Warren, 1992). Disneyworld is likened to a drug trip; a World's Fair was felt to strengthen family identity rather than provoke wonder at our now technological 'global' village (Ley and Olds, 1988). This geographical knowledge does not rely on the figural, but uses the figural as accessory. Neither the caravan sites nor the leisure practices of smallholders uses what Zukin identifies as a 'dreamscape of visual consumption'; the market can be bypassed (Zukin, 1990).

Ironically, one of my key conclusions must be that the signs of commodified country are the 'others', out of touch and unable to connect with the way the rural is worked in people's lives, and its own fragments are contextualized or rejected; marginalized by that everyday, ordinary and also extraordinary, cultural practice - mobilized especially through leisure. Geographical knowledge is much more socially situated in the intersubjectivities of lives than contemporary interpretations suggest, mainly because those interpretations read the signs of the 'market' and the one-dimensional survey data on consumption (Tyrrel, 1990; CPRE, 1994). The caravan site and the Dale are texts we can read, but for caravanners we discover this grossly limits our understanding of their knowledge, their practices, processes of geographical knowledge and the positioning of place in cultural identity.

Similarly, the commodified countryside is validated by the academy only by its self-production and self-presentation, not in the complexity of its consumption. Thus, commodified countryside enhances its position of control and becomes asserted and registered as inevitable (Gramsci, 1971). I have already suggested the selective choices that emerge from this process - a contestation of myth, a metaphor and marketing articulated around their appropriation and particular versions of 'choice' and empowerment.

Contemporary 'leisure' is arguably all about 'playfulness', 'fun', and experimentation. Transgression, diversity, flickering images, surprise and celebration are all acceptable if they are contained within a clearly situated and contextualized frame, both materially and metaphorically. Changes in the political economy of the rural, the commodification of places and promotional imaging and reimaging challenge our case study opportunities of empowerment. Theming caravan sites, removing 'others', and driving for versions of 'tidiness' and powerful promotion of versions for the figural - accompanied by the shifting legal ownership of land - provide different contexts and structures of cultural practice.

This is where the concerns of Murdoch and Pratt (1993) re-emerge. The possibility of empowerment through practices like those of our case studies confronts an emerging hegemony in production and in organizing consumption. This commodification of space may reduce room for making multiple meanings (polysemy - Fiske, 1990) as we consume space in the countryside. It may reduce the chances for diverse and empowering production of leisure places in the countryside, however temporary that production may be. As well as consuming countryside, we are enormously productive in both polysemy and in shaping and reshaping the material itself.

Notes

1. Twelve rally caravanners from a range of national and local clubs were interviewed during 1994. A further 15 were joined on rallies of the Caravan Club and Camping and Caravanning Club over weekends during 1994. A questionnaire was sent to 100 members of the Caravanning Club, of which 38 responded, and a further six households were interviewed on a commercial caravan site during summer 1994. This research was funded by an Anglia University Research Grant.
2. This section draws on interviews with seven smallholders in middle and upper Weardale carried out between 1993–94 which was funded by a Nuffield Small Social Science Grant.

References

Berger, J. (1984) *About Looking*. London: Writers and Readers.
Blyton, E. (1946) *Five go off in a Caravan*. London: Hodder and Stoughton.
Bourdieu, P. (1984) *Distinction: A Social Critique of the Judgement of Taste*. London: Routledge.
Caravan Club (1994) *Members' Information Caravan Club*. East Grinstead: Caravan Club.
Chambers, I. (1986) *Popular Culture: The Metropolitan Experience*. London: Methuen.
Chambers, I. (1994) *Migrancy, Culture, Identity*. London: Routledge.
Clouston, E. (1992) Anti-caravan club declares war on snails on the road. *Guardian*, 6 August, 4.
Cohen, A. (ed.) (1982) *Belonging: Identity and Social Organisation in British Rural Cultures*. Manchester: Manchester University Press.
Cosgrove, D. and Daniels, S. (1989) *The Iconography of Landscape*. Cambridge: Cambridge University Press.
Council for the Protection of Rural England (1994) *Leisure Landscapes*. Lancaster University: CPRE.
Countryside Commission (1992) *Enjoying the Countryside: People and Policies*. Cheltenham: Countryside Commission.
Cresswell, T. (1993) Mobility as resistance; a geographical reading of Kerouac's *On The Road*. *Transactions of the Institute of British Geographers*, 18 (2), 249–62.
Crouch, D. (1992) Popular culture and what we make of the rural: the case of village allotments. *Journal of Rural Studies*, 8 (3), 229–40.
Crouch, D. (1994) *Signs, Places and Lives*. Working Paper. Odense University.
Crouch, D. and Matless, D. (1996) Refiguring geography: the parish maps of Common Ground, *Transactions of the Institute of British Geographers*, 21 (1), 236–55.
Crouch, D. and Tomlinson, A. (1994) Self-generated consumption; leisure, space and cultural identity. In I. Henry (ed.) *Leisure, Modernity, Postmodernity and Lifestyles*. Brighton: Leisure Studies Association.
Crouch, D. and Ward, C. (1994) (2nd edition) *The Allotment: Its Culture and Landscape*. Nottingham: Mushroom Press.
Crowe, G. and Allan, G. (1994) *Community Life: An Introduction to Local Social Relations*. London: Harvester Wheatsheaf.
Deleuze, G. (1990) *The Logic of Sense*. New York: Columbia University Press.
East Anglia Tourist Board (1984) *Towards a Design for Coastal Caravan Parks*. Hadleigh, Suffolk: East Anglia Tourist Board.
East Anglia Tourist Board (1990) *Caravanscape Design*. Hadleigh, Suffolk: East Anglia Tourist Board.
Eyerman, R. and Lofgren, O. (1995) Romancing the road: road movies and images of mobility. *Theory, Culture and Society*. 12, 53–79.
Fiske, J. (1990) *Understanding Popular Culture*. London: Routledge.
Giddens, A. (1990) *The Consequences of Modernity*. Cambridge: Polity Press.
Grahame, K. (1908) *The Wind in the Willows*. London: Methuen.
Gramsci, A. (1971) *Selections from the Prison Notebooks*. London: Lawrence and Wishart.

Gutman, R. and Kaufman, E. (1979) *American Diner*. New York: Harper and Row.
Hannerz, U. (1992) *Cultural Complexity: Studies in the Social Organisation of Meaning*. London: Columbia University Press.
Hardy, D. and Ward, C. (1984) *Arcadia for All*. London: Mansell.
Harper, S. (1989) The British rural community; an overview of perspectives. *Journal of Rural Studies*, 5, 161–84.
Hemingway, J. (1995) Leisure studies and interpretative social enquiry. *Leisure Studies*, 14 (1), 32–47.
Hetherington, K. (1992) Stonehenge and its festival; spaces of consumption. In R. Shields (ed.) *Lifestyle Shopping*. London: Routledge.
Heywood, I. (1994) Urgent dreams: climbing, rationalisation and ambivalence. *Leisure Studies*, 13, 179–94.
House of Commons Environment Committee (1995) *Fourth Report (Vol. 1)*. London: HMSO.
Howkins, A. (1989) Peace of the country. *New Society*, August.
Jackson, P. (1988) Street Life: the politics of carnival. *Environment and Planning D: Society and Space*, 6, 213–27.
Katz, C. and Kirby, A. (1991) In the Nature of things; the environment and everyday life. *Transactions of the Institute of British Geographers*. NS 16, 259–77.
Lash, S. (1993) Reflexive modernities: the aesthetic dimension. *Theory, Culture and Society*, 10, 1–23.
Lash, S. and Urry, J. (1994) *Economies of Signs and Space*. London: Sage.
Ley, D. and Olds, K. (1988) Landscape as spectacle: world's fairs and the culture of heroic consumption. *Environment and Planning D: Society and Space*, 6, 191–212.
McNaghten, P. (1993) Landscapes of discipline and transgression. Paper to the De-traditionalization conference, University of Lancaster.
Miller, D. (1987) *Mass Consumption and Consumer Culture*. Cambridge: Cambridge University Press.
Murdoch, J. and Pratt, A. (1993) Rural studies: modernism, post-modernism and the 'post-rural'. *Journal of Rural Studies*, 9 (4), 411–27.
Nielsen, N. (1993) Sports between rationalism and romanticism: about patterns of movement and conflict. Paper to the Geography and Sport conference, University of Keele.
Okeley, J. (1980) Trading stereotypes; the case of English Gypsies. In S. Wallman (ed.) *Ethnicity at Work*. Basingstoke: Macmillan.
Orwell, G. (1949) *Coming up for Air*. London: Gollancz.
Philo, C. (1992) Neglected rural geographies: a review. *Journal of Rural Studies*, 8 (2), 193–207.
Putnam, T. (1993) Beyond the modern home; shifting the parameters of residence. In J. Bird, B. Curtis, T. Putnam, G. Robertson and L. Tickner (eds) *Mapping the Futures*. London: Routledge.
Reville, G. (1993) Reading Rosehill: community, identity and inner city Derby. In M. Keith and S. Pile (eds) *Place and the Politics of Cultural Identity*. London: Routledge.
Ricouer, P. (1981) The model of the text: meaningful action considered in the text. In J.B. Thompson (ed.) *Hermeneutics and the Human Sciences*. Cambridge: Cambridge University Press.

Sack, R. (1988) The consumer's world; place as context. *Annals of the Association of American Geographers*, 81 (4), 642–64.
Savage, M. (1992) Cultural consumption and lifestyle. In T. Barlow, P. Dickens, T. Fielding and M. Savage *Property, Bureaucracy and Lifestyle: Middle-Class Formations in Contemporary Britain*. London: Routledge.
Shields, R. (1992) (ed.) *Lifestyle Shopping*. London: Routledge.
Shoard, M. (1982) The lure of the moors. In J. Goldand and J. Burgess (eds) *Valued Environments*. London: Allen and Unwin.
Short, J. (1992) *Imagined Country*. London: Routledge.
Shurmer-Smith, P. and Hannam, K. (1994) *Worlds of Desire: Realms of Power*. London: Edward Arnold.
Sibley, D. (1980) *Outsiders in Urban Societies*. Oxford: Basil Blackwell.
Smith, M. (1983) The pub: a sociological perspective. In A. Tomlinson (ed.) *Leisure and Popular Cultural Forms*. Brighton: Leisure Studies Association.
Smith, S. (1993) Bounding the borders: claiming space and making place in Scotland. *Transactions of the Institute of British Geographers*, NS 18, 291–308.
South Lakeland District Council (1979) *South Lakeland District Plan: Caravan and Camping Subject Plan*. Kendal: South Lakeland District Council.
Stables, G. (1886) The Voyage of the Land Yacht Wanderer. London: Hodder and Stoughton.
Taylor, C. (1979) Interpretation and the science of man. In P. Rainbow and W. Sullivan (eds) *Interpretative Social Science: A Reader*. Berkeley: University of California Press.
Thrift, N. (1987) Manufacturing rural geography? *Journal of Rural Studies*, 3, 77–81.
Thrift, N. (1994) Inhuman geographies: landscapes of speed, light and power. In P. Cloke, D. Matlass, M. Phillips and N. Thrift, *Writing the Rural: Five Cultural Geographies*. London: Paul Chapman Publishing.
Tyrrel, R. (1990) *Leisure Futures*. Henley Centre for Forecasting.
Urry, J. (1995) *Consuming Places*. London: Routledge.
Ward, C. and Hardy, D. (1986) *Goodnight Campers! The History of the British Holiday Camp*. London: Mansell.
Warren, S. (1992) This heaven gives me migraine: the problems and promise of landscapes of leisure. In J. Duncan and D. Ley (eds) *Place/Culture/ Representation*. London: Routledge.
Whitt, L. and Slack, J. (1994) Communities, environments, and cultural studies. *Cultural Studies*, 8, 5–31.
Williams, R. (1973) *The Country and the City*. London: Chatto and Windus.
Williams, R. (1976) *Keywords*. London: Fontana.
Williams, R. (1990) *The People of the Black Mountains:1, The Beginning*. London: Paladin.
Wright, P. (1985) *On Living in an Old Country*. London: Verso.
Zukin, S. (1990) *Landscapes of Power*. Berkeley: University of California Press.

Index